COUNTY COLLEGE OF **MORRIS**

Practical C++ Design

From Programming to Architecture

Adam B. Singer

Apress®

Practical C++ Design: From Programming to Architecture

Adam B. Singer
The Woodlands, Texas, USA

ISBN-13 (pbk): 978-1-4842-3056-5

ISBN-13 (electronic): 978-1-4842-3057-2

DOI 10.1007/978-1-4842-3057-2

Library of Congress Control Number: 2017954981

Cover image by Freepik (www.freepik.com)

Managing Director: Welmoed Spahr
Editorial Director: Todd Green
Acquisitions Editor: Steve Anglin
Development Editor: Matthew Moodie
Technical Reviewer: Michael Thomas
Coordinating Editor: Mark Powers
Copy Editor: Mary Behr

Distributed to the book trade worldwide by Springer Science+Business Media New York, 233 Spring Street, 6th Floor, New York, NY 10013. Phone 1-800-SPRINGER, fax (201) 348-4505, e-mail orders-ny@springer-sbm.com, or visit www.springeronline.com. Apress Media, LLC is a California LLC and the sole member (owner) is Springer Science + Business Media Finance Inc (SSBM Finance Inc). SSBM Finance Inc is a **Delaware** corporation.

For information on translations, please e-mail rights@apress.com, or visit www.apress.com/rights-permissions.

Apress titles may be purchased in bulk for academic, corporate, or promotional use. eBook versions and licenses are also available for most titles. For more information, reference our Print and eBook Bulk Sales web page at www.apress.com/bulk-sales.

Any source code or other supplementary material referenced by the author in this book is available to readers on GitHub via the book's product page, located at www.apress.com/9781484230565. For more detailed information, please visit www.apress.com/source-code.

Printed on acid-free paper

For Terri, Caroline, and Rebecca

Table of Contents

About the Author

Adam B. Singer graduated first in his class at the Georgia Institute of Technology in 1999 with a bachelor's degree in chemical engineering. He subsequently attended the Massachusetts Institute of Technology on a National Defense, Science, and Engineering Graduate Fellowship. He graduated from MIT with a Ph.D. in chemical engineering in 2004 after defending his thesis titled "Global Dynamic Optimization." Since graduation, Adam has been a member of the research and engineering staff at the ExxonMobil Upstream Research Company,[1] where he has worked in software development, design, and project management in areas such as optimization, reservoir simulation, decision support under uncertainty, basin modeling, well log modeling, and process stratigraphy. He has also served on and chaired committees designing in-house training in the areas of technical software development and computational and applied mathematics. He currently holds a joint supervisory position in both the Computational Sciences and Stratigraphic and Reservoir Systems Functions. Adam additionally held the title of adjunct assistant professor in the Department of Computational and Applied Mathematics at Rice University from 2007-2012. In both 2006 and 2007, he taught a graduate level course, CAAM 520, on computational science. The course focused on the design and implementation of high performance parallel programs.

---

[1] The advice, information, and conclusions discussed in this book are those of the author and have not been endorsed by, or reflect the opinions or practices of, ExxonMobil Corporation or its affiliates.

About the Technical Reviewer

Michael Thomas has worked in software development
for more than 20 years as an individual contributor, team
lead, program manager, and vice president of engineering.
Michael has more than 10 years of experience working with
mobile devices. His current focus is in the medical sector,
using mobile devices to accelerate information transfer
between patients and health care providers.

Preface

Throughout my career, I have mentored both students and fellow employees in programming, and many of them have suggested that I write my thoughts down in book form. However, I have typically responded with the rebuttal that I felt I had nothing novel to present. Being a largely self-taught programmer, I have always been able to rattle off a long list of books from which I have derived most of my knowledge. Therefore, what could I write about that has not already been said?

I came to realize, however, that the majority of books that I encounter tend to focus only on pieces of design or implementation rather than taking a holistic approach. For example, if one wants to learn the C++ language, Stroustrup [24] or Lippman and Lajoie [15] are excellent references. For learning C++ best practices, one need only read the books by Sutter [25, 26, 27], Sutter and Alexandrescu [28], or Meyers [18, 17, 19]. Of course, learning to program extends well beyond C++. For data structures and algorithms, there are always the classics by Knuth [11, 12, 13] or the more accessible and concise book by Cormen *et al* [6]. To learn object-oriented analysis and design, the book by Booch *et al* [4] is an excellent reference. Of course, design patterns can be learned from Gamma *et al* [7], and general programming practices can be learned from many books such as those by McConnell [16], Spinellis [23], or Kernighan and Pike [10].

Certainly, the deeper the specialty one seeks, the more esoteric the book one can find (and should eventually read). This book is not such a book. Rather, I have striven to write a book that operates from the premise that the reader already possesses a working knowledge of the information encased in works such as the aforementioned titles. In this book, I instead attempt to ground the reader's theoretical knowledge of design through practice using a single case study.

Target Audience

As mentioned above, the goal of this book is not to present any specific topic but rather to explore the interrelationship of often compartmentalized subjects. The successful combination of these components to form a cohesive, maintainable, elegant piece of software is, in essence, design. As such, this book is intended to target practicing professionals, in particular those who have several years of development experience but who do not yet possess sufficient experience to architect independently a large software project.

Because my intent is to emphasize the utilization of one's existing knowledge effectively to design software, I make little effort to explain individual topics in great depth. I believe too many books classified as intermediate to advanced fail because the author devotes too much content describing prerequisites. The result is a massive tome filled with unnecessary detail for the advanced reader, while the beginner is left with a long and complicated exposition that is still inaccessible because the beginner does not possess sufficient knowledge or experience to grasp the subject regardless of the amount of detail devoted to the description. I have, therefore, aimed for conciseness over completeness. Often, I simply refer the reader to relevant material rather than myself describing a background topic in great detail. While this strategy may indeed make this book difficult for beginners, I hope experienced professionals appreciate both the brevity of the book and its tone, which assumes the reader is competent at his or her craft.

Structure of the Book

Learning most tasks in programming requires hands-on experience and repetition; design is no exception. My opinion is that design is best learned through a combination of self-exploration and mentoring from an expert. For this reason, I have chosen to organize this book as a study in design through the detailed working of a case study. Instead of discussing design elements in the abstract, we will instead examine the concrete application of design principles as they relate to the design and construction of a simplistic (but not too simplistic) software project. Importantly, we will not only examine successful results that led to the final implementation, but we will also spend time considering alternatives, some of which are viable and others which are not. Where multiple solutions may suffice, choosing one over the other is often either a matter of context or just taste. Regardless, experience is usually the arbiter of such decisions, and hopefully this book will enable the reader to learn from the author's experiences without having to repeat his mistakes. That is, I hope I have created a book that can serve as a self-contained master class in design.

Language Selection

Design as an abstract concept can be taught in the absence of a particular programming language. However, once committed to a concrete example, a specific language must be chosen for the implementation. I decided to write the case study exclusively using C++. While every line of the program does not appear in the text, all of the source code is available for the reader to examine. Despite this book's primary focus on design, reading the source code is a good way to learn how implementation details in a specific language enable or, at least, facilitate a chosen design. The source code also serves as a high quality (I hope) exemplar of a modern C++ implementation of a complete user application. I highly recommend reading and modifying the source code in conjunction with reading the text.

The decision to use C++ does not imply that C++ is the best choice for all programs, and, in fact, it may not even be the best choice for the program examined in this book. However, to ground the abstraction, a concrete language had to be selected. I chose C++ because it is standardized, widely deployed, and available at zero cost on many platforms. Selfishly, I also chose C++ because it is my most proficient language. While I could, perhaps, have chosen another language meeting the aforementioned objective criteria (e.g., Java), the resulting code would probably have been functional but non-idiomatic due to my relative lack of expertise.

During the writing of this book, C++0x was ratified as C++11 and then updated as C++14. Soon we will have C++17. This progression of standards occurring while I was writing this book should give the reader an idea of how long it takes to write a book in one's "free time" at night! The ratification of these standards and the relative paucity of design literature focused on using these new language and library features give me the unique opportunity to highlight how these new language elements can be used effectively in the design of a large scale program. That said, I have not gone out of my way to incorporate modern C++ features where they are inappropriate just to demonstrate usage. In some cases, new language features provide syntactic convenience (e.g., the auto keyword), and, in these instances, I use these features without further mention as they are now established elements of modern C++. In other instances, new language features imply new design semantics afforded by the language (e.g., smart pointers). Where new, modern C++ language or library features enable new design paradigms expressible in the language, I have chosen to highlight these points in a sidebar.

The above said, the reader should not expect this to be a book that simply focuses on various modern C++ features and how to use them effectively. Of particular note will be the relative sparseness of templated classes and the complete lack of some advanced features such as template metaprogramming. This intentional omission is not meant to be a commentary on the importance of these language features or a critique of their usefulness as design constructs. In fact, they are essential for specific domains, particularly where efficiency and genericity dominate (e.g., the standard library, boost). Rather, the lack of usage of any particular feature reflects my pragmatic approach toward design: the appropriate language subset for a particular project should reflect only those features required to express clearly and efficiently the developer's intent. If your favorite language feature is missing, it may be because I felt that its use in this context was less clear than my chosen alternative. After all, we write programs in higher level languages to be read and understood by other programmers. The task of designing, implementing, maintaining, and extending code in a production environment is quite difficult in its own right. Displays of unnecessary cleverness are generally neither warranted nor appreciated.

GUI Framework and Platforms

While graphical user interfaces (GUI) are not the primary focus of this book, our program will eventually acquire one; hence, selecting a particular GUI framework was necessary. I selected Qt for this purpose and have successfully tested the code with versions 4 and 5. As with C++, Qt is widely deployed, cross platform, and free. As with C++, again, selfishly, I chose Qt because I am experienced using desktop Qt and personally enjoy using it. A big advantage of using Qt is that it makes nearly all of the source code for the project platform-independent. Where platform independence was not achievable, I encapsulated the platform-dependent code behind an abstract interface. We'll explore this design pattern, in depth, in Chapter 7.

In general, I always strive to write standards-conforming, platform-independent code. The source code in this book should compile with any C++14-compliant compiler and on any platform where Qt is supported. That said, every platform and every compiler somehow manage to have their own unique idiosyncrasies, and testing every possible combination of platform and compiler is impossible. I personally have tested the source code for this book on Windows 7, Windows 10, and Linux using gcc (the mingw variant on Windows). I do not own an Apple computer, so I have not tested the source code on Mac OS X. However, the code should work as is or require only very minor changes to get it to compile there if that is your platform of choice. Any known platform-specific code is compartmentalized and encapsulated; extension to other platforms should be straightforward.

The Case Study

To this point, I have not yet mentioned the subject of the case study central to this book. In my opinion, an ideal problem would be one that is not too daunting and yet not so trivial that it needs no design. Additionally, the domain of the problem should be readily understandable to any reader. For this reason, I have chosen to implement a stack-based, Reverse Polish Notation (RPN) calculator that I named pdCalc, short for Practical Design Calculator. Functionally, pdCalc was inspired by the HP48S calculator, an old favorite calculator of mine from high school and college (that still sits on my desk today). I cannot imagine any reader being unfamiliar with the basic operations of a calculator, and making the calculator use RPN adds a little twist that I hope will make the project interesting.

The Source Code

The source code (and supporting unit tests) for pdCalc is available, in its entirety, from Apress's GitHub repository. The easiest way to find the repository is via the **Download Source Code** button located at www.apress.com/9781484230565. Appendix A describes, in detail, how to download and build the source code. Although most readers will likely prefer to download the source using a git client, the entire source code is also available from GitHub as a single zip file.

The source code itself is licensed under the GNU Public License (GPL) version 3. I hope you find the source code useful for learning about design and implementation. Beyond its use as an educational aide for this book, you are, of course, free to do anything you like with the source code within the rights granted to you by the GPL.

This book uses two distinct fonts, the standard font you are reading now and a fixed width font used for source code. The fixed width font is demonstrated in the following list of standard template library containers: `vector`, `list`, and `map`. When clear from context, to save space, I often omit namespaces and template arguments. When the discussion requires a block of source code, it will be offset from the rest of the text as follows:

```
class ExampleClass
{
public:
  // your implementation here
};
```

In general, I tried to reproduce the code in the text identically to the code in the repository. However, in some cases, parts of the source were deliberately omitted in the text either for brevity or clarity. I have tried to note instances where the differences are significant. Where the two differ, assume the code in the repository is the more correct and complete version.

Contacting the Author

I suspect that as you read this book and explore the source code, you will invariably have questions. Please feel free to contact me with questions about the content of the book, questions about the source code, errors, or improvements to my design or implementation. I can be contacted at `PracticalDesignBook@gmail.com`. I will make my best effort to reply to all reasonable email related to pdCalc, but without knowing the volume of email I'll receive, I can make no ironclad guarantee that I will be able to respond to every request. If I find that there is a significant interest in a community discussion of pdCalc and its design, I'll investigate establishing a web page to accompany this book. Again, I can offer no promises.

Parting Advice

Finally, in addition to learning something, I hope that you, the reader, have fun with the subject. My personal suggestion is to try to think about the design decisions yourself before reading my solutions. If you are truly industrious, you may even want to implement your own calculator using a completely different, possibly better design. After all, as I said before, design is ultimately about both experience and taste, and your experience and taste may differ significantly from mine.

CHAPTER 1

Defining the Case Study

1.1 A Brief Introduction

This book is about programming design. However, unlike many books on this topic, this book teaches design by exploration rather than design by instruction. Typically, most authors writing about some aspect of design establish principles they wish to convey, lay out these principles in the abstract, and then proceed to give examples supporting the current points. This is not such a book. Rather, this book defines a practical problem to be solved, and proceeds to examine its solution in detail. That is, instead of deciding on a topic and creating trivial examples to support its teaching, I have defined a hard problem and then let the solution of this problem dictate what topics should be discussed.

Interestingly enough, the above approach is exactly how I would tell someone *not* to learn a subject. I always stress that people should learn broad fundamentals first and subsequently apply these principles to solving problems. However, this is not a book meant to teach the principles of design. Rather, this is a book meant for someone who already knows the fundamentals but wishes to deepen his knowledge of practice. This is a book meant to teach someone the craft of designing and implementing a realistic, albeit small, program from start to finish. This process involves more than knowing elements of design. It involves understanding when and how to use what you know, understanding how to decide between seemingly equivalent approaches, and understanding the long-term implications of various decisions. This book is not comprehensive in its coverage of data structures, algorithms, design patterns, or C++ best practices; volumes of books exist to cover these topics. This is a book about learning how to apply this knowledge to write code that is organized, cohesive, sensible, purposeful, and pragmatic. In other words, this book is about learning to write code that both gets the job done now (development) and allows others to continue to get the job done in the future (maintenance). This, I have termed *practical design*.

© Adam B. Singer 2017
A. B. Singer, *Practical C++ Design*, DOI 10.1007/978-1-4842-3057-2_1

1

In order to explore practical design, we need a case study. Ideally, the case study problem should be

- Large enough to be more than trivial,

- Small enough to be tractable,

- Familiar enough to not require domain specific expertise, and

- Interesting enough to maintain the reader's attention for the duration of the book.

After taking the above criteria into consideration, I decided to select a stack-based, Reverse Polish Notation (RPN) calculator as the case study. The details of the calculator's requirements will be defined below. I believe that the code for a fully functioning calculator is significant enough that the detailed study of its design provides sufficient material to cover a book. Yet, the project is small enough that the book can be a reasonable length. Certainly, specialized domain expertise is not required. I suspect every reader of this book has used a calculator and is well-versed in its basic functionality. Finally, I hope that making the calculator RPN provides a suitable twist to stave off boredom.

1.2 A Few Words About Requirements

No matter how big or how small, all programs have requirements. Requirements are those features, whether explicit or implicit, to which the program must comply. Entire books have been written on gathering and managing software requirements (see, for example, [28] or [21]). Typically, despite one's best efforts, it is practically impossible to gather all of the requirements upfront. Sometimes, the effort required is economically infeasible. Sometimes, domain experts overlook what seem like obvious requirements to them, and they simply neglect to relate all of their requirements to the development team. Sometimes, requirements only become apparent after the program begins to take shape. Sometimes, the customer does not understand his or her own requirements well enough to articulate them to the development team. While some of these dilemmas may be mitigated using agile development methods, the fact remains that many design decisions, some of which may have far reaching implications, must occur before all of the requirements are known.

In this book, you will not study techniques for gathering requirements; rather, the requirements are simply given upfront. Well, most of them will be given upfront. A few of the requirements have been explicitly reserved until a later chapter so that you can study how your design might change to accommodate unknown future expansion. Certainly, one could justly argue that since the author knows how the requirements will change, the initial design will correctly "predict" the unforeseen features. While this criticism is fair, I nonetheless argue that the thought process and discussion behind the design decisions is still relevant. As a software architect, part of your job will be to anticipate future requests. Although any request is possible, incorporating too much flexibility at the outset is not economical. Designing for future expansion must always be considered as a tradeoff between the cost difference for expressly accommodating expandability upfront versus modifying the code later if a change is requested. Where a design should land in the spectrum between simplicity and flexibility must ultimately be measured against the likelihood of a feature request materializing and the feasibility of adding a new feature if its incorporation is not considered at the beginning.

1.3 Reverse Polish Notation

I presume that anyone reading this book is familiar with the typical operation of a calculator. However, unless you grew up using a Hewlett Packard calculator, you may be unfamiliar with how a stack-based RPN calculator functions (see [5] if you are unfamiliar with how a stack works). Simply stated, input numbers are pushed onto a stack, and operations are performed on the numbers already on the stack. A binary operator, such as addition, pops the top two numbers from the stack, adds the two numbers, and then pushes the result onto the stack. A unary operator, such as the sine function, pops one number from the top of the stack, uses this number as the operand, and pushes the result onto the stack. For those familiar with basic compiler lingo, RPN functions as the postfix notation of the operation (see [1] for a detailed discussion of postfix notation). The following list describes my opinion of just a few of the advantages of Reverse Polish Notation over conventional syntax:

- All operations can be expressed parentheses free.

- Multiple inputs and outputs can be visualized simultaneously.

- Large calculations can be trivially decomposed into multiple, simple operations.

- Intermediate results can be trivially retained and reused.

While RPN will likely seem incredibly awkward at first, once you've become accustomed to it, you will curse every calculator that does not employ it when you are tasked with performing anything more complicated than simple arithmetic.

To ensure that the operation of an RPN calculator is clear, let's examine a short example. Suppose we wish to evaluate the following expression:

$$\frac{(4+7)*3+2}{7}$$

On a typical, non-RPN calculator, we would type $((4 + 7) * 3 + 2)/7$ and then press the = key. On an RPN calculator, we would instead type $4\ 7 + 3 * 2 + 7 /$, where there is an enter command following each number in order to push the input onto the stack. Note that for many calculators, to reduce key entry, operations such as + may also function to implicitly enter the previous number on the stack. Figure 1-1 shows the above calculation performed step-by-step on an RPN calculator.

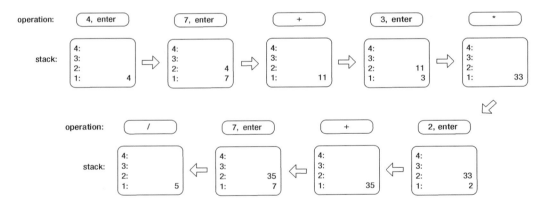

Figure 1-1. *An example calculation performed on an RPN calculator showing intermediate steps. Counterintuitively, the top of the stack is at the bottom of the screen.*

1.4 The Calculator's Requirements

Once you understand the nature of Reverse Polish Notation, the rest of the calculator's functionality should be straightforward from the requirements description. If RPN is still unclear, I recommend spending some time clarifying this concept before proceeding. Given that caveat, the requirements of the calculator are now defined as follows:

- The calculator will be stack-based; the stack size should not be hard coded.

- The calculator will use RPN to perform operations.

- The calculator will exclusively operate on floating point numbers; a technique for entering input numbers (including scientific notation) should be implemented.

- The calculator will have the ability to undo and redo operations; the undo/redo stack sizes should be unlimited.

- The calculator will have the ability to swap the top two elements of the stack.

- The calculator will be able to drop (erase) an element from the top of the stack.

- The calculator will be able to clear the entire stack.

- The calculator will be able to duplicate the element from the top of the stack.

- The calculator will be able to negate the element from the top of the stack.

- The calculator will implement the four basic arithmetic operations: addition, subtraction, multiplication, and division. Division by 0 is impermissible.

- The calculator will implement the three basic trigonometric functions and their inverses: sin, cos, tan, arcsin, arccos, and arctan. Arguments to the trigonometric functions will be given in radians.

- The calculator will implement functions for y^x and $\sqrt[x]{y}$.

- The calculator will implement a runtime plugin structure to expand the operations the calculator can perform.

- The calculator will implement both a command line interface (CLI) and a graphical user interface (GUI).

- The calculator will not support infinity or imaginary numbers.

- The calculator will be fault tolerant (i.e., will not crash if the user gives bad input) but does not need to handle floating point exceptions.

Now that the calculator has requirements, it deserves a name. I chose to call the calculator pdCalc, short for Practical Design Calculator. Please accept my apologies to you for my lack of naming creativity.

The remainder of this book will examine, in detail, the complete design of a calculator that satisfies the above requirements. In addition to describing the decisions made for the final design, I will also discuss alternatives so you can understand why the final decisions were made and what could have been the consequences of different decisions. Note that the final design presented in this book is not the only design that will meet the requirements, and it may not even be the best design that meets the requirements. I encourage the ambitious reader to experiment with alternate designs and extend the calculator to meet his or her own needs and interests.

1.5 The Source Code

Throughout the text of this book, you will be examining a lot of code snippets as we design our calculator. Most of these code snippets are taken directly from pdCalc's GitHub source repository (see Appendix A for instruction for downloading the source code). I will point out any significant differences between the code in the text and the code in the repository. Occasionally, code snippets are comprised of small, contrived examples. These code snippets are not part of pdCalc's source repository. All of the code is made available under the GPL version 3 [7]. I highly encourage you to experiment with the source code and modify it in any way you see fit.

In order to build pdCalc, you will need access to a C++14 compliant compiler and Qt (version 4 or 5). Since the project has an intrinsic Qt dependency (and because I like the Qt Creator IDE), I used Qt project files for the build system and Qt Test for the unit testing framework. I have built and tested the program on both Linux and Windows using gcc/mingw, but the code should also build and execute on additional systems or with additional compilers with little or no source code modification. Some tweaks to the qmake project files will be necessary for porting to a different platform. Because I expect that the audience for this book leans toward developers with years of experience, I suspect that building the code from source will be a fairly trivial task. However, for completeness, I have included build guidance in Appendix A. Additionally, I have included Appendix B to explain the organization of pdCalc's source code, libraries, and executables. Although these two Appendices appear at the end of the book, you may wish to read them first if you intend to build pdCalc and explore its full implementation while reading the text.

CHAPTER 2

Decomposition

Software is complex, one of the most complex endeavors humankind has ever undertaken. When you first read the requirements document for a large-scale programming project, you may feel overwhelmed. That's expected; the task is overwhelming! For this reason, largescale programming projects typically begin with analysis.

The analysis phase of a project consists of the time spent exploring the problem domain in order to understand the problem completely, clarify the requirements, and resolve any ambiguities between the client's and developer's domains. Without fully understanding the problem, you, as the architect or developer, have absolutely no chance of developing a maintainable design. For the case study chosen for this book, however, the domain should be familiar (if not, you may wish to pause here and partake in an analysis exercise). Therefore, we will skip a formal, separate analysis phase. That said, aspects of analysis can never be skipped entirely, and we will explore several analysis techniques during the construction of our design. This intentional coupling of analysis and design emphasizes the interplay between these two activities to demonstrate that even for the simplest of problem domains, producing a good design requires some formal techniques for analyzing the problem.

One of the most important techniques we have as software designers for addressing inherent problem complexity is hierarchical decomposition. Most people tend to decompose a problem in one of two ways: top down or bottom up. A top-down approach starts by looking at the whole picture and subsequently subdividing the problem until reaching the bottom-most level. In software design, the absolute bottom-most level is individual function implementations. However, a top-down design might stop short of implementation and conclude by designing objects and their public interfaces. A bottom-up approach would start at the individual function or object level and combine components repeatedly until eventually encompassing the entire design.

For our case study, both top-down and bottom-up approaches will be used at various stages of the design. I find it practical to begin decomposition in a top-down

© Adam B. Singer 2017
A. B. Singer, *Practical C++ Design*, DOI 10.1007/978-1-4842-3057-2_2

fashion until bulk modules and their interfaces are defined, and then actually design these modules from the bottom up. Before tackling the decomposition of our calculator, let's first begin by examining the elements of a good decomposition.

2.1 The Elements of a Good Decomposition

What makes a decomposition good? Obviously, we could just randomly split functionality into different modules and group completely unconnected components. Using the calculator as an example, we could place arithmetic operators and the GUI in one module while placing trigonometric functions with the stack and error handling in another module. This is a decomposition, just not a very useful one.

In general, a good design will display attributes of modularity, encapsulation, cohesion, and low coupling. Many developers will have already seen many of the principles of a good decomposition in the context of object-oriented design. After all, breaking code into objects is itself a decomposition process. Let's first examine these principles in an abstract context. Subsequently, I'll ground the discussion by applying these principles to pdCalc.

Modularity, or breaking components into independently interacting parts (modules), is important for several reasons. First, it immediately allows one to partition a large, complex problem into multiple, smaller, more tractable components. While trying to implement code for the entire calculator at once would be difficult, implementing an independently functioning stack is quite reasonable. Second, once components are split into distinct modules, unit tests can be defined that validate individual modules instead of requiring the entire program to be completed before testing commences. Third, for large projects, if modules with clear boundaries and interfaces are defined, the development effort can be divided between multiple programmers, preventing them from constantly interfering with each others' progress by needing to modify the same source files.

The remaining principles of good design, encapsulation, cohesion, and low coupling all describe characteristics that modules should possess. Basically, they prevent spaghetti code. Encapsulation, or information hiding, refers to the idea that once a module is defined, its internal implementation (data structures and algorithms) remains hidden from other modules. Correspondingly, a module should not make use of the private implementation of any other module. That is not to say that modules should not interact with each other. Rather, encapsulation insists that modules interact with each other only through clearly defined, and, preferably, limited interfaces. This distinct separation ensures that internal module implementation can be independently modified without concern for breaking external, dependent code, provided the interfaces remain fixed and the contracts guaranteed by the interfaces are met.

Cohesion refers to the idea that the code inside a module should be self-consistent or, as the name implies, cohesive. That is, all of the code within a module should logically fit together. Returning to our example of a poor calculator design, a module mixing arithmetic code with user interface code would lack cohesion. No logical ties bind the two concepts together (other than that they are both components of a calculator). While a small code, like our calculator, would not be completely impenetrable if it lacked cohesion, in general, a large, noncohesive code base is very difficult to understand, maintain, and extend.

Poor cohesion can manifest in one of two ways: either code that should not be together is crammed together or code that should be together is split apart. In the first instance, code functionality is almost impossible to decompose into mentally manageable abstractions because no clear boundaries exist between logical subcomponents. In the latter situation, reading or debugging unfamiliar code (especially for the first time) can be very frustrating because a typical execution path through the code jumps from file to file in a seemingly random fashion. Either manifestation is counterproductive, and I thus prefer cohesive code.

Finally, we'll examine coupling. Coupling represents the interconnectedness of components, be it functional coupling or data coupling. Functional coupling occurs when the logical flow of one module requires calling another module to complete its action. Conversely, data coupling is when data is shared between individual modules either via direct sharing (e.g., one or more modules point to some set of shared data) or via passing of data (e.g., one module returning a pointer to an internal data structure to another module). To argue for zero coupling is clearly absurd because this state would imply that no module could communicate in any way with any other module. However, in good design, we do strive for low coupling. How low should low be? The glib answer is as low as possible while still maintaining the ability to function as necessary. The reality is that minimizing coupling without detrimentally complicating code is a skill acquired with experience. As with encapsulation, low coupling is enabled by ensuring that modules communicate with each other only through cleanly defined, limited interfaces. Code that is highly coupled is difficult to maintain because small changes in one module's design may lead to many unforeseen, cascading changes through seemingly unrelated modules. Note that whereas encapsulation protects module A from internal implementation changes to module B, low coupling protects module A from changes to the interface of module B.

2.2 Selecting an Architecture

Although it is now tempting to follow the above guidelines and simply start decomposing our calculator into what seem like sensible constituent components, it's best to first see if someone else has already solved our problem. Because similar problems tend to arise frequently in programming, software architects have created a catalog of templates for solving these problems; these archetypes are called patterns. Patterns typically come in multiple varieties. Two categories of patterns that will be examined in this book are design patterns [6] and architectural patterns.

Design patterns are conceptual templates used to solve similar problems that arise during software design; they are typically applied to local decisions. We will encounter design patterns repeatedly throughout this book during the detailed design of our calculator. Our first top level of decomposition, however, requires a pattern of global scope that will define the overarching design strategy, or, software architecture. Such patterns are naturally referred to as architectural patterns.

Architectural patterns are conceptually similar to design patterns; the two differ primarily in their domains of applicability. Whereas design patterns are typically applied to particular classes or sets of related classes, architectural patterns typically outline the design for an entire software system. Note that I refer to a software system rather than a program because architectural patterns can extend beyond simple program boundaries to include interfaces to hardware or the coupling of multiple independent programs. Two architectural patterns of particular interest for our case study are the multi-tiered architecture and the model-view-controller (MVC) architecture. We'll examine each of these two patterns in the abstract before applying them to pdCalc. The successful application of an architectural pattern to our case study will represent the first level of decomposition for the calculator.

2.2.1 Multi-Tiered Architecture

In a multi-tiered, or n-tiered, architecture, components are arranged sequentially in tiers. Communication is bidirectional via adjacent tiers, but nonadjacent tiers are not permitted to communicate directly. An n-tiered architecture is depicted in Figure 2-1.

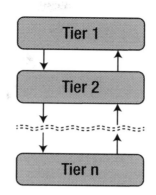

Figure 2-1. *A multi-tiered architecture with arrows indicating communication*

The most common form of the multi-tiered architecture is the three-tiered architecture. The first tier is the presentation layer, which consists of all of the user interface code. The second tier is the logic layer, which captures the so-called "business logic" of the application. The third tier is the data layer, which, as the name implies, encapsulates the data for the system. Very often, the three-tiered architecture is applied as an enterprise-level platform, where each tier could represent not only a different local process, but possibly a different process operating on a different machine. In such a system, the presentation layer would be the client interface, whether it be a traditional desktop application or a browser-based interface. The logic layer of the program could run on either the client or server side of the application or, possibly, on both. Finally, the data layer would be represented by a database that could be running locally or remotely. However, as you shall see with pdCalc, the three-tiered architecture can also be applied to a single desktop application.

Let's examine how the three-tiered architecture obeys our general decomposition principles. First and foremost, at the highest level of decomposition, the architecture is modular. At least three modules, one for each tier, exist. However, the three-tiered architecture does not preclude multiple modules from existing at each tier. If the system were large enough, each of the primary modules would warrant subdivision. Second, this architecture encourages encapsulation, at least between tiers. While one could foolishly design a three-tiered architecture where adjacent tiers accessed private methods of neighboring tiers, such a design would be counterintuitive and very brittle. That said, in applications where the tiers coexist in the same process space, it is very easy to intertwine the layers, and care must be taken to ensure this situation does not arise. This separation is achieved by clearly delineating each layer via definitive interfaces. Third, the three-tiered architecture is cohesive. Each tier of the architecture has a distinct task, which is not commingled with the tasks of the other tiers. Finally, the three-tiered architecture truly shines as an example of limited coupling. By separating each of the tiers via clearly defined interfaces, each tier can change independently of the others. This feature is particularly important for applications that must execute on multiple platforms (only the presentation layer changes platform to platform) or applications that undergo unforeseen replacement of a given tier during their lifetimes (e.g., the database must be changed due to a scalability problem).

2.2.2 Model-View-Controller (MVC) Architecture

In the Model-View-Controller architecture, components are decomposed into three distinct elements aptly named the model, the view, and the controller. The model abstracts the domain data, the view abstracts the user interface, and the controller manages the interaction between the model and the view. Often, the MVC pattern is applied locally to individual GUI widgets at the framework level where the design goal is to separate the data from the user interface in situations where multiple distinct views may be associated with the same data. For example, consider a scheduling application with the requirement that the application must be able to store dates and times for appointments, but the user may view these appointments in a calendar that can be viewed by day, week, or month. Applying MVC, the appointment data is abstracted by a model module (likely a class in an object-oriented framework), and each calendar style is abstracted by a distinct view (likely three separate classes). A controller is introduced to handle user events generated by the views and to manipulate the data in the model.

At first glance, MVC seems no different than the three-tiered architecture with the model replacing the data layer, the view replacing the presentation layer, and the controller replacing the business logic layer. The two architectural patterns are different, however, in their interaction pattern. In the three-tiered architecture, the communication between layers is rigidly linear. That is, the presentation and data layers talk only bidirectionally to the logic layer, never to each other. In MVC, the communication is triangular. While different MVC implementations differ in their exact communication patterns, a typical implementation is depicted in Figure 2-2. In this figure, the view can both generate events to be handled by the controller and get the data to be displayed directly from the model. The controller handles events from the view, but it can also directly manipulate either the model or the controller. Finally, the model can be acted upon directly by either the view or the controller, but it can also generate events to be handled by the view. A typical such event would be a state change event that would cause the view to update its presentation to the user.

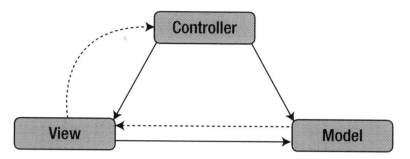

Figure 2-2. *An MVC architecture with arrows indicating communication. Solid lines indicate direct communication. Dashed lines indicate indirect communication (e.g., via eventing) [30].*

As we did with the three-tiered architecture, let's now examine how MVC obeys the general decomposition principles. First, an MVC architecture will usually be broken into at least three modules: model, view, and controller. However, as with the three-tiered architecture, a larger system will admit more modules because each of the model, view, and controller will require subdivision. Second, this architecture also encourages encapsulation. The model, view, and controller should only interact with each other through clearly defined interfaces, where events and event handling are defined as part of an interface. Third, the MVC architecture is cohesive. Each component has a distinct, well-defined task. Finally, we ask if the MVC architecture is loosely coupled. By inspection, this architectural pattern is more tightly coupled than the three-tiered architecture because the presentation layer and the data layer are permitted to have direct dependencies. In practice, these dependencies are often limited either through loosely coupled event handling or via polymorphism with abstract bases classes. Typically, however, this added coupling does usually relegate the MVC pattern to applications in one memory space. This limitation directly contrasts with the flexibility of the three-tiered architecture, which may span applications over multiple memory spaces.

2.2.3 Architectural Patterns Applied to the Calculator

Let's now return to our case study and apply the two architectural patterns discussed above to pdCalc. Ultimately we'll select one as the architecture for our application. As previously described, a three-tiered architecture consists of a presentation layer, a logic layer, and a data layer. For the calculator, these tiers are clearly identified as entering commands and viewing results (via either a graphical or command line user interface), the execution of the commands, and the stack, respectively. For the MVC architecture, we have the stack as the model, the user interface as the view, and the command dispatcher as the controller. Both calculator architectures are depicted in Figure 2-3. Note that in both the three-tiered and MVC architectures, the input aspects of the presentation layer or view are responsible only for accepting the commands, not interpreting or executing them. Enforcing this distinction alleviates a common problem developers create for themselves: the mixing of the presentation layer with the logic layer.

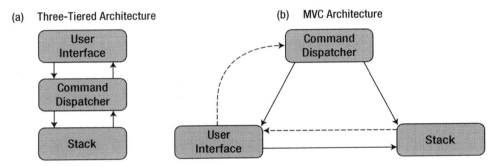

Figure 2-3. *Calculator architecture options*

2.2.4 Choosing the Calculator's Architecture

From Figure 2-3, one quickly identifies that the two architectures partition the calculator into identical modules. In fact, at the architectural level, these two competing architectures differ only in their coupling. Therefore, in selecting between these two architectures, we only need to consider the design tradeoffs between their two communication patterns.

Obviously, the main difference between the three-tiered architecture and the MVC architecture is the communication pattern between the user interface (UI) and the stack. In the three-tiered architecture, the UI and stack are only allowed to communicate indirectly through the command dispatcher. The biggest benefit of this separation is a decrease in coupling in the system. The UI and the stack need to know nothing about the interface of the other. The disadvantage, of course, is that if the program requires significant direct UI and stack communication, the command dispatcher will be required to broker this communication, which decreases the cohesion of the command dispatcher module. The MVC architecture has the exact opposite tradeoff. That is, at the

16

expense of additional coupling, the UI can directly exchange messages with the stack, avoiding the awkwardness of the command dispatcher performing added functionality unrelated to its primary purpose. Therefore, the architecture decision reduces to examining whether or not the UI frequently needs a direct connection to the stack.

In an RPN calculator, the stack acts as the repository for both the input and output for the program. Frequently, the user will wish to see both the input and output exactly as it appears on the stack. This situation favors the MVC architecture with its direct interaction between the view and the data. That is, the calculator's view does not require the command dispatcher to translate the communication between the data and the user because no transformation of the data is required. Therefore, I selected the model-view-controller as the architecture for pdCalc. The advantages of the MVC architecture over the three-tiered architecture are, admittedly, small for our case study. Had I instead chosen to use the three-tiered architecture, pdCalc still would have had a perfectly valid design.

2.3 Interfaces

Although it might be tempting to declare the first level of decomposition complete with the selection of the MVC architecture, we cannot yet declare victory. While we have defined our three highest level modules, we must also define their public interfaces. However, without utilizing some formal method for capturing all the data flows in our problem, we are very likely to miss key necessary elements of our interface. We therefore turn to an object-oriented analysis technique, the use case.

A use case is an analysis technique that generates a description of a specific action a user has with a system. Essentially, a use case defines a workflow. Importantly, a use case does not specify an implementation. The customer should be consulted during use case generation, particularly in instances where a use case uncovers an ambiguity in the requirements. Details concerning use cases and use case diagrams can be found in Booch *et al* [4].

For the purpose of designing interfaces for pdCalc's high-level modules, we will first define the use cases for an end user interacting with the calculator. Each use case should define a single workflow, and we should provide enough use cases to satisfy all of the technical requirements for the calculator. These use cases can then be studied to discover the minimal interactions required between the modules. These communication patterns will define the modules' public interfaces. An added benefit of this use case analysis is that if our existing modules are insufficient to implement all of the workflows, we will have uncovered the need for additional modules in our top-level design.

2.3.1 Calculator Use Cases

Let's create the use cases for our requirements. For consistency, use cases are created in the order in which they appear in the requirements.

2.3.1.1 Use Case: User Enters a Floating Point Number onto the Stack

Scenario: The user enters a floating point number onto the stack. After entry, the user can see the number on the stack.

Exception: The user enters an invalid floating point number. An error condition is displayed.

2.3.1.2 Use Case: User Undoes Last Operation

Scenario: The user enters the command to undo the last operation. The system undoes the last operation and displays the previous stack.

Exception: There is no command to undo. An error condition is displayed.

2.3.1.3 Use Case: User Redoes Last Operation

Scenario: The user enters the command to redo the last operation. The system redoes the last operation and displays the new stack.

Exception: There is no command to redo. An error condition is displayed.

2.3.1.4 Use Case: User Swaps Top Stack Elements

Scenario: The user enters the command to swap the top two elements on the stack. The system swaps the top two elements on the stack and displays the new stack.

Exception: The stack does not have at least two numbers. An error condition is displayed.

2.3.1.5 Use Case: User Drops the Top Stack Element

Scenario: The user enters the command to drop the top element from the stack. The system drops the top element from the stack and displays the new stack.

Exception: The stack is empty. An error condition is displayed.

2.3.1.6 Use Case: User Clears the Stack

Scenario: The user enters the command to clear the stack. The system clears the stack and displays the empty stack.

Exception: None. Let clear succeed even for an empty stack (by doing nothing).

2.3.1.7 Use Case: User Duplicates the Top Stack Element

Scenario: The user enters the command to duplicate the top element on the stack. The system duplicates the top element on the stack and displays the new stack.

Exception: The stack is empty. An error condition is displayed.

2.3.1.8 Use Case: User Negates the Top Stack Element

Scenario: The user enters the command to negate the top element on the stack. The system negates the top element on the stack and displays the new stack.

Exception: The stack is empty. An error condition is displayed.

2.3.1.9 Use Case: User Performs an Arithmetic Operation

Scenario: The user enters the command to add, subtract, multiply, or divide. The system performs the operation and displays the new stack.

Exception: The stack size is insufficient to support the operation. An error condition is displayed.

Exception: Division by zero is detected. An error condition is displayed.

19

2.3.1.10 Use Case: User Performs a Trigonometric Operation

Scenario: The user enters the command for sin, cos, tan, arcsin, arccos, or arctan. The system performs the operation and displays the new stack.

Exception: The stack size is insufficient to support the operation. An error condition is displayed.

Exception: The input for the operation is invalid (e.g., arctan(-50) produces an imaginary result). An error condition is displayed.

2.3.1.11 Use Case: User Performs y^x

Scenario: The user enters the command for y^x. The system performs the operation and displays the new stack.

Exception: The stack size is insufficient to support the operation. An error condition is displayed.

Exception: The input for the operation is invalid (e.g., $-1^{0.5}$ produces an imaginary result). An error condition is displayed.

2.3.1.12 Use Case: User Performs $\sqrt[x]{y}$

Scenario: The user enters the command for $\sqrt[x]{y}$. The system performs the operation and displays the new stack.

Exception: The stack size is insufficient to support the operation. An error condition is displayed.

Exception: The input for the operation is invalid (e.g., $\sqrt[4]{-1}$ produces an imaginary result). An error condition is displayed.

2.3.1.13 Use Case: User Loads a Plugin

Scenario: The user places a plugin into the plugins directory. The system loads the plugin on startup, making the plugin functionality available.

Exception: The plugin cannot be loaded. An error condition is displayed.

2.3.2 Analysis of Use Cases

We will now analyze the use cases for the purpose of developing C++ interfaces for pdCalc's modules. Keep in mind that the C++ language does not formally define a module concept. Therefore, think of an interface conceptually as the publicly facing function signatures to a collection of classes and functions grouped logically to define a module. For the sake of brevity, the std namespace prefix is omitted in the text.

Let's examine the use cases in order. As the public interface is developed, it will be entered into Table 2-2. The exception will be for the first use case, whose interface will be described in Table 2-1. By using a separate table for the first use case, we'll be able to preserve the errors we'll make on the first pass for comparison to our final product. By the end of this section, the entire public interface for all of the modules will have been developed and cataloged.

We begin with the first use case: entering a floating point number. The implementation of the user interface will take care of getting the number from the user into the calculator. Here, we are concerned with the interface required to get the number from the UI onto the stack.

Regardless of the path the number takes from the UI to the stack, we must eventually have a function call for pushing numbers onto the stack. Therefore, the first part of our interface is simply a function on the stack module, push(), for pushing a double precision number onto the stack. We enter this function into Table 2-1. Note that the table contains the complete function signature, while the return type and argument types are omitted in the text.

Now, we must explore our options for getting the number from the user interface module to the stack module. From Figure 2-3b, we see that the UI has a direct link to the stack. Therefore, the simplest option would be to push the floating point number onto the stack directly from the UI using the push() function we just defined. Is this a good idea?

By definition, the command dispatcher module, or the controller, exists to process commands the user enters. Should entering a number be treated differently than, for example, the addition command? Having the UI bypass the command dispatcher and directly enter a number onto the stack module violates *the principle of least surprise* (also referred to as *the principle of least astonishment*). Essentially, this principle states that when a designer is presented with multiple valid design options, the correct choice is the one that conforms to the user's intuition. In the context of interface design, the user is another programmer or designer. Here, any programmer working on our system would expect all commands to be handled identically, so a good design will obey this principle.

To avoid violating the principle of least surprise, we must build an interface that routes a newly entered number from the UI through the command dispatcher. We again refer to Figure 2-3b. Unfortunately, the UI does not have a direct connection to the command dispatcher, making direct communication impossible. It does, however, have an indirect pathway. Thus, our only option is for the UI to raise an event (you'll study events in detail in Chapter 3). Specifically, the UI must raise an event indicating that a number has been entered, and the command dispatcher must be able to receive this event (eventually, via a function call in its public interface). Let's add two more functions to Table 2-1, one for the numberEntered() event raised by the UI and one for the numberEntered() event handling function in the command dispatcher.

Once the number has been accepted, the UI must display the revised stack. This is accomplished by the stack signaling that it has changed, and the view requesting n elements from the stack and displaying them to the user. We must use this pathway because the stack only has an indirect communication channel to the UI. We add three more functions to Table 2-1: a stackChanged() event on the stack module, a stackChanged() event handler on the UI, and a getElements() function on the stack module (see the "Modern C++ Design Note" sidebar on move semantics to see options for the getElements() function signature). Unlike the entering of the number itself, it is reasonable to have the UI directly call the stack's function for getting elements in response to the stackChanged() event. This is, in fact, precisely how we want a view to interact with its data in the MVC pattern.

Of course, the aforementioned workflow assumes the user entered a valid number. For completeness, however, the use case also specifies that error checking must be performed on number entry. Therefore, the command dispatcher should actually check the validity of the number before pushing it onto the stack, and it should signal the user interface if an error has occurred. The UI should correspondingly be able to handle error events. That's two more functions for Table 2-1: an error() event on the command dispatcher, and a function, displayError(), on the UI, for handling the error event. Note that we could have selected an alternative error handling design by leaving the UI to perform its own error checking and only raise a number entered event for valid numbers. However, for improved cohesion, I prefer placing the "business logic" of error checking in the controller rather than in the interface.

Phew! That completes our analysis of the first use case. In case you got lost, remember that all of the functions and events just described are summarized in Table 2-1. Now just 12 more exciting use cases to go to complete our interface analysis! Don't worry, the drudgery will end shortly. We will soon derive a design that can consolidate almost all of the use cases into a unified interface.

Table 2-1. *Public Interfaces Derived from the Analysis of the Use Case for Entering a Floating Point Number onto the Stack*

	Functions	Events
User Interface	`void displayError(const string&)` `void stackChanged()`	`numberEntered(double)`
Command Dispatcher	`void numberEntered(double)`	`error(string)`
Stack	`void push(double)` `void getElements(n, vector<double>&)`	`stackChanged()`

Before proceeding immediately to the next use case, let's pause for a moment and discuss two decisions we just implicitly made about error handling. First, the user interface handles errors by catching events rather than by catching exceptions. Because the user interface cannot directly send messages to the command dispatcher, the UI can never wrap a call to the command dispatcher in a try block. This communication pattern immediately eliminates using C++ exceptions for inter-module error handling (note that it does not preclude using exceptions internally within a single module). In this case, since number entry errors are trapped in the command dispatcher, we could have notified the UI directly using a callback. However, this convention is not sufficiently general, for it would break down for errors detected in the stack since the stack has no direct communication with the UI. Second, we have decided that all errors, regardless of cause, will be handled by passing a string to the UI describing the error rather than making a class hierarchy of error types. This decision is justified because the UI never tries to differentiate between errors. Instead, the UI simply serves as a conduit to display error messages verbatim from other modules.

MODERN C++ DESIGN NOTE: MOVE SEMANTICS

In Table 2-1, the stack has the function `void getElements(n, vector<double>&)`, which enables callers to fill a `vector` with the top *n* elements from the stack. However, the interface of the function tells us nothing about how the elements are actually added to the vector. Are they added at the front? Are they added at the back? Is it presumed that the vector is already sized correctly and the new elements are entered using `operator[]`? Are old elements erased from the vector before the new ones are added? Hopefully, this ambiguity will be resolved by developer documentation (good luck with that one). In the absence of further information, one would likely conclude that new elements were simply pushed to the back of the `vector`.

Beginning with C++11, however, the above interface ambiguity can be resolved semantically by the language itself. Rvalue references and move semantics allow us to make this interface decision very explicit. We can now efficiently (that is, without copying the `vector` or relying on the compiler to implement the return value optimization) implement the function `vector<double> getElements(n)`. A temporary `vector` is created internally in the function, and its contents are moved into the caller on function return. The interface contract is now explicit: A new `vector` of size *n* will be returned and filled with the top *n* elements on the stack.

To not bloat the interface in the text, both variants of the function do not explicitly appear in the tables defining the interface. However, both variants do appear in the source code. This convention will often be used in this book. Where multiple helper calls performing the same operation are useful in the implementation, both appear there, but only one variant appears in the text. This omission is acceptable for the illustrative purposes of this book, but this omission would not be acceptable for a detailed design specification for a real project.

The next two use cases, undo and redo of operations, are sufficiently similar that we can analyze them simultaneously. First, we must add two new events to the user interface: one for undo and one for redo. Correspondingly, we must add two event handling functions in the command dispatcher for undo and redo, respectively. Before simply adding these functions to Table 2-2, let's take a step back and see if we can simplify.

Table 2-2. *Public Interfaces for the Entire First Level Decomposition*

	Functions	Events
User Interface	`void postMessage(const string&)` `void stackChanged()`	`commandEntered(string)`
Command Dispatcher	`void commandEntered(const string&)`	`error(string)`

Stack	`void push(double)`
	`void getElements(n, vector<double>&)`
	`double pop()`
	`void swapTop()`
		`stackChanged()`
		`error(string)`

At this point, you should begin to see a pattern emerging from the user interface events being added to the table. Each use case adds a new event of the form `commandEntered()`, where command has thus far been replaced by number, undo, or redo. In subsequent use cases, command might be replaced with operations such as swap, add, sin, exp, etc. Rather than continue to bloat the interface by giving each command a new event in the UI and a corresponding event handler in the command dispatcher, we instead replace this family of commands with the rather generic sounding UI event `commandEntered()` and the partner event handler `commandEntered()` in the command dispatcher. The single argument for this event/handler pair is a `string`, which encodes the given command. In the case of a number entered, the argument is the ASCII representation of the number.

Combining all of the UI command events into one event with a string argument instead of issuing each command as an individual event serves several design purposes. First, and most immediately evident, this choice declutters the interface. Rather than needing individual pairs of functions in the UI and the command dispatcher for each individual command, we now need only one pair of functions for handling events from all commands. This includes the known commands from the requirements and any unknown commands that might derive from future extensions. However, more importantly, this design promotes cohesion because now the UI does not need to understand anything about any of the events it triggers. Instead, the deciphering of the command events is placed in the command dispatcher, where this logic naturally belongs. Creating one `commandEntered()` event for commands even has direct implications on the implementations of commands, graphical user interface buttons, and plugins. I will reserve those discussions for when you encounter those topics in Chapters 4, 6, and 7.

We now return to our analysis of the undo and redo use cases. As described above, we will forgo adding new command events in Table 2-2 for each new command we encounter. Instead, we add the `commandEntered()` event to the UI and the `commandEntered()` event handler to the command dispatcher. This event/handler pair will suffice for all commands in all use cases. The stack, however, does not yet possess all of the necessary functionality to implement every command. For example, in order to undo pushes onto the stack, we will need to be able to pop numbers from the stack. Let's add a `pop()` function to the stack in Table 2-2. Finally, we note that a stack error could occur if we attempted to pop an empty stack. We, therefore, add a generic `error()` event to the stack to mirror the error event on the command dispatcher.

We move to our next use case, swapping the top of the stack. Obviously, this command will reuse the `commandEntered()` and `error()` patterns from the previous use cases, so we only need to determine if a new function needs to be added to the stack's interface. Obviously, swapping the top two elements of the stack could either be implemented via a `swapTop()` function on the stack or via the existing `push()` and `pop()` functions. Somewhat arbitrarily, I chose to implement a separate `swapTop()` function, so I added it to Table 2-2. This decision was probably subconsciously rooted in my natural design tendency to maximize efficiency (the majority of my professional projects are high-performance numerical simulations) at the expense of reuse. In hindsight, that might not be the better design decision, but this example demonstrates that sometimes design decisions are based on nothing more than the instincts of a designer as colored by his or her individual experiences.

At this point, a quick scan of the remaining use cases shows that, other than loading a plugin, the existing module interfaces defined by Table 2-2 are sufficient to handle all user interactions with the calculator. Each new command only adds new functionality internal to the command dispatcher, the logic of which will be detailed in Chapter 4. Therefore, the only remaining use case to examine concerns loading plugins for pdCalc. The loading of plugins, while complex, is minimally invasive to the other modules in the calculator. Other than command and user interface injection (you'll encounter these topics in Chapter 7), the plugin loader is a standalone component. We therefore defer the design of its interface (and the necessary corresponding changes to the other interfaces) until we are ready to implement plugins.

Deferring the design of a significant portion of the top-level interface is a somewhat risky proposition, and one to which design purists might object. Pragmatically, however, I have found that when enough of the major elements have been designed, you need to start coding. The design will change as the implementation progresses anyway, so seeking perfection by overworking the initial design is mostly futile. Of course, neither should one completely abandon all upfront design in an agile frenzy!

The above said, a few caveats exist for adopting a strategy of delaying the design of a major component. First, if the delayed portion of the design will materially impact the architecture, the delay may potentially cause significant rework later. Second, delaying parts of the design prolongs the stabilization of the interfaces. Such delays may or may not be problematic on large teams working independently on connected components. Knowing what can and what cannot be deferred comes only with experience. If you are uncertain as to whether the design of a component can be safely deferred or not, you are much better off erring on the side of caution and performing a little extra design and analysis work upfront to minimize the impact to the overall architecture. Poor designs impacting the architecture of a program will impact development for the duration of a project. They cause much more significant rework than poor implementations, and in the worst case scenario, poor design decisions become economically infeasible to fix. Sometimes, they can only be fixed in a major rewrite, which may never occur.

Before completing the analysis of the use cases, let's compare the interface developed in Table 2-1 for the first use case with the interface developed in Table 2-2 encompassing all of the use cases. Surprisingly, Table 2-2 is only marginally longer than Table 2-1. This is a testament to the design decision to abstract commanding into one generic function instead of individual functions for each command. Simplifying the communication patterns between modules is one of the many time-saving advantages of designing code instead of just hacking away. The only other differences between the first interface and the complete interface are the addition of a few stack functions and the modification of a few function names (e.g., renaming the `displayError()` function to `postMessage()` to increase the generality of the operation).

2.3.3 A Quick Note on Actual Implementation

For the purposes of this text, the interfaces developed, as exemplified by Table 2-2, represent idealizations of the actual interfaces deployed in the code. The actual code may differ somewhat in the syntax, but the semantic intent of the interface will always be preserved. For example, in Table 2-2, we have defined the interface to get n elements as `void getElements(n, vector<double>&)`, which is a perfectly serviceable interface. However, using new features of modern C++ (see the sidebar on move semantics), the implementation makes use of rvalue references and move construction by also providing `vector<double> getElements(n)` as a logically equivalent, overloaded interface.

Defining good C++ interfaces is a highly nontrivial task; I know of at least one excellent book dedicated entirely to this subject [20]. Here in this book, I only provide a sufficient level of detail about the interfaces needed to clearly explain the design. The available source code demonstrates the intricacies necessary for developing efficient C++ interfaces. In a very small project, allowing developers some latitude in adapting the interface can usually be tolerated and is often beneficial as it allows implementation details to be delayed until they can be practically determined. However, in a large-scale development, in order to prevent absolute chaos between independent teams, it is wise to finalize the interfaces as soon as practical before implementation begins.

2.4 Assessment of Our Current Design

Before beginning the detailed design of our three major components, let's stop and assess our current design against the criteria we identified in the beginning of this chapter. First, having defined three distinct modules, our design is clearly modular. Second, each module acts as a cohesive unit, with each module dedicated to one specific task. User interface code belongs to one module, operational logic belongs to another, and data management belongs to yet another, separate module. Additionally, each module encapsulates all its own features. Finally, the modules are loosely coupled, and where coupling is necessary, it is through a set of clearly defined, concise, public interfaces. Not only does our top-level architecture meet our good design criteria, but it also conforms to a well-known and well-studied architectural design pattern that has been successfully used for decades. At this point, we have reaffirmed the quality of our design and should feel very comfortable proceeding to the next step in our decomposition, the design of the individual components.

2.5 Next Steps

Where do we go from here? We have now established the overall architecture of our calculator, but how do we tackle the task of choosing which component to design and implement first? In a corporate setting, with a large-scale project, the likelihood would be that many modules would be designed and coded simultaneously. After all, isn't that one of the primary reasons for creating distinct modules separated cleanly by interfaces? Of course, for our project, the modules will be handled sequentially, with some level of iteration to make *a posteriori* improvements. Therefore, we must choose one module to design and build first.

Of the three modules, the most logical starting point is the module with the fewest dependencies on the other modules. From Figure 2-3, we see that, in fact, the stack is the only module that has no dependencies on the interfaces of the other modules. The only outward pointing arrow from the stack is dashed, which means that the communication is indirect via eventing. Although the figure makes this decision pictorially obvious, one would likely reach the same conclusion without the architecture diagram. The stack is essentially an independent data structure that is easy to implement and test in isolation. Once the stack has been completed and tested, it can be integrated into the design and testing of the remaining modules. We therefore begin our next level of decomposition by designing and implementing the stack.

CHAPTER 3

The Stack

The stack is the first module of the calculator that we will design and implement. Although I defined the module's public interface in Chapter 2, I said very little about its implementation. In C++, the module is not a defined language concept. Therefore, we are essentially left to decompose the stack into a logical grouping of functions and classes and call this our module. Hence, this is where we begin. If you're a little rusty on the mechanics of the stack data structure, now would be a great time to consult your favorite data structures and algorithms book. My personal favorite is the one by Cormen *et al* [5].

3.1 Decomposition of the Stack Module

The first question to ask in decomposing the stack module is, "Into how many pieces should the stack be divided?" In object-oriented parlance, we ask, "How many objects do we need, and what are they?" In this case, the answer is fairly obvious: one, the stack itself. Essentially, the entire stack module is the manifestation of a single data structure, which can easily be encapsulated by a single class. The public interface for this class was already described in Chapter 2.

The second question one might ask is, "Do I even need to build a class at all or can I just use the Standard Template Library (STL) stack class directly?" This is actually a very good question. All design books preach that you should never write your own data structure when you can use one from a library, especially when the data structure can be found in the STL, which is guaranteed to be a part of a standards-conforming C++ distribution. Indeed, this is sage advice, and we should not rewrite the mechanics of the stack data structure. However, neither should we use the STL stack directly as the stack in our system. Instead, we will write our own stack class that encapsulates an STL container as a private member.

© Adam B. Singer 2017
A. B. Singer, *Practical C++ Design*, DOI 10.1007/978-1-4842-3057-2_3

Suppose we chose to implement our stack module using an STL `stack`. Several reasons exist for preferring encapsulating an STL container (or a data structure from any vendor) versus direct utilization. First, by wrapping the STL `stack`, we put in an interface guard for the rest of the calculator. That is, we are insulating the other calculator modules from potential changes to the underlying stack implementation by separating the stack's interface from its implementation (remember encapsulation?). This precaution can be particularly important when using vendor software because this design decision localizes changes to the wrapper's implementation rather than to the stack module's interface. In the event that the vendor modifies its product's interface (vendors are sneaky like that) or you decide to exchange one vendor's product for another's, these changes will only locally impact your stack module's implementation and not affect the stack module's callers. Even when the underlying implementation is standardized, such as the ISO standardized STL `stack`, the interface guard enables you to change the underlying implementation without affecting dependent modules. For example, what if you changed your mind and later decided to reimplement your stack module using, for example, a `vector` instead of a `stack`.

The second reason to wrap an STL container instead of using it directly is that this decision allows us to limit the interface to exactly match our requirements. In Chapter 2, we expended a significant amount of effort designing a limited, minimal interface for the stack module capable of satisfying all of pdCalc's use cases. Often, an underlying implementation may provide more functionality than you actually wish to expose. If we were to choose the STL `stack` directly as our stack module, this problem would not be severe because the STL `stack`'s interface is, not surprisingly, very similar to the interface we have defined for the calculator's stack. However, suppose we selected Acme Corporation's `RichStack` class with its 67 public member functions to be used unwrapped as our stack module. A junior developer who neglected to read the design spec may unknowingly violate some implicit design contract of our stack module by calling a `RichStack` function that should not have been publicly exposed in the application's context. While such abuse may be inconsistent with the module's documented interface, one should never rely on other developers actually reading or obeying the documentation (sad, but true). If you can forcibly prevent a misuse from occurring via a language construct that the compiler can enforce (e.g., access limitation), do so.

The third reason to wrap an STL container is to expand or modify the functionality of an underlying data structure. For example, for pdCalc, we need to add two functions (`getElements()` and `swapTop()`) not present on the STL `stack` class and transform the error handling from standard exceptions to our custom error events. Thus, the wrapper class enables us to modify the STL's standard container interface so that we can conform to our own internally designed interface rather than being bound by the functionality provided to us by the STL.

As one might expect, the encapsulation scenario described above occurs quite frequently and has therefore been codified as a design pattern, the adapter (wrapper) pattern [6]. As described by Gamma *et al*, the adapter pattern is used to convert the interface of a class into another interface that clients expect. Often, the adapter provides some form of transformational capabilities, thereby also serving as a broker between otherwise incompatible classes.

In the original description of the pattern, the adapter is abstracted to allow a single message to wrap multiple distinct adaptees via polymorphism using an adapter class hierarchy. For the needs of pdCalc's stack module, one simple concrete adapter class suffices.

Remember, design patterns exist to assist in design and communication. Try not to get caught in the trap of implementing patterns exactly as they are prescribed in texts. Use the literature as a guide to help clarify your design, but, ultimately, prefer to implement the simplest solution that fits your application rather than the solution that most closely resembles the academic ideal.

A final question we should ask is, "Should my stack be generic (i.e., templated)?" The answer here is a resounding maybe. In theory, designing an abstract data structure to encapsulate any data type is sound practice. If the end goal of the data structure is to appear in a library or to be shared by multiple projects, the data structure should be generalized. However, in the context of a single project, I do not recommend making data structures generic, at least not at first. Generic code is harder to write, more difficult to maintain, and more difficult to test. Unless multiple type usage scenarios exist upfront, I find writing generic code to not be worth the bother. I've finished too many projects where I spent extra time designing, implementing, and testing a generic data structure only to use it for one type. Realistically, if you have a non-generic data structure and suddenly discover you do need to use it for a different type, the refactoring necessary is not usually more difficult than had the class been designed to be generic from the outset. Furthermore, the existing tests will be easily adapted to the generic interface, providing a baseline for correctness established by a single type. We will, therefore, design our stack to be `double` specific.

3.2 The Stack Class

Now that we have established that our module will consist of one class, an adapter for an underlying stack data structure, let's design it. One of the first questions to be asked when designing a class is, "How will this class be used?" For example, are you designing an abstract base class to be inherited and thus be used polymorphically? Are you designing a class primarily as a plain old data (POD) repository? Will many different instances of this class exist at any given time? What is the lifetime of any given instance? Who will typically own instances of this class? Will instances be shared? Will this class be used concurrently? By asking these and other similar questions, we uncover the following list of functional requirements for our stack:

- Only one stack should exist in the system.

- The stack's lifetime is the lifetime of the application.

- Both the UI and the command dispatcher need to access the stack; neither should own the stack.

- Stack access is not concurrent.

Anytime the first three criteria above are met, the class is an excellent candidate for the singleton pattern [6].

3.2.1 The Singleton Pattern

The singleton pattern is used to create a class where only one instance should ever exist in the system. The singleton class is not owned by any of its consumers, but neither is the single instance of the class a global variable (however, some argue that the singleton pattern is global data in disguise). In order to not rely on the honor system, language mechanics are employed to ensure only a single instantiation can ever exist.

Additionally, in the singleton pattern, the lifetime of the instance is often from the time of first instantiation until program termination. Depending on the implementation, singletons can be created either to be thread safe or suitable for single threaded applications only. An excellent discussion concerning different C++ singleton implementations can be found in Alexandrescu [2]. For our calculator, we'll use the simplest implementation that satisfies our goals.

In order to derive a simple singleton implementation, we refer to our knowledge of the C++ language. First, as previously discussed, no other class owns a singleton instance nor is the singleton's instance a global object. This implies that the singleton class needs to own its single instance, and the ownership access should be private. In order to prevent other classes from instantiating our singleton, we will also need to make its constructors and assignment operators either private or deleted. Second, knowing that only one instance of the singleton should exist in the system immediately implies that our class should hold its instance statically. Finally, other classes will need access to this single instance, which we can provide via a public static function. Combining the above points, we construct the shell for the singleton class shown in Listing 3-1.

Listing 3-1. The Shell for the Singleton Class

```
class Singleton
{
public:
  static Singleton& Instance
  {
    static Singleton instance;
    return instance;
  }

  void foo(){ /* does foo things */ }

private:
  // prevent public instantiation, copying, assignment, movement,
  // & destruction
  Singleton() { /* constructor */ }
  Singleton(const Singleton&) = delete;
  Singleton& operator=(const Singleton&) = delete;
  Singleton(Singleton&&) = delete;
  Singleton&& operator=(Singleton&&) = delete;
  ~Singleton() { /* destructor */ }
};
```

The static instance of the Singleton class is held at function scope instead of class scope to prevent uncontrollable instantiation order conflicts in the event that one singleton class's constructor depends on another singleton. The details of C++'s instantiation ordering rules are beyond the scope of this book, but a detailed discussion in the context of singletons can be found in Alexandrescu [2].

Note that due to the lack of locking surrounding the access to the one instance, our model singleton is currently only suitable for a single threaded environment. In this age of multicore processors, is such a limitation wise? For pdCalc, absolutely! Our simple calculator has no need for multi-threading. Programming is hard. Multi-threaded programming is much harder. Never turn a simpler design problem into a harder one unless it's absolutely necessary.

Now that we have the shell of a `Singleton` class, let's see how to use it. In order to access the instance and call the `foo()` function, we simply use the following code:

```
Singleton::Instance().foo();
```

On the first function call to the `Instance()` function, the `instance` variable is statically instantiated and a reference to this object is returned. Because objects statically allocated at function scope remain in memory until program termination, the `instance` object is not destructed at the end of the `Instance()` function's scope. On future calls to `Instance()`, instantiation of the `instance` variable is skipped (it's already constructed and in memory from the previous function call), and a reference to the `instance` variable is simply returned. Note that while the underlying singleton instance is held statically, the `foo()` function itself is not static.

The inquisitive reader may now question, "Why bother holding an instance of the class at all? Why not instead simply make all data and all functions of the `Singleton` class static?" The reason is because the singleton pattern allows us to use the `Singleton` class where instance semantics are required. One particular important usage of these semantics is in the implementation of callbacks. For example, take Qt's signals and slots mechanism (you'll encounter signals and slots in Chapter 6), which can be loosely interpreted as a powerful callback system. In order to connect a signal in one class to a slot in another, we must provide pointers to both class instances. If we had implemented our singleton without a private instantiation of the `Singleton` class (that is, utilizing only static data and static functions), using our `Singleton` class with Qt's signals and slots would be impossible.

3.2.2 The Stack Module as a Singleton Class

We now possess the basic design for our stack module. We have decided that the entire module will be encapsulated in one class, which essentially acts as an adapter for an STL container. We have decided that our one class fits the model criteria for a singleton, and this singleton class will have the public interface designed in Chapter 2. Combining each of these design elements gives us the initial declaration for our class, shown in Listing 3-2.

Listing 3-2. The Stack as a Singleton

```
class Stack
{
  class StackImpl;
public:
  static Stack& Instance();
  void push(double);
  double pop();
  void getElements(int, vector<double>&) const;
  void swapTop();

private:
  Stack();
  ~Stack();
  // appropriate blocking of copying, assigning, moving...
  unique_ptr<StackImpl> pimpl_;
};
```

Because the focus of this book is on design, the implementation for each member function is not provided in the text unless the details are particularly instructive or highlight a key element of the design. As a reminder, the complete implementation for pdCalc can be downloaded from the GitHub repository. Occasionally, the repository source code will be a more sophisticated variant of the idealized interfaces appearing in the text. This will be the general format for the remainder of this book.

For those readers unfamiliar with the pimpl idiom (placing the implementation of one class in a separate private implementation class), the pimpl member variable will seem very mysterious. Don't fret. You'll review this principle in a section below.

Before temporarily departing the discussion of the Stack class's design, let's take a brief detour and discuss a relevant implementation detail. We spent a lot of time reviewing the importance of using the adapter pattern in the Stack's design to hide the underlying data structure. One of the justifications for this decision was that it offered the ability to seamlessly alter the underlying implementation without impacting classes dependent upon the Stack's interface. The question is, "Why might the underlying implementation of the Stack change?"

In my first version of the Stack's implementation, I selected the obvious choice for the underlying data structure, the STL stack. However, I quickly encountered an efficiency problem using the STL stack. Our Stack class's interface provides a getElements() function that enables the user interface to view the contents of the calculator's stack. Unfortunately, the STL stack's interface provides no similar function. The only way to see an element other than the top element of an STL stack is to successively pop the stack until the element of interest is reached. Obviously, because we are only trying to see the elements of the stack and not alter the stack itself, we'll need to immediately push all the entries back onto the stack. Interestingly enough, for our purposes, the STL stack turns out to be an unsuitable data structure to implement a stack! There must be a better solution.

Fortunately, the STL provides another data structure suitable for our task, the double-ended queue, or deque. The deque is an STL data structure that behaves similarly to a vector, except the deque permits pushing elements onto both its front and its back. Whereas the vector is optimized to grow while still providing a contiguity guarantee, the deque is optimized to grow and shrink rapidly by sacrificing contiguity. This feature is precisely the design tradeoff necessary to implement a stack efficiently. In fact, the most common method to implement an STL stack is simply to wrap an STL deque (yes, just like our Stack, the STL's stack is also an example of the adapter pattern). Fortuitously, the STL deque also admits nondestructive iteration, the additional missing requirement from the STL stack that we needed to implement our Stack's getElements() method. It's good that I used encapsulation to hide the Stack's implementation from its interface. After realizing the limitations of visualizing an STL stack, I was able to change the Stack class's implementation to use an STL deque with no impact to any of pdCalc's other modules.

3.2.2.1 The Pimpl Idiom

If you choose to look at the GitHub repository version of pdCalc's implementation, you will notice that many of the actual class implementations are hidden by the pimpl idiom (a C++ specialization of the bridge pattern). For those unfamiliar with this term, it is shorthand notation for pointer to implementation. In practice, instead of declaring all of a class's implementation in a header file, you instead forward declare a pointer to a "hidden" implementation class, and fully declare and define this "hidden" class in the implementation file. Containing and using an incomplete type (the pimpl variable) is permissible provided the pimpl variable is only dereferenced in the source file containing its complete declaration. For example, consider class A below with a public interface consisting of functions f() and g(); a private implementation with functions u(), v(), and w(); and private data v_ and m_:

```
class A
{
public:
  void f();
  void g();

private:
  void u();
  void v();
  void w();
  vector<double> v_;
  map<string, int> m_;
};
```

Instead of visually exposing the private interface of A to consumers of this class, using the pimpl idiom, we write

```
class A
{
  class AImpl;
public:
  void f();
  void g();

private:
  unique_ptr<AImpl> pimpl_;
};
```

where u, v, w, v_, and m_ are now all part of class AImpl, which is both declared and defined only in the implementation file associated with class A. To ensure AImpl cannot be accessed by any other classes, we declare this implementation class to be a private class wholly defined within A. Sutter and Alexandrescu [27] give a brief explanation of the advantages of the pimpl idiom. One of the main advantages is that by moving the private interface of class A from A.h to A.cpp, we no longer need to recompile any code consuming class A when only A's private interface changes. For large-scale software projects, the time savings during compilation can be significant.

Personally, I use the pimpl idiom in the majority of the code that I write. The exception to my general rule is for code that has a very limited private interface or code that is computationally intensive (i.e., code where the indirection overhead of the pimpl is significant). In addition to the compilation benefits of not having to recompile files including `A.h` when only class `AImpl` changes, I find that the pimpl idiom adds significant clarity to the code. This clarity derives from the ability to hide helper functions and classes in implementation files rather than listing them in header files. In this manner, header files truly reflect only the bare essentials of the interface and thus prevent class bloat, at least at the visible interface level. For any other programmer simply consuming your class, the implementation details are visually hidden and therefore do not distract from your hopefully well-documented, limited, public interface.

Before moving on to completing the `Stack`'s interface, note that the use of the pimpl idiom here completely hides the selection of the underlying stack data structure from a user of the `Stack` class. This selection is an implementation detail and should be hidden from the user. The pimpl idiom enables us to hide it completely, even from visual inspection. The pimpl idiom truly is the epitome of encapsulation.

3.3 Adding Events

The final element necessary to build a `Stack` conforming to the stack interface from Chapter 2 is the implementation of events. Eventing is a form of weak coupling that enables one object, the notifier or publisher, to signal any number of other objects, the listeners or subscribers, that something interesting has occurred. The coupling is weak because neither the notifier nor the listener need to know directly about the other's interface. How events are implemented is both language and library dependent, and even within a given language, multiple options may exist. For example, in C#, events are part of the core language, and event handling is relatively easy. In C++, we are not so lucky and must implement our own eventing system or rely on a library providing this facility.

The C++ programmer has several published library options for handling events; prominent among these choices are boost and Qt. The boost library supports signals and slots, a statically typed mechanism for a publisher to signal events to subscribers via callbacks. Qt, on the other hand, provides both a full event system and a dynamically typed event callback mechanism, which, coincidentally, is also referred to as signals and slots. Both libraries are well-documented, well-tested, well-respected, and available for open source and commercial use. Either library would be a viable option for implementing events in our calculator. However, for both instructive purposes and to minimize the dependency of our calculator's backend on external libraries, we will instead implement our own eventing system. The appropriate decision to make when designing your own software is very situationally dependent, and you should examine the pros and cons of using a library versus building custom event handling for your individual application. That said, the default position, unless you have a compelling reason to do otherwise, should be to use a library.

3.3.1 The Observer Pattern

Because eventing is such a commonly implemented C++ feature, you can rest assured that a design pattern describing eventing exists; this pattern is the observer. The observer pattern is a standard method for the abstract implementation of publishers and listeners. As the name of the pattern implies, here, the listeners are referred to as observers.

In the pattern as described by Gamma *et al* [6], a concrete publisher implements an abstract publisher interface, and concrete observers implement an abstract observer interface. Notionally, the implementation is via public inheritance. Each publisher owns a container of its observers, and the publisher's interface permits attaching and detaching observers. When an event occurs (is raised), the publisher iterates over its collection of observers and notifies each one that an event has occurred. Via virtual dispatch, each concrete observer handles this notify message according to its own implementation.

Observers can receive state information from publishers in one of two ways. First, a concrete observer can have a pointer to the concrete publisher it is observing. Through this pointer, the observer can query the publisher's state at the time the event occurred. This mechanism is known as pull semantics. Alternatively, push semantics can be implemented, whereby the publisher pushes state information to the observer along with the event notification. A simplified class diagram for the observer pattern exhibiting push semantics is found in Figure 3-1.

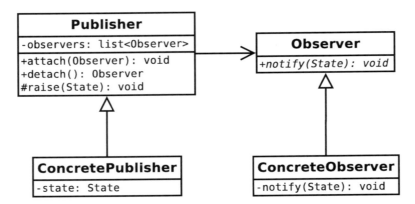

Figure 3-1. *A simplified version of the class diagram for the observer pattern as it is implemented for pdCalc. The diagram illustrates push semantics for event data.*

3.3.1.1 Enhancing the Observer Pattern Implementation

In the actual implementation for our calculator, several additional features have been added beyond the abstraction depicted in Figure 3-1. First, in the figure, each publisher owns a single list of observers that are all notified when an event occurs. However, this implementation implies either that publishers have only one event or that publishers have multiple events, but no way of disambiguating which observers get called for each event. A better publisher implementation instead holds an associative array to lists of observers. In this manner, each publisher can have multiple distinct events, each of which only notifies observers interested in watching that particular event. While the key in the associative array can technically be any suitable data type that the designer chooses, I chose to use strings for the calculator. That is, the publisher distinguishes individual events by a name. This choice enhances readability and enables runtime flexibility to add events (versus, say, choosing enumeration values as keys).

Once the publisher class can contain multiple events, the programmer needs the ability to specify the event by name when attach() or detach() is called. These method signatures must therefore be modified appropriately from how they appear in Figure 3-1 to include an event name. For attachment, the method signature is completed by adding the name of the event. The caller simply calls the attach() method with the concrete observer instance and the name of the event to which this observer is attaching. Detaching an observer from a publisher, however, requires slightly more sophisticated mechanics. Since each event within a publisher can contain multiple observers, the programmer requires the ability to differentiate observers for detachment. Naturally, this requirement leads to naming observers, as well, and the detach() function signature must be modified to accommodate both the observer's and event's names.

In order to facilitate detaching observers, observers on each event should be stored indirectly and referenced by their names. Thus, rather than storing an associative array of lists of observers, we instead choose to use an associative array of associative arrays of observers.

In modern C++, the programmer has a choice of using either a map or an unordered_ map for a standard library implementation of an associative array. The canonical implementation of these two data structures are the red-black tree and the hash table, respectively. Since the ordering of the elements in the associative array is not important, I selected the unordered_map for pdCalc's Publisher class. However, for the likely small number of observers subscribing to each event, either data structure would have been an equally valid choice.

To this point, we have not specified precisely how observers are stored in the publisher, only that they are somehow stored in associative arrays. Because observers are used polymorphically, language rules require them to be held by either pointer or reference. The question then becomes, should publishers own the observers or simply refer to observers owned by some other class? If we choose the reference route (by either reference or raw pointer), a class other than the publisher would be required to own the memory for the observers. This situation is problematic because it is not clear who should own the observers in any particular instance. Therefore, every developer would probably choose a different option, and the maintenance of the observers over the long term would descend into chaos. Even worse, if the owner of an observer released the observer's memory without also detaching the observer from the publisher, triggering the publisher's event would cause a crash because the publisher would hold an invalid reference to the observer. For these reasons, I prefer having the publisher own the memory for its observers.

Having eschewed referencing, we must use owning semantics, and, because of the C++ mechanics of polymorphism, we must implement ownership via pointers. In modern C++, unique ownership of a pointer type is achieved via the unique_ptr (see the "Modern C++ Design Note" sidebar on owning semantics to understand the design implications). Putting all of the above advice together, we are able to design the final public interface for the Publisher class, as shown in Listing 3-3.

Listing 3-3. The Final Public Interface for the Publisher Class

```cpp
// Publisher.h
class Observer;

class Publisher
{
  class PublisherImpl
public:
  void attach(const string& eventName,
              unique_ptr<Observer> observer);
  unique_ptr<Observer> detach(const string& eventName,
                              const string& observerName);
  // ...
private:
  unique_ptr<PublisherImpl> publisherImpl_;
};
```

The implementation details of event storage become

```cpp
// Publisher.cpp
class Publisher::PublisherImpl
{
  // ...
private :
  using ObserversList = unordered_map<string, unique_ptr<Observer>>;
  using Events = unordered_map<string, ObserversList>;
  Events events_;
};
```

The interface for the Observer class is quite a bit simpler than the interface for the Publisher class. However, because I have not yet described how to handle event data, we are not yet ready to design the Observer's interface. I will address both event data and the Observer class's interface in Section 3.3.1.2 below.

```
MODERN C++ DESIGN NOTE: OWNING SEMANTICS AND UNIQUE_PTR
```

In C++, the notion of owning an object implies the responsibility for deleting its memory when the object is no longer required. Prior to C++11, although anyone could implement his own smart pointer (and many did), the language itself expressed no standard semantics for pointer ownership (excepting `auto_ptr`, which has since been deprecated). Passing memory by native pointers was more of a trust issue. That is, if you "newed" a pointer and passed it via raw pointer to a library, you hoped the library deleted the memory when it was finished with it. Alternatively, the documentation for the library might inform you to delete the memory after certain operations were performed. Without a standard smart pointer, in the worst case scenario, your program leaked memory. In the best case scenario, you had to interface to a library using a nonstandard smart pointer.

C++11 corrected the problem of unknown pointer ownership by standardizing a set of smart pointers largely borrowed from the boost libraries. The `unique_ptr` finally allows programmers to implement unique ownership correctly (hence the deprecation of `auto_ptr`). Essentially, the `unique_ptr` ensures that only one instance of a pointer exists at any one time. For the language to enforce these rules, copy and non-moving assignment for `unique_ptrs` are not implemented. Instead, move semantics are employed to ensure transfer of ownership (explicit function calls can also be used to manage the memory manually). Josuttis [8] provides an excellent detailed description of the mechanics of using the `unique_ptr`. An important point to remember is not to mix pointer types between `unique_ptrs` and raw pointers.

From a design perspective, the `unique_ptr` implies that we can write interfaces, using standard C++, that unequivocally express unique ownership semantics. As was seen in the discussion of the observer pattern, unique ownership semantics are important in any design where one class creates memory to be owned by another class. For example, in the calculator's eventing system, while the publisher of an event should own its observers, a publisher will rarely have enough information to create its observers. It is therefore important to be able to create the memory for the observers in one location but be able to pass ownership of that memory to another location, the publisher. The `unique_ptr` provides that service. Because the observers are passed to the publisher via a `unique_ptr`, ownership is transferred to the publisher, and the observer's memory is deleted by the smart pointer when the publisher no longer needs the observer. Alternatively, any class may reclaim an observer from the publisher. Since the `detach()` method returns the observer in a `unique_ptr`, the publisher clearly relinquishes ownership of the observer's memory by transferring it back to the caller.

The above implementation of the observer pattern explicitly enforces a design where the publisher owns its observers. The most natural way to use this implementation involves creating small, dedicated, intermediary Observer classes that themselves hold pointers or references to the actual classes that should respond to an event. For example, from Chapter 2, we know that pdCalc's user interface is an observer of the Stack class. However, do we really want the user interface to be an (publicly inherit from) Observer that is owned by the Stack as depicted in Figure 3-2a? No. A better solution is depicted in Figure 3-2c. Here, the Stack owns a stack ChangeEvent observer, which in turn notifies the UserInterface when the stack changes. This pattern enables the Stack and the UserInterface to remain truly independent. More will be said about this topic when you study our first user interface in Chapter 5.

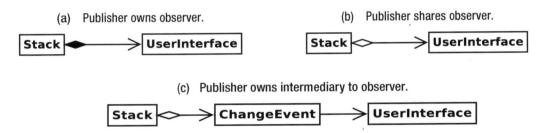

Figure 3-2. *Different ownership strategies for the observer pattern*

Modern C++ does admit yet another sensible alternative for the ownership semantics of the observer pattern: shared ownership. As stated above, it is unreasonable for the Stack to own the user interface. Some, however, might consider it equally unreasonable to create an extra ChangeEvent intermediary class instead of directly making the user interface an observer. The only middle ground option available seems to be for the Stack to refer to the user interface. Previously, though, I stated that having a publisher refer to its observers is unsafe because the observers could disappear from under the publisher, leaving a dangling reference. Can this dangling reference problem be solved?

Fortunately, modern C++ once again comes to the rescue with shared semantics (as depicted in Figure 3-2b). In this scenario, observers are shared using a shared_ptr (see the sidebar on shared_ptrs below), while the publisher retains a reference to observers with a weak_ptr (a relative of the shared_ptr). weak_ptrs are designed specifically to mitigate the problem of dangling references to shared objects. This design for shared observer ownership by publishers is described by Meyers [19] in Item 20. Personally, I prefer the design that uses owning semantics and a lightweight, dedicated observer class.

3.3.1.2 Handling Event Data

In describing the observer pattern, I mentioned that two distinct paradigms exist for handling event data: pull and push semantics. In pull semantics, the observer is simply notified that an event has occurred. The observer then has the additional responsibility of acquiring any additional data that might be required. The implementation is quite simple. The observer maintains a reference to any object from which it might need to acquire state information, and the observer calls member functions to acquire this state in response to the event.

Pull semantics have several advantages. First, the observer can choose at the time of handling the event exactly what state it wants to acquire. Second, no unnecessary resources are consumed in passing potentially unused arguments to observers. Third, pull semantics are easy to implement because events do not need to carry data. However, pull semantics also have disadvantages. First, pull semantics increase coupling because observers need to hold references to and understand the state acquisition interfaces of publishers. Second, observers only have access to the public interfaces of publishers. This access restriction precludes observers from obtaining private data from publishers.

In contrast to pull semantics, push semantics are implemented by having the publisher send state data relevant to an event when that event is raised. Observers then receive this state data as the arguments to the notify callback. The interface enforces push semantics by making the notify function pure virtual in the abstract `Observer` base class.

Push semantics for event handling also have both advantages and disadvantages. The first advantage is that push semantics decrease coupling. Neither publishers nor observers need to know about each others' interfaces. They need only obey the abstract eventing interface. Second, the publisher can send private information to the observers when it pushes state. Third, the publisher, as the object raising the event, can send precisely the data needed to handle the event. The main disadvantages of push semantics are that they are slightly more difficult to implement and potentially carry unnecessary overhead in situations where the observer does not require the state data that the publisher pushes. Finally, note that a design that uses push semantics can always be trivially augmented with pull semantics for special cases by adding a callback reference to the pushed data. The reverse is not true since push semantics require dedicated infrastructure within the event handling mechanism.

Based on the tradeoffs between push and pull semantics described above, I chose to implement push semantics for the event handling for pdCalc. The main disadvantage of push semantics is the potential computational overhead of the implementation. However, since our application is not performance intensive, the decreased coupling this pattern exhibits and the argument control the publisher maintains outweigh the slight performance overhead. Our task now becomes designing an implementation for passing event data via push semantics.

In order to implement push semantics for event handling, one must standardize the interface for passing arguments from publisher to observer when an event is raised. Ideally, each publisher/observer pair would agree on the types of the arguments to be passed, and the publisher would call the appropriate member function on the observer when an event was raised. However, this ideal situation is effectively impossible within our publisher/observer class hierarchy because concrete publishers are not aware of the interfaces of concrete observers. Concrete publishers can only raise events generically by calling the `raise()` function in the `Publisher` base class. The `raise()` function, in turn, polymorphically notifies a concrete observer through the `Observer` base class's virtual `notify()` function. We, therefore, seek a generic technique for passing customized data via the abstract raise/notify interface.

The solution to our dilemma is rather simple. We create a parallel object hierarchy for event data and pass the event data from publisher to observer via this abstract state interface. The base class in this hierarchy, `EventData`, is an empty class that contains only a virtual destructor. Each event that requires arguments then subclasses this base class and implements whatever data handling scheme is deemed appropriate. When an event is raised, the publisher passes the data to the observer through an `EventData` base class pointer. Upon receipt of the data, the concrete observer downcasts the state data to the concrete data class and subsequently extracts the necessary data via the derived class's concrete interface. While the concrete publisher and concrete observer do have to agree on the interface for the data object, neither concrete publisher nor concrete observer is required to know the interface of the other. Thus, we maintain loose coupling.

To solidify the ideas above, let's examine how the calculator's `Stack` implements state data. Recall from Chapter 2 that the `Stack` implements two events, the `stackChanged()` event and the `error(string)` event. The `stackChanged()` event is uninteresting in this context since the event carries no data. The error event, however, does carry data. Consider the class hierarchy for the `Stack`'s error condition shown in Listing 3-4.

Listing 3-4. The Event Data Hierarchy

```
// Publisher.h
class EventData
{
public:
    virtual ~EventData();
};

// Stack.h
class StackEventData : public EventData
{
public:
  enum class ErrorConditions { Empty, TooFewArguments };
  StackEventData(ErrorConditions e) : err_(e) { }

  static const char* Message(ErrorConditions ec);
  const char* message() const;
  ErrorConditions error() const { return err_; }

private:
  ErrorConditions err_;
};
```

The StackEventData class defines how the Stack's event data is packaged and sent to classes observing the Stack. When an error occurs within the stack module, the Stack class raises an event and pushes information about that event to its observers. In this instance, the Stack creates an instance of StackEventData specifying the type of error in the constructor. This enumerated type comprising the finite set of error conditions can be converted to a string using the message() function. The observers are then free to use or ignore this information when they are notified about the event's occurrence. If you were paying attention, yes, I subtly just changed the signature for the error() interface from string to EventData.

As a concrete example, suppose an error is triggered because an empty stack is popped. In order to raise this event, the Stack calls the following code (the actual implementation is slightly different because the Stack is wrapped in a pimpl):

```
parent_.raise(Stack::StackError, make_shared<StackEventData>(
  StackEventData::ErrorConditions::Empty));
```

The first argument to the raise() function is a static string that resolves to "error". Recall that in order to handle multiple events, the publisher names each event. Here, the Stack::StackError static variable holds the name of this event. A variable is used instead of directly using the string to prevent runtime errors being caused by mistyping the event name. The second argument to the raise() function creates the StackEventData instance and initializes it with the empty stack error condition. Note that the implementation passes event data using a shared_ptr. This decision is discussed below in the sidebar concerning sharing semantics. Although the StackObserver class has not yet been introduced, I note for completeness that an event can be interpreted with code typified by the following:

```
StackObserver::notify(shared_ptr<EventData> d)
{
   shared_ptr<StackEventData> p = dynamic_pointer_cast<StackEventData>(d);

   if(p)
   {
     // do something with the data
   }
   else
   {
     // uh oh, what event did we just catch?!
   }
}
```

MODERN C++ DESIGN NOTE: SHARING SEMANTICS AND SHARED_PTR

Whereas unique_ptr enables the programmer to express, safely, unique ownership, shared_ptr enables the programmer to express, safely, shared ownership. Prior to the C++11 standard, C++ enabled data sharing by either raw pointer or reference. Because references for class data could only be initialized during construction, for late binding data, only raw pointers could be used. Therefore, often two classes shared a single piece of data by each containing a raw pointer to a common object. The problem with that scenario is, of course, that it is unclear which object owns the shared object. In particular, this ambiguity implies uncertainty about when such a shared object can safely be deleted and which owning object ultimately should free the memory. shared_ptrs rectify this dilemma at the standard library level.

shared_ptr implements sharing semantics via reference counting. As new objects point to a shared_ptr, the internal reference count increases (enforced via constructors and assignment). When a shared_ptr goes out of scope, its destructor is called, which decrements the internal reference count. When the count goes to zero, the destruction of the final shared_ptr triggers reclamation of the underlying memory. As with unique_ptr, explicit member function calls can also be used to manage memory manually. Josuttis [8] provides an excellent detailed description of the mechanics of using shared_ptr. As with unique_ptr, one must be careful not to mix pointer types. The exception to this rule, of course, is mixed usage with weak_ptr. Additionally, reference counting carries both time and space overhead, so the reader should familiarize himself with these tradeoffs before deploying shared pointers.

In terms of design considerations, the shared_ptr construct enables the programmer to share heap memory without directly tracking the ownership of the objects. For the calculator, passing event data by value is not an option. Because the event data objects exist in a hierarchy, passing event data objects by value would cause slicing. However, using raw pointers (or references) to pass event data would also be problematic because the lifetime of these data objects cannot be known among the classes sharing them. Naturally, the publisher allocates the memory when it raises an event. Since an observer may wish to retain the memory after completion of event handling, the publisher cannot simply deallocate the memory after the event has been handled. Moreover, because multiple observers can be called for any given event, neither can the publisher transfer unique ownership of the data to any given observer. Therefore, the shared_ptr standardized in C++11 offers the ideal semantics for handling this situation.

Now that you understand event data, let's finally write the abstract Observer interface. It is, unsurprisingly, exactly what you might have been expecting. See Listing 3-5.

Listing 3-5. The Abstract Observer Interface

```
class Observer
{
public :
  explicit Observer(const string& name);
  virtual ~Observer();

  virtual void notify(shared_ptr<EventData>) = 0;
};
```

3.3.2 **The Stack as an Event Publisher**

The final step in constructing the Stack is simply to put all of the pieces together. Listing 3-1 shows the Stack as a singleton. In order to implement events, we simply modify this code to inherit from the Publisher base class. We now must ask ourselves, should this inheritance be public or private?

Typically, in object-oriented programming, one uses public inheritance to indicate the *is-a* relationship. That is, public inheritance expresses the relationship that a derived class is a type of or specialization of a base class. More precisely, the *is-a* relationship obeys the Liskov Substitutability Principle (LSP) [29], which states that (via polymorphism) a function that takes a base class pointer (reference) as an argument must be able to accept a derived class pointer (reference) without knowing it. Succinctly, a derived class must be usable wherever a base class can be used, interchangeably. When people refer to inheritance, they are generally referring to public inheritance.

Private inheritance is used to express the *implements-a* relationship. Private inheritance, simply, is used to embed the implementation of one class into the private implementation of another. It does not obey the LSP, and, in fact, the C++ language does not permit substitution of a derived class for a base class if the inheritance relationship is private. For completeness, the closely related protected inheritance is semantically the same as private inheritance. The only difference is that in private inheritance, the base class implementation becomes private in the derived class while in protected inheritance, the base class implementation becomes protected in the derived class.

Our question has now been refined to, *is* the Stack *a* Publisher or does the Stack *implement a* Publisher? The answer is yes and yes. That was unhelpful, so how do we choose?

In order to disambiguate whether we should use public or private inheritance in this instance, we must delve deeper into the usage of the Stack class. Public inheritance, or the *is-a* relationship, would indicate our intent to use the stack polymorphically as a publisher. However, this is not the case. While the Stack class is a publisher, it is not a publisher in the context that it could be substituted for a Publisher in an LSP sense. Therefore, we should use private inheritance to indicate the intent to use the implementation of the Publisher within the Stack. Equivalently, we can state that the Stack provides the Publisher service. If you've been following along with the repository source code, you might have noticed a big hint that private inheritance was the answer. The Publisher class was implemented with a nonvirtual, protected destructor, making it unusable for public inheritance.

Readers familiar with object-oriented design may wonder why I didn't ask the ubiquitous *has-a* question, which indicates ownership or the aggregation relationship. That is, why shouldn't the Stack simply own a Publisher and reuse its implementation instead of privately inheriting from it? Many designers prefer almost exclusively to use aggregation in place of private inheritance, arguing that when given an equivalent choice between these two, one should always prefer the language feature leading to looser coupling (inheritance is a stronger relationship than aggregation). This opinion has merit. Personally, though, I simply prefer to accept the technique that trades off stronger coupling for greater clarity. I believe that private inheritance more clearly states the design intent of implementing the Publisher service than does aggregation. This decision has no right or wrong answer. In your code, you should prefer the style that suits your tastes.

An additional consequence of privately inheriting from the Publisher class is that the attach() and detach() methods of the Publisher become private. However, they need to be part of the public interface for the Stack if any other class intends to subscribe to the Stack's events. Thus, the implementer must choose to utilize either using statements or forwarding member functions to hoist attach() and detach() into the public interface of the Stack. Either approach is acceptable in this context, and the implementer is free to use his or her personal preference.

3.3.3 The Complete Stack Interface

We are finally ready to write the complete Stack public interface. See Listing 3-6.

Listing 3-6. The Complete Stack Public Interface

```
class Stack : private Publisher
{
public:
  static Stack& Instance();

  void push(double, bool suppressChangeEvent = false);
  double pop(bool suppressChangeEvent = false);
  void swapTop();
  vector<double> getElements(size_t n) const;

  using Publisher::attach;
  using Publisher::detach;
};
```

As described in this chapter, the `Stack` is a singleton class (note the `Instance()` method) that implements the `Publisher` service (note the private inheritance of the `Publisher` class and the hoisting of the `attach()` and `detach()` methods into the public interface). The `Stack` class's public section, in conjunction with the `EventData` class described in Listing 3-2, encompasses the complete interface of the stack module introduced in Table 2-2 in Chapter 2. While I have not yet described any concrete observers for the `Stack`, we have fully defined our event system for pdCalc, which is based on the tried and true observer pattern. At this point, we are ready to design pdCalc's next component, the command dispatcher module.

3.4 A Quick Note on Testing

Before concluding this first chapter introducing source code for pdCalc, I should pause a moment and say a few words about testing. Although testing is by no means a central exploratory topic of this book, it is nonetheless an integral part of any high quality implementation. Alongside the source code for the calculator found on GitHub, I have also included all of my automated unit testing code. Because I chose to use Qt for the graphic user interface framework for pdCalc (see Chapter 6), the Qt Test framework was a natural choice on which to build pdCalc's unit test suite. Primarily, this choice does not add any additional library dependencies on the project, and the test framework is guaranteed to work on all platforms to which Qt has been ported. That said, any one of the many high quality C++ unit test frameworks would have sufficed equally well.

Personally, I find unit testing to be indispensable when programming even small projects. First and foremost, unit tests provide a means to ensure your code functions as expected. Second, unit testing enables you to see a module working correctly long before a user interface is developed. Early testing enables early bug detection, and a well-known fact of software engineering is that earlier bug detection leads to exponentially cheaper bug fixing costs. I also find that seeing modules fully working early in the development cycle is oddly motivational. Finally, unit tests also enable you to know that your code functions the same before and after code changes. As iteration is an essential element of design and implementation, your code will change numerous times, even after you think you've completed it. Running comprehensive unit tests automatically at every build will ensure that new changes have not unpredictably broken any existing functioning units.

Because I value testing very highly (it's one of the first lessons I try to teach to new professional developers), I strove to ensure completeness in the testing of pdCalc's code. Not only does the test code provide an exemplar (I hope) for the reader, but it also assured me that my code was correct throughout the code development portion of writing this book. However, despite my best intentions to write error free code, and even after an irrational number of reviews of the source code, I am certain that bugs still exist in the final product. Please feel free to email me any and all errors that you find. I will make my best effort to incorporate corrections in real time to the code in the GitHub repository and give proper attribution to the first reader who reports any of my bugs to me.

CHAPTER 4

The Command Dispatcher

The command dispatcher is the centerpiece of the calculator. As the controller in the MVC framework, the command dispatcher is responsible for the entire business logic of the application. This chapter addresses not only the specific design of the command dispatcher module for the calculator but also, more broadly, the flexible design of a loosely coupled command infrastructure.

4.1 Decomposition of the Command Dispatcher

The first question we asked when decomposing the stack was, "Into how many components should the stack be divided?" We ask the same question now for the command dispatcher. To answer this question, let's consider the functionality that the command dispatcher must encapsulate. The function of the command dispatcher is to

1. Store a collection of known commands,

2. Receive and interpret requests for these commands,

3. Dispatch command requests (including the ability to undo and redo), and

4. Perform the actual operation (including updating the calculator's state).

In Chapter 2, I discussed the principle of cohesion. At the class level, designing for cohesion implies that each class should only do one thing, and, presumably, do it well. At the topmost decomposition level, the command dispatcher indeed does only one thing: it interprets commands. At the task level, however, from our list of functionality above, it clearly must execute multiple tasks. Therefore, we decompose the command

© Adam B. Singer 2017
A. B. Singer, *Practical C++ Design*, DOI 10.1007/978-1-4842-3057-2_4

dispatcher into several distinct classes, one for each major task it must perform. Hence, we have the following classes:

1. `CommandRepository`: Stores the list of available commands

2. `CommandDispatcher`: Receives and interprets requests to execute commands

3. `CommandManager`: Dispatches commands and manages undo and redo

4. `Command` hierarchy: Executes commands

The remainder of this chapter is devoted to describing the design and salient implementation details for the above list of classes and class hierarchies.

4.2 The Command Class

At this stage in the decomposition, I find it more useful to switch to a bottom-up approach to design. In a strictly top-down approach, we would probably start with the `CommandDispatcher`, the class that receives and interprets command requests, and work our way down to the commands themselves. However, in this bottom-up approach, we will begin by studying the design of the commands themselves. We begin with the abstraction known as the command pattern.

4.2.1 The Command Pattern

The command pattern is a simple, but very powerful, behavioral pattern that encapsulates a request in the form of an object. Structurally, the pattern is implemented as an abstract command base class that provides an interface for executing a request. Concrete commands simply implement the interface. In the most trivial case, the abstract interface consists solely of a command to execute the request that the command encapsulates. The class diagram for the trivial implementation is shown in Figure 4-1.

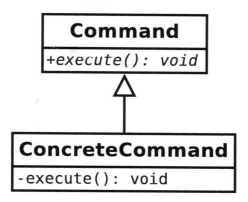

Figure 4-1. *The simplest hierarchy for the command pattern*

Essentially, the pattern does two things. First, it decouples the requester of a command from the dispatcher of the command. Second, it encapsulates the request for an action, which might otherwise be implemented by a function call, into an object. This object can carry state and posses an extended lifetime beyond the immediate lifetime of the request itself.

Practically, what do these two features give us? First, because the requester is decoupled from the dispatcher, the logic for executing a command does not need to reside in the same class or even the same module as the class responsible for executing the command. This obviously decreases coupling, but it also increases cohesion since a unique class can be created for each unique command the system must implement. Second, because requests are now encapsulated in command objects with a lifetime distinct from the lifetime of the action, commands can be both delayed in time (for example, queuing commands) and undone. The undo operation is made possible because already executed commands can be retained with sufficient data to restore the state to the instant before the command was executed. Of course, combining the queuing ability with the undo ability permits the creation of an unlimited undo/redo for all requests implementing the command pattern.

4.2.2 More on Implementing Undo/Redo

One of the requirements for pdCalc is to implement unlimited undo and redo operations. Most books state that undo can be implemented via the command pattern by merely augmenting the abstract command interface with an undo command. However, this simplistic treatment glosses over the actual details necessary to properly implement the undo feature.

Implementing undo and redo involves two distinct steps. First (and obviously), undo and redo must be implemented correctly in the concrete command classes. Second, a data structure must be implemented to track and store the command objects as they are dispatched. Naturally, this data structure must preserve the order in which the commands were executed and be capable of dispatching a request to undo, redo, or execute a new command. This undo/redo data structure is described in detail in Section 4.4 below. The implementation of undo and redo are discussed presently.

Implementing undo and redo operations themselves is usually straightforward. The redo operation is the same as the command's execute function. Provided that the state of the system is the same before the first time a command is executed and after undo has been called, then implementing the redo command is essentially free. This, of course, immediately implies that implementing undo is really about reverting the state of the system to immediately before the command was first executed.

Undo can be implemented by two similar but slightly distinct mechanisms, each responsible for restoring the system's state in different ways. The first mechanism does exactly what the name undo implies: it takes the current state of the system and literally reverses the process of the forward command. Mathematically, that is, undo is implemented as the inverse operation to execute. For example, if the forward operation were to take the square root of the number on the top of the stack, then the undo operation would be to take the square of the number on the top of the stack. The advantage of this method is that no extra state information needs to be stored in order to be able to implement undo. The disadvantage is that the method does not work for all possible commands. Let's examine the converse of our previous example. That is, consider taking the square of the number on the top of the stack. The undo operation would be to take the square root of the result of the squaring operation. However, was the original number the positive or negative root of the square? Without retaining additional state information, the inversion method breaks down.

The alternative to implementing undo as an inverse operation is to preserve the state of the system before the command is first executed and then implement the undo as a reversion to this prior state. Returning to our example of squaring a number, the forward operation would both compute the square, but also save the top number on the stack. The undo operation would then be implemented by dropping the result from the stack and pushing the saved state from before the forward operation was performed. This procedure is enabled by the command pattern since all commands are implemented as instantiations of concrete command classes that are permitted to carry state. An interesting feature of this method of implementing undo is that the operation itself need not have a mathematical inverse. Notice that in our example, the undo did not even need to know what the forward operation was. It simply needed to know how to replace the top element from the stack with the saved state.

Which mechanism to use in your application really depends on the distinct operations your application performs. When operations have no inverses, storing the state is the only option. When the inverse operation is overly expensive to compute, storing the state is usually the better implementation. When storage of the state is expensive, implementing undo via inversion is preferred, assuming an inverse operation exists. Of course, since each command is implemented as a separate class, a global decision for how undo is implemented need not be made for the entire system. The designer of a given command is free to choose the method most appropriate for that particular operation on a command-by-command basis. In some cases, even a hybrid approach (both storing and inverting separate parts of the operation) may be optimal. In the next section, we will examine the choice that I made for pdCalc.

4.2.3 The Command Pattern Applied to the Calculator

In order to execute, undo, and redo all of the operations in the calculator, we will implement the command pattern, and each calculator operation will be encapsulated by its own concrete class deriving from an abstract Command class. From the discussion above concerning the command pattern, we can see that two decisions must be made in order to apply the pattern to the calculator. First, we must decide what operations must be supported by every command. This collection of operations will define the abstract interface of the Command base class. Second, we must choose a strategy for how undo will be supported. To be precise, this decision is always deferred to the implementer of a particular concrete command. However, by choosing either state reconstruction or command inversion upfront, we can implement some infrastructure to simplify undo for command implementers. We'll tackle these two issues consecutively.

4.2.3.1 The Command Interface

Choosing what public functions to include in the abstract Command class is identical to defining the interface for all commands in the calculator. Therefore, this decision must not be taken lightly. While each concrete command will perform a distinct function, all concrete commands must be substitutable for each other (recall the LSP). Because we want interfaces to be minimal but complete, we must determine the fewest number of functions that can abstractly express the operations needed for all commands.

The first two commands to be included are the most obvious and easiest to define. They are execute() and undo(), the functions for performing the forward and inverse operations of the command, respectively. These two functions return void and require no arguments. No arguments are needed because all of the data for the calculator is handled via the Stack class, which is globally accessible via the singleton pattern. Additionally, the Command class will need a constructor and a destructor. Because the class is intended to be an interface class with virtual functions, the destructor should be virtual. Listing 4-1 illustrates our first attempt at an interface.

Listing 4-1. A First Attempt at the Command Interface

```
class Command
{
public:
  virtual ~Command();
  void execute();
  void undo();

protected:
  Command();

private:
  virtual void executeImpl() = 0;
  virtual void undoImpl() = 0;
};
```

In Listing 4-1, the reader will immediately notice that the constructor is protected, both execute() and undo() are public and nonvirtual, and separate executeImpl() and undoImpl() virtual functions exist. The reason the constructor is protected is to signal to an implementer that the Command class cannot be directly instantiated. Of course, because the class contains pure virtual functions, the compiler prevents direct instantiation of the Command class anyway. Making the constructor protected is somewhat superfluous. Defining the public interface using a combination of virtual and nonvirtual functions, on the other hand, deserves a more detailed explanation.

Defining the public interface for a class via a mixture of public nonvirtual functions and private virtual functions is a design principle known as the non-virtual interface (NVI) pattern. The NVI pattern states that polymorphic interfaces should always be defined using non-virtual public functions that forward calls to private virtual functions.

The reasoning behind this pattern is quite simple. Since a base class with virtual functions acts as an interface class, clients should be accessing derived class functionality only through the base class's interface via polymorphism. By making the public interface non-virtual, the base class implementer reserves the ability to intercept virtual function calls before dispatch in order to add preconditions or postconditions to the execution of all derived class implementations. Making the virtual functions private forces consumers to use the non-virtual interface. In the trivial case where no precondition or postcondition is needed, the implementation of the non-virtual function reduces to a forwarding call to the virtual function. The additional verbosity of insisting on the NVI pattern even in the trivial case is warranted because it preserves design flexibility for future expansion at zero computational overhead since the forwarding function call can be inlined. A more in-depth rationale behind the NVI pattern is discussed in detail in Sutter [27].

Let's now consider if either execute() or undo() requires preconditions or postconditions; we start with execute(). From a quick scan of the use cases in Chapter 2, we can see that many of the actions pdCalc must complete can only be performed if a set of preconditions are first satisfied. For example, to add two numbers, we must have two numbers on the stack. Clearly, addition has a precondition. From a design perspective, if we trap this precondition before the command is executed, we can handle precondition errors before they cause execution problems. We'll definitely want to check preconditions as part of our base class execute() implementation before calling executeImpl().

What precondition or preconditions must be checked for all commands? Maybe, as with addition, all commands must have at least two numbers on the stack? Let's examine another use case. Consider taking the sine of a number. This command only requires one number to be on the stack. Ah, preconditions are command-specific. The correct answer to our question concerning the general handling of preconditions is to ask derived classes to check their own preconditions by having execute() first call a checkPreconditionsImpl() virtual function.

What about postconditions for execute()? It turns out that if the preconditions for each command are satisfied, then all of the commands are mathematically well-defined. Great, no postcondition checks are necessary! Unfortunately, mathematical correctness is insufficient to ensure error-free computations with floating point numbers. For example, floating point addition can result in positive overflow when using the double precision numbers required by pdCalc even when the addition is mathematically defined. Fortunately, however, our requirements from Chapter 1 stated that floating point errors can be ignored. Therefore, we are technically excepted from needing to handle floating point errors and do not need a postcondition check after all.

To keep the code relatively simple, I chose to adhere to the requirements and ignore floating point exceptions in pdCalc. If I had instead wanted to be proactive in the design and trap floating point errors, a checkPostconditions() function could have been used. Because floating point errors are generic to all commands, the postcondition check could have been handled at the base class level.

Understanding our precondition and postcondition needs, using the NVI pattern, we are able to write the following simple implementation for execute() shown in Listing 4-2.

Listing 4-2. A Simple Implementation for execute()

```
void Command::execute()
{
  checkPreconditionsImpl();
  executeImpl();
  return;
}
```

Given that checkPreconditionsImpl() and executeImpl() must both be consecutively called and handled by the derived class, couldn't we just lump both of these operations into one function call? We could, but that decision would lead to a suboptimal design. First, by lumping these two operations into one executeImpl() function call, we would lose cohesion by asking one function to perform two distinct operations. Second, by using a separate checkPreconditionsImpl() call, we could choose either to force derived class implementers to check for preconditions (by making checkPrecodnitionsImpl() pure virtual) or to provide, optionally, a default implementation for precondition checks. Finally, who is to say that checkPreconditionsImpl() and executeImpl() will dispatch to the same derived class? Remember, hierarchies can be multiple levels deep.

Analogously to the execute() function, one might assume that precondition checks are needed for undoing commands. However, it turns out that we never actually have to check for undo preconditions because they will always be true by construction. That is, since an undo command can only be called after an execute command has successfully completed, the precondition for undo() is guaranteed to be satisfied (assuming, of course, a correct implementation of execute()). As with forward execution, no postcondition checks are necessary for undo().

The analysis of preconditions and postconditions for execute() and undo() resulted in the addition of only one function to the virtual interface, checkPreconditionImpl(). However, in order for the implementation of this function to be complete, we must determine the correct signature of this function. First, what should be the return value for the function? Either we could choose to make the return value void and handle failure of the precondition via an exception or make the return value a type that could indicate that the precondition was not met (e.g., a boolean returning false on precondition failure or an enumeration indicating the type of failure that occurred). For pdCalc, I chose to handle precondition failures via exceptions. This strategy enables a greater degree of flexibility because the error does not need to be handled by the immediate caller, the execute() function. Additionally, the exception can be designed to carry a customized, descriptive error message that can be extended by a derived command. This contrasts with using an enumerated type, which would have to be completely defined by the base class implementer.

The second item we must address in specifying the signature of checkPrecondition Impl() is to choose whether the function should be pure virtual or have a default implementation. While it is true that most commands will require some precondition to be satisfied, this is not true of every command. For example, entering a new number onto the stack does not require a precondition. Therefore, checkPreconditionImpl() should not be a pure virtual function. Instead, it is given a default implementation of doing nothing, which is equivalent to stating that preconditions are satisfied.

Because errors in commands are checked via the checkPreconditionImpl() function, a proper implementation of any command should not throw an exception except from checkPreconditionImpl(). Therefore, for added interface protection, each pure virtual function in the Command class should be marked noexcept. For brevity, I often skip this keyword in the text; however, noexcept does appear in the implementation. This specifier is really only important in the implementation of plugin commands, which are discussed in Chapter 7.

The next set of functions to be added to the Command class are functions for copying objects polymorphically. This set includes a protected copy constructor, a public non-virtual clone() function, and a private cloneImpl() function. At this point in the design, the rationale for why commands must be copyable cannot be adequately justified. However, the reasoning will become clear when we examine the implementation of the CommandRepository. For continuity's sake, however, I'll discuss the implementation of the copy interface presently.

For class hierarchies designed for polymorphic usage, a simple copy constructor is insufficient, and copies of objects must be performed by a cloning virtual function. Consider the following abbreviated command hierarchy showing only the copy constructors:

```
class Command
{
protected:
  Command(const Command&);
};

class Add : public Command
{
public:
  Add(const Add&);
};
```

Our objective is to copy Commands that are used polymorphically. Let's take the following example where we hold an Add object via a Command pointer:

```
Command* p = new Add;
```

By definition, a copy constructor takes a reference to its own class type as its argument. Because in a polymoprhic setting we do not know the underlying type, we must attempt to call the copy constructor as follows:

```
auto p2 = new Command{*p};
```

The above construction is illegal and will not compile. Because the Command class is abstract (and its copy constructor is protected), the compiler will not allow the creation of a Command object. However, not all hierarchies have abstract base classes, so one might be tempted to try this construction in those cases where it is legal. Beware. This construction would slice the hierarchy. That is, p2 would be constructed as a Command instance, not an Add instance, and any Add state from p would be lost in the copy.

Given that we cannot directly use a copy constructor, how do we copy classes in a polymorphic setting? The solution is to provide a virtual clone operation that can be used as follows:

```
Command* p2 = p->clone();
```

Here, the nonvirtual clone() function dispatches the cloning operation to the derived class's cloneImpl() function, whose implementation is simply to call its own copy constructor with a dereferenced this pointer as its argument. For the example above, the expanded interface and implementation would be as follows:

```
class Command
{
public:
  Command* clone() const { return cloneImpl(); }

protected:
  Command(const Command&) { }

private:
  virtual Command* cloneImpl() const = 0;
};

class Add : public Command
{
public:
  Add(const Add& rhs) : Command{rhs} { }

private:
  Add* cloneImpl() const { return new Add{*this}; }
};
```

The only interesting implementation feature here is the return type for the cloneImpl() function. Notice that the base class specifies the return type as Command*, while the derived class specifies the return type as Add*. This construction is called return type covariance, a rule which states that an overriding function in a derived class may return a type of greater specificity than the return type in the virtual interface. Covariance allows a cloning function to always return the specific type appropriate to the hierarchy level from which cloning was called. This feature is important for implementations that have public cloning functions and allow cloning calls to be made from all levels in the hierarchy.

I chose to round out the command interface with a help message function and a corresponding virtual implementation function. The intent of this help function is to enforce that individual command implementers provide brief documentation for the commands that can be queried through a help command in the user interface. The help function is not essential to the functionality of the commands, and its inclusion as part of the design is optional. However, it's always nice to provide some internal documentation for command usage, even in a program as simplistic as a calculator.

Combining all of the above information, we can finally write the complete abstract interface for our Command class; see Listing 4-3.

Listing 4-3. The Complete Abstract Interface for the Command Class

```
class Command
{
public:
  virtual ~Command();
  void execute();
  void undo();
  Command* clone() const;
  const char* helpMessage() const;

protected:
  Command();
  Command(const Command&);

private:
  virtual void checkPreconditionsImpl() const;
  virtual void executeImpl() noexcept = 0;
  virtual void undoImpl() noexcept = 0;
  virtual Command* cloneImpl() const = 0;
  virtual const char* helpMessageImpl() const noexcept = 0;
};
```

If you look at the source code in Command.h, you will also see a virtual deallocate() function. This function is exclusively used for plugins, and its addition to the interface will be discussed in Chapter 7.

MODERN C++ DESIGN NOTE: THE OVERRIDE KEYWORD

The override keyword was introduced in C++11. Functionally, it prevents a common error that is often surprising to new C++ programmers. Consider the following code snippet:

```
class Base
{
public:
  virtual void foo(int);
};

class Derived : public Base
{
public:
  void foo(double);
};

Base* p = new Derived;
p->foo(2.1);
```

Which function is called? Most novice C++ programmers assume that Derived::foo() is called because they expect that Derived's foo() is overriding Base's implementation. However, because the signature of the foo() function differs between the base and derived classes, Base's foo() actually hides Derived's implementation since overloading cannot occur across scope boundaries. Therefore, the call, p->foo(), will call Base's foo() regardless of the argument's type. Interestingly enough, for the same reason

```
Derived d;
d->foo(2);
```

can never call anything but Derived's foo().

In C++03 and C++11, the above code behaves in exactly the same confusing, but technically correct, way. However, starting in C++11, a derived class may optionally mark overriding functions with the override keyword:

```
class Derived : public Base
{
public:
  void foo(double) override;
};
```

Now, the compiler will flag the declaration as an error because the programmer explicitly declared that the derived function should override. Thus, the addition of the override keyword prevents a perplexing bug from occurring by allowing the programmer to disambiguate his intentions.

From a design perspective, the override keyword explicitly marks the function as being an override. While this may not seem important, it is quite useful when working on a large code base. When implementing a derived class whose base class is in another distinct part of the code, it is convenient to know which functions override base class functions and which do not without having to look at the base class's declaration.

4.2.3.2 The Undo Strategy

Having defined the abstract interface for our commands, we next move on to designing the undo strategy. Technically, because the undo() command in our interface is a pure virtual, we could simply waive our hands and claim that the implementation of undo is each concrete command's problem. However, this would be both inelegant and inefficient. Instead, we seek some functional commonality for all commands (or at least groupings of commands) that might enable us to implement undo at a higher level than at each leaf node in the command hierarchy.

As previously discussed, undo can be implemented either via command inversion or state reconstruction (or some combination of the two). Command inversion was already shown to be problematic because the inverse problem is ill-posed (specifically, it has multiple solutions) for some commands. Let's therefore examine state reconstruction as a generalized undo strategy for pdCalc.

We begin our analysis by considering a use case, the addition operation. Addition removes two elements from the stack, adds them together, and returns the result. A simple undo could be implemented by dropping the result from the stack and restoring the original operands, provided these operands were stored by the execute() command. Now, consider subtraction, or multiplication, or division. These commands can also be undone by dropping their result and restoring their operands. Could it be so simple to implement undo for all commands that we would simply need to store the top two values from the stack during execute() and implement undo by dropping the command's result and restoring the stored operands? No. Consider sine, cosine, and tangent. They each take one operand from the stack and return a single result. Consider swap. It takes two operands from the stack and returns two results (the operands in the opposite order). A perfectly uniform strategy for undo cannot be implemented over all commands. That said, we shouldn't just give up hope and return to implementing undo individually for every command.

Just because all commands in our calculator must descend from the Command class, no rule requires this inheritance to be the direct inheritance depicted in Figure 4-1. Consider, instead, the command hierarchy depicted in Figure 4-2. While some commands still directly inherit from the Command base class, we have created two new subclasses from which more specialized commands can be inherited. In fact, as will be seen shortly, these two new base classes are themselves abstract.

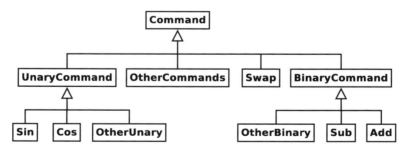

Figure 4-2. *A multi-level hierarchy for the calculator's command pattern*

Our preceding use case analysis identified two significant subcategories of operations that implement undo uniformly for their respective members: binary commands (commands that take two operands and return one result) and unary commands (commands that take one operand and return one result). Thus, we can simplify our implementation significantly by generically handling undo for these two classes of commands. While commands not fitting into either the unary or binary

command family will still be required to implement undo() individually, these two
subcategories account for about 75% of the core commands of the calculator. Creating
these two abstractions will save a significant amount of work.

Let's examine the UnaryCommand class. By definition, all unary commands require
one argument and return one value. For example, $f(x) = \sin(x)$ takes one number, x, from
the stack and returns the result, $f(x)$, onto the stack. As previously stated, the reason for
considering all unary functions together as a family is because regardless of the function,
all unary commands implement both forward execution and undo identically, differing
only in the functional form of f. Additionally, they also all must minimally meet the same
precondition. Namely, there must be at least one element on the stack.

In code, the above common traits of unary commands are enforced by overriding
executeImpl(), undoImpl(), and checkPreconditionsImpl() in the UnaryCommand
base class and creating a new unaryOperation() pure virtual that delegates the
precise implementation of each command to a further derived class. The result is a
UnaryCommand class with the following declaration in Listing 4-4.

Listing 4-4. The UnaryCommand Class

```
class UnaryCommand : public Command
{
public:
  virtual ~UnaryCommand();

protected:
  void checkPreconditionsImpl() const override;
  UnaryCommand() { }
  UnaryCommand(const UnaryCommand&);

private:
  void executeImpl() override;
  void undoImpl() override;
  virtual double unaryOperation(double top) const = 0;

  double top_;
};
```

For completeness, let's examine the implementation of the three overridden functions from `Command`. Checking the precondition is trivial; we ensure at least one element is on the stack. If not, an exception is thrown:

```
void UnaryCommand::checkPreconditionsImpl() const
{
  if(Stack::Instance().size() < 1)
    throw Exception{"Stack must have one element"};
}
```

The `executeImpl()` command is also quite straightforward:

```
void UnaryCommand::executeImpl()
{
  top_ = Stack::Instance().pop(true);
  Stack::Instance().push( unaryOperation(top_) );
}
```

The top element is popped from the stack and stored in the `UnaryCommand`'s state for the purposes of undo. Remember, because we have already checked the precondition, we can be assured that `unaryOperation()` will complete without an error. Commands with special preconditions will still need to implement `checkPreconditionsImpl()`, but they can at least delegate the unary precondition check upward to `UnaryCommand`'s `checkPreconditionImpl()` function. In one fell swoop, we then dispatch the unary function operation to a further derived class and push its result back onto the stack.

The only peculiarity in `UnaryCommand`'s `executeImpl()` function is the boolean argument to the stack's `pop` command. This boolean optionally suppresses the emission of a stack changed event. Because we know that the following push command to the stack will immediately alter the stack again, there is no need to issue two subsequent stack changed events. The suppression of this event permits the command implementer to lump the action of the command into one user-apparent event. Although this boolean argument to `Stack`'s `pop()` was not part of the original design, this functionality can be added to the `Stack` class now as a convenience. Remember, design is iterative.

The final member function to examine is `undoImpl()`:

```
void UnaryCommand::undoImpl()
{
  Stack::Instance().pop(true);
  Stack::Instance().push(top_);
}
```

This function also has the expected obvious implementation. The result of the unary operation is dropped from the stack, and the previous top element, which was stored in the `top_` member of the class during the execution of `executeImpl()`, is restored to the stack.

As an example of using the `UnaryCommand` class, we present a partial implementation of the sine command:

```
class Sine : public UnaryCommand
{
private:
  double unaryOperation(double t) const override { return std::sin(t); }
};
```

Clearly, the advantage of using the `UnaryCommand` as a base class instead of the highest level `Command` class is that we have removed the need to implement `undoImpl()` and `checkPreconditionsImpl()`, and we replaced the implementation of `executeImpl()` with the slightly simpler `unaryOperation()`. Not only do we need less code overall, but because the implementations of `undoImpl()` and `checkPreconditionsImpl()` would be identical over all unary commands, we reduce code repetition as well, which is always a positive.

Binary commands are implemented in an analogous manner to unary commands. The only difference is that the function for executing the operation takes two commands as operands and correspondingly must store both of these values for undo. The complete definition for the `BinaryCommand` class can be found alongside the `Command` and `UnaryCommand` classes in the `Command.h` header file found in the source code from the GitHub repository.

4.2.3.3 Concrete Commands

Defining the `Command`, `UnaryCommand`, and `BinaryCommand` classes above completed the abstract interface for using the command pattern in the calculator. Getting these interfaces correct encompasses the lion's share of the design for commands. However, at this point, our calculator is yet to have a single concrete command (other than the partial `Sine` class implementation). This section will finally rectify that problem, and the core functionality of our calculator will begin to take shape.

The core commands of the calculator are all defined in the `CoreCommands.h` file, and their implementations can be found in the corresponding `CoreCommands.cpp` file. What are core commands? I have defined the core commands to be the set of commands that encompass the functionality distilled from the requirements listed in Chapter 1. A unique core command exists for each distinct action the calculator must perform. Why did I term these the core commands? They are the core commands because they are compiled and linked alongside the calculator and are therefore available immediately when the calculator loads. They are, in fact, an intrinsic part of the calculator. This is in contrast to plugin commands, which may be optionally loaded by the calculator dynamically during runtime. Plugin commands are discussed in detail in Chapter 7.

While one might suspect that we now need to perform an analysis to determine the core commands, it turns out that this analysis has already been done. Specifically, the core commands were defined by the actions described in the use cases from Chapter 2. The astute reader will even recall that the exception listings in the use cases define each command's precondition. Therefore, with reference to the use cases as necessary, one can trivially derive the core commands. For convenience, they are all listed in Table 4-1.

Table 4-1. *The Core Commands Listed by Their Immediate Abstract Base Class*

Command	UnaryCommand	BinaryCommand
EnterCommand	Sine	Add
SwapTopOfStack	Cosine	Subtract
DropTopOfStack	Tangent	Multiply
Duplicate	Arcsine	Divide
ClearStack	Arccosine	Power
	Arctangent	Root
	Negate	

In comparing the list of core commands above to the use cases from Chapter 2, one notes the conspicuous absence of undo and redo as commands even though they are both actions the user can request the calculator to perform. These two "commands" are special because they act on other commands in the system. For this reason, they are not implemented as commands in the command pattern sense. Instead, they are handled intrinsically by the yet-to-be-discussed CommandManager, which is the class responsible for requesting commands, dispatching commands, and requesting undo and redo actions. The undo and redo actions (as opposed to the undo and redo operations defined by each command) will be discussed in detail in Section 4.4 below.

The implementation of each core command, including the checking of preconditions, the forward operation, and the undo implementation, is relatively straightforward. Most of the command classes can be implemented in about 20 lines of code. The interested reader is referred to the repository source code if he or she wishes to examine the details.

4.2.3.4 An Alternative to Deep Command Hierarchies

Creating a separate Command class for each operation is a very classical way of implementing the command pattern. Modern C++, however, gives us a very compelling alternative that enables us to flatten the hierarchy. Specifically, we can use lambda expressions (see sidebar) to encapsulate operations instead of creating additional derived classes and then use the standard function class (see sidebar) to store these operations in a class at the UnaryCommand or BinaryCommand level. To make the discussion concrete, let's consider an alternative partial design to the BinaryCommand class, shown in Listing 4-5.

Listing 4-5. An Alternative Partial Design

```
class BinaryCommandAlternative final : public Command
{
  using BinaryCommandOp = double(double, double);
public:
  BinaryCommandAlternative(const string& help,
    function<BinaryCommandOp> f);
```

```
private:
  void checkPreconditionsImpl() const override;
  const char* helpMessageImpl() const override;
  void executeImpl() override;
  void undoImpl() override;

  double top_;
  double next_;
  string helpMsg_;
  function<BinaryCommandOp> command_;
};
```

Now, instead of an abstract BinaryCommand that implements executeImpl() by deferral to a binaryOperation() virtual function, we declare a concrete and final (see sidebar) class that accepts a callable target and implements executeImpl() by invoking this target. In fact, the only material difference between BinaryCommand and BinaryCommandAlternative is a subtle difference in the implementation of the executeImpl() command; see Listing 4-6.

Listing 4-6. A Subtle Difference

```
void BinaryCommandAlternative::executeImpl()
{
  top_ = Stack::Instance().pop(true);
  next_ = Stack::Instance().pop(true);
  // invoke callable target instead of virtual dispatch:
  Stack::Instance().push( command_(next_, top_) );
}
```

Now, as an example, instead of declaring a Multiply class and instantiating a Multiply object, like

```
auto mult = new Multiply;
```

we create a BinaryCommandAlternative capable of multiplication, as in

```
auto mult = new BinaryCommandAlternative{ "help msg",
  [](double d, double f){ return d * f; } };
```

For completeness, I mention that because no classes further derive from `BinaryCommandAlternative`, we must handle help messages directly in the constructor rather than in a derived class. Additionally, as implemented, `BinaryCommandAlternative` only handles the binary precondition. However, additional preconditions could be handled in an analogous fashion to the handling of the binary operation. That is, the constructor could accept and store a lambda to execute the precondition test after the test for two stack arguments in `checkPreconditionImpl()`.

Obviously, unary commands could be handled similarly to binary commands through the creation of a `UnaryCommandAlternative` class. With enough templates, I'm quite certain you could even unify binary and unary commands into one class. Be forewarned, though. Too much cleverness, while impressive at the water cooler, does not usually lead to maintainable code. Keeping separate classes for binary commands and unary commands in this flattened command hierarchy probably strikes an appropriate balance between terseness and understandability.

The implementation difference between `BinaryCommand`'s `executeImpl()` and `BinaryCommandAlternative`'s `executeImpl()` is fairly small. However, you should not understate the magnitude of this change. The end result is a significant design difference in the implementation of the command pattern. Is one better than the other in the general case? I do not think such a statement can be made unequivocally; each design has tradeoffs. The `BinaryCommand` strategy is the classic implementation of the command pattern, and most experienced developers will recognize it as such. The source code is very easy to read, maintain, and test. For every command, exactly one class is created that performs exactly one operation. The `BinaryCommandAlternative`, on the other hand, is very concise. Rather than having *n* classes for *n* operations, only one class exists, and each operation is defined by a lambda in the constructor. If paucity of code is your objective, this alternative style is hard to beat. However, because lambdas are, by definition, anonymous objects, some clarity is lost by not naming each binary operation in the system.

Which strategy is better for pdCalc, the deep command hierarchy or the shallow command hierarchy? Personally, I prefer the deep command hierarchy because of the clarity that naming each object brings. However, for such simple operations, like addition and subtraction, I think one could make a good argument that the reduced line count improves clarity more than what is lost through anonymity. Because of my personal preference, I implemented most of the commands using the deep hierarchy and the `BinaryCommand` class. Nonetheless, I did implement multiplication via the `BinaryCommandAlternative` to illustrate the implementation in practice. In a production system, I would highly recommend choosing one strategy or the other. Implementing both patterns in the same system is certainly more confusing than adopting one, even if the one chosen is deemed suboptimal.

MODERN C++ DESIGN NOTE: LAMBDAS, STANDARD FUNCTION, AND THE FINAL KEYWORD

Lambdas, standard `function`, and the `final` keyword are actually three independent modern C++ concepts. I'll therefore address them separately.

Lambdas:

Lambdas (more formally, lambda expressions) can be thought of as anonymous function objects. The easiest way to reason about lambdas is to consider their function object equivalent. The syntax for defining a lambda is given by the following:

$$[capture\text{-}list](argument\text{-}list)\{function\text{-}body\}$$

The above lambda syntax identically equates to a function object that stores the *capture-list* as member variables via a constructor and provides an `operator() const` member function with arguments provided by *argument-list* and a function body provided by *function-body*. The return type of the `operator()` is generally deduced from the function body, but it can be manually specified using the alternative function return type syntax (i.e., `-> ret` between the argument list and the function body), if desired.

Given the equivalence between a lambda expression and a function object, lambdas do not actually provide new functionality to C++. Anything that can be done in C++11 with a lambda can be done in C++03 with a different syntax. What lambdas do provide, however, is a compelling, concise syntax for the declaration of inline, anonymous functions. Two very common use cases for lambdas are as predicates for STL algorithms and targets for C++11 asynchronous tasks. Some have even argued that the lambda syntax is so compelling that there is no longer a need to write `for` loops in high-level code since they can be replaced with a lambda and an algorithm. Personally, I find this point of view too extreme.

In the alternative design to binary commands, you saw yet another use for lambdas. They can be stored in objects and then called on demand to provide different options for implementing algorithms. In some respects, this paradigm encodes a micro-application of the strategy pattern. To avoid confusion with the command pattern, I specifically did not introduce the strategy pattern in the main text. The interested reader is referred to Gamma et al [6] for details.

Standard `function`**:**

The `function` class is part of the C++ standard library. This class provides a generic wrapper around any callable target converting this callable target into a function object. Essentially, any C++ construct that can be called like a function is a callable target. This includes functions, lambdas, and member functions.

Standard `function` provides two very useful features. First, it provides a generic facility for interfacing with any callable target. That is, in template programing, storing a callable target in a `function` object unifies the calling semantics on the target independent of the underlying type. Second, `function` enables the storage of otherwise difficult-to-store types, like lambda expressions. In the design of the `BinaryCommandAlternative`, we made use of the `function` class to store lambdas to implement small algorithms to overlay the strategy pattern onto the command pattern. Although not actually utilized in pdCalc, the generic nature of the `function` class actually enables the `BinaryCommandAlternative` constructor to accept callable targets other than lambdas.

The `final` **Keyword:**

The final keyword, introduced in C++11, enables a class designer to declare either that a class cannot be inherited from or a virtual function may not be further overridden. For those programmers coming from either C# or Java, you'll know that C++ is late to the game in finally (pun intended) adding this facility.

Before C++11, nasty hacks needed to be used to prevent further derivation of a class. Beginning with C++11, the `final` keyword enables the compiler to enforce this constraint. Prior to C++11, many C++ designers argued that the `final` keyword was unnecessary. A designer wanting a class to be non-inheritable could just make the destructor non-virtual, thereby implying that deriving from this class was outside the designer's intent. Anyone who has seen code inheriting from STL containers will know how well developers tend to follow intent not enforced by the compiler. How often have you heard a fellow developer say, "Sure, that's a bad idea, in general, but, don't worry, it's fine in my special case." This oft-uttered comment is almost inevitably followed by a week-long debugging session to track down obscure bugs.

Why might you want to prevent inheriting from a class or overriding a previously declared virtual function? Likely because you have a situation where inheritance, while being well-defined by the language, simply makes no sense logically. A concrete example of this is pdCalc's `BinaryCommandAlternative` class. While you could attempt to derive from it and override the executeImpl() member function (without the final keyword in place, that is), the intent of the class is to terminate the hierarchy and provide the binary operation via a callable target. Inheriting from BinaryCommandAlternative is outside the scope of its design. Preventing derivation is therefore likely to prevent subtle semantic errors.

4.3 The Command Repository

Our calculator now has all of the commands required to meet its requirements. However, we have not yet defined the infrastructure necessary for storing commands and subsequently accessing them on demand. In this section, we'll explore several design strategies for storing and retrieving commands.

4.3.1 The CommandRepository Class

At first glance, instantiating a new command seems like a trivial problem to solve. For example, if a user requests the addition of two numbers, the following code will perform this function:

```
Command* cmd = new Add;
cmd->execute();
```

Great! Problem solved, right? Not really. How is this code called? Where does this code appear? What happens if new core commands are added (i.e., requirements change)? What if new commands are added dynamically (as in plugins)? What seems like an easy problem to solve is actually more complex than initially expected. Let's explore possible design alternatives by answering the above questions.

First, we ask the question of how the code is called. Part of the calculator's requirements are to have both a command line interface (CLI) and a graphical user interface (GUI). Clearly, the request to initialize a command will derive somewhere in the user interface in response to a user's action. Let's consider how the user interface would handle subtraction. Suppose that the GUI has a subtraction button, and when this button is clicked, a function is called to initialize and execute the subtraction command (we'll ignore undo, momentarily). Now consider the CLI. When the subtraction token is recognized, a similar function is called. At first, one might expect that we could call the same function, provided it existed in the business logic layer instead of in the user interface layer. However, the mechanism for GUI callbacks makes this impossible because it would force an undesired dependency in the business logic layer on the GUI's widget library (e.g., in Qt, a button callback is a slot in a class, which requires the callback's class to be a Q_OBJECT). Alternatively, the GUI could deploy double indirection to dispatch each command (each button click would call a function which would call a function in the business logic layer). This scenario seems both inelegant and inefficient.

While the above strategy appears rather cumbersome, this initialization scheme has a structural deficit much deeper than inconvenience. In the model-view-controller architecture we have adopted for pdCalc, the views are not permitted direct access to the controller. Since the commands rightly belong to the controller, direct initialization of commands by the UI violates our foundational architecture.

How do we solve this new problem? Recall from Table 2-2 that the command dispatcher's only public interface is the event handling function commandEntered(const string&). This realization actually answers the first two questions we originally posed: how is the initialization and execution code called and where does it reside? This code must be triggered indirectly via an event from the UI to the command dispatcher with the specific command encoded via a string. The code itself must reside in the command dispatcher. Note that this interface has the additional benefit of removing duplication between the CLI and the GUI in creating new commands. Now both user interfaces can simply create commands by raising the commandEntered event and specifying the command by string. You'll see how each user interface implements raising this event in Chapters 5 and 6, respectively.

From the above analysis, we are motivated to add a new class to the command dispatcher with the responsibility of owning and allocating commands. We'll call this class the CommandRepository. For the moment, we'll assume that another part of the command dispatcher (the CommandDispatcher class) receives the commandEntered() event and requests the appropriate command from the CommandRepository (via the commandEntered()'s string argument), and yet another component of the command dispatcher (the CommandManager class) subsequently executes the command (and handles undo and redo). That is, we have decoupled the initialization and storage of commands from their dispatch and execution. The CommandManager and CommandDispatcher classes are the subjects of upcoming sections. For now, we'll focus on command storage, initialization, and retrieval.

We begin with the following skeletal interface for the `CommandManager` class:

```
class CommandRepository
{
public:
  unique_ptr<Command> allocateCommand(const string&) const;
};
```

From the interface above, we see that given a string argument, the repository allocates the corresponding command. The interface employs a smart pointer return type to make explicit that the caller owns the memory for the newly constructed command.

Let's now consider what an implementation for `allocateCommand()` might look like. This exercise will assist us in modifying the design for more flexibility.

```
unique_ptr<Command> CommandRepository::allocateCommand(const string& c)
const
{
  if(c == "+") return make_unique<Add>();
  else if(c == "-") return make_unique<Subtract>();
  // ... all known commands ...
  else return nullptr;
}
```

The above interface is simple and effective, but it is limited by requiring *a priori* knowledge of every command in the system. In general, such a design would be highly undesirable and inconvenient for several reasons. First, adding a new core command to the system would require modifying the repository's initialization function. Second, deploying runtime plugin commands would require a completely different implementation. Third, this strategy creates unwanted coupling between the instantiation of specific commands and their storage. Instead, we would prefer a design where the `CommandRepository` relies only on the abstract interface defined by the `Command` base class.

The above problem is solved by application of a simple pattern known as the prototype pattern [6]. The prototype pattern is a creational pattern where a prototype object is stored, and new objects of this type are created simply by copying the prototype. Now, consider a design that treats our `CommandRepository` as merely a container of command prototypes. Furthermore, let the prototypes all be stored by `Command` pointer, say, in a hash table, using a string as the key (maybe the same string raised in the commandEntered() event). Then, new commands could be added (or removed) dynamically by adding (or removing) a new prototype command. To implement this strategy, we make the following additions to our CommandRepository class:

```
class CommandRepository
{
public:
  unique_ptr<Command> allocateCommand(const string&) const;
  void registerCommand(const string& name, unique_ptr<Command> c);

private:
  using Repository = unordered_map<string, unique_ptr<Command>>;
  Repository repository_;
};
```

The implementation for registering a command is quite simple:

```
void CommandRepository::registerCommand(const string& name,
unique_ptr<Command> c)
{
  if( repository_.find(name) != repository_.end() )
    // handle duplicate command error
  else
    repository_.emplace( name, std::move(c) );
}
```

Here, we check whether or not the command is already in the repository. If it is, then we handle the error. If not, then we move the command argument into the repository, where the command becomes the prototype for the command name. Note that the use of unique_ptr indicates that registering a command transfers ownership of this prototype to the command repository. In practical usage, the core commands are all registered via a function in the CoreCommands.cpp file, and a similar function exists inside each plugin to register the plugin commands (we'll see this interface when we examine the construction of plugins in Chapter 7). These functions are called during initialization of the calculator and during plugin initialization, respectively. Optionally, the command repository can be augmented with a deregister command with the obvious implementation.

Using our new design, we can rewrite the allocateCommand() function as follows:

```
unique_ptr<Command> CommandRepository::allocateCommand(const string& name)
const
{
  auto it = repository_.find(name);
  if( it != repository_.end() )
  {
    return unique_ptr<Command>( it->second->clone() );
  }
  else return nullptr;
}
```

Now, if the command is found in the repository, a copy of the prototype is returned. If the command is not found, a nullptr is returned (alternatively, an exception could be thrown). The copy of the prototype is returned in a unique_ptr, indicating that the caller now owns this copy of the command. Note the use of the clone() function from the Command class. The clone function was originally added to the Command class with the promise of future justification. As is now evident, we require the clone() function in order to copy Commands polymoprhically for our implementation of the prototype pattern. Of course, had we not had the foresight to implement a cloning function for all commands at the time that the Command class was designed, it could easily be added now. Remember, you won't get the design perfect on the first pass, so get used to the idea of iterative design.

Essentially, registerCommand() and allocateCommand() embody the minimally complete interface for the CommandRepository class. However, if you examine the included source code for this class, you will see some differences. First, additional functions have been added to the interface. The additional functions are mostly convenience and syntactic sugar. Second, the entire interface is hidden behind a pimpl. Third, I use an alias, CommandPtr, instead of directly using unique_ptr<Command>. For the purposes of this chapter, just think of CommandPtr as being defined by the following using statement:

```
using CommandPtr = std::unique_ptr<Command>;
```

The real alias, which can be found in Command.h, is slightly more complicated. It will be explained in detail in Chapter 7. Correspondingly, I use a function MakeCommandPtr() rather than make_unique<Command>() to create CommandPtrs.

Finally, the only other part of the interface from the repository code not already discussed that impacts the design is the choice to make the CommandRepository a singleton. The reason for this decision is simple. Regardless of how many different command dispatchers exist in the system (interestingly enough, we'll eventually see a case for having multiple command dispatchers), the prototypes for functions never change. Therefore, making the CommandRepository a singleton centralizes the storage, allocation, and retrieval of all commands for the calculator.

MODERN C++ DESIGN NOTE: UNIFORM INITIALIZATION

You might have noticed that I routinely use curly braces for initialization. For developers who have been programming in C++ for a long time, the use of curly braces to initialize a class (i.e., call its constructor) may appear odd. While we are accustomed to a list syntax for initializing arrays, as in

```
int a[] = { 1, 2, 3 };
```

using curly braces to initialize classes is a new feature in C++11. While parentheses may still be used for calling constructors, the new syntax using curly braces, called *uniform initialization*, is the preferred syntax for modern C++. While the two initialization mechanisms functionally perform the same task, the new syntax has three advantages:

1. Uniform initialization is non-narrowing:

    ```
    class A { A(int a); };
    A a(7.8); // ok, truncates
    A a{7.8}; // error, narrows
    ```

2. Uniform initialization (combined with initializer lists) permits initializing user defined types with lists:

    ```
    vector <double> v{ 1.1, 1.2, 1.3 }; // valid since C++11;
        initializes vector with 3 doubles
    ```

3. Uniform initialization is never mistakenly parsed as a function:

    ```
    struct B { B(); void foo(); };
    B b(); // Are you declaring a function that returns a B?
    b.foo(); // error, requesting foo() in non-class type b
    ```

```
B b2{}; // ok, default construction
b2.foo(); // ok, call B::foo()
```

There is only one big caveat when using uniform initialization: a list constructor is always called before any other constructor. The canonical example comes from the STL `vector` class, which has an initializer list constructor and a separate constructor accepting an integer to define the vector's size. Because initializer list constructors are called before any other constructor if curly braces are used, there are the following different behaviors:

```
vector<int> v(3); // vector, size 3, all elements initialized to 0
vector<int> v{3}; // vector with 1 element initialized to 3
```

Fortunately, the above situation does not arise often. However, when it does, you must understand the difference between uniform initialization and function style initialization.

From a design perspective, the main advantage of uniform initialization is that user defined types may be designed to accept lists of identically typed values for construction. Therefore, containers, such as `vectors`, may be statically initialized with a list of values rather than default initialized followed by successive assignment. This modern C++ feature enables initialization of derived types to use the same syntax for initialization as built-in array types, a syntactical feature missing in C++03.

4.3.2 Registering Core Commands

We have now defined the core commands of the calculator and a class for loading and serving the commands on demand. However, we have not discussed a method for loading the core commands into the CommandRepository. In order to function properly, the loading of all the core commands must only be performed once, and it must be performed before the calculator is used. Essentially, this defines an initialization requirement for the command dispatcher module. A finalization function is not needed since deregistering the core commands when exiting the program is unnecessary.

The best place to call an initialization operation for the command dispatcher is in the main() function of the calculator. Therefore, we simply create a global RegisterCoreCommands() function, declare it in the CoreCommands.h header, implement it in the CoreCommands.cpp file, and call it from main(). The reason to create a global function instead of registering the core commands in the CommandRepository's constructor is to avoid coupling the CommandRepository with the derived classes of the command hierarchy. The registration function, of course, could be called something like `InitCommandDispatcher()`, but I prefer a name that more specifically describes the functionality.

Implicitly, we have just extended the interface to the command dispatcher (originally defined in Table 2-2), albeit fairly trivially. Should we have been able to anticipate this part of the interface in advance? Probably not. This interface update was necessitated by a design decision at a level significantly more detailed than the high-level decomposition of Chapter 2. I find slightly modifying a key interface during development to be an acceptable way of designing a program. A design strategy requiring immutability is simply too rigid to be practical. However, note that easy acceptance of a key interface modification during development is in contrast with the acceptance of a key interface modification after release, a decision that should only be made after significant consideration for how the change will affect clients already using your code.

4.4 The Command Manager

Having designed the command infrastructure and created a repository for the storage, initialization, and retrieval of commands in the system, we are now ready to design a class with responsibility for executing commands on demand and managing undo and redo. This class is called the `CommandManager`. Essentially, it manages the lifetime of commands by calling the `execute()` function on each command and subsequently retaining each command in a manner appropriate for implementing unlimited undo and redo. We'll start by defining the interface for the `CommandManager` and conclude the section by discussing the strategy for implementing unlimited undo and redo.

4.4.1 The Interface

The interface for the `CommandManager` is remarkably simple and straightforward. The `CommandManager` needs an interface for accepting commands to be executed, for undoing commands, and for redoing commands. Optionally, one could also include an interface for querying the available number of undo and redo operations, which might be important for the implementation of a GUI (e.g., for redo size equals zero, grey out the redo button). Once a command is passed to the `CommandManager`, the `CommandManager` owns the lifetime of the command. Therefore, the interface for the `CommandManager` should enforce owning semantics. Combining, we have the following complete interface for the CommandManager:

```
class CommandManager
{
public:
  size_t getUndoSize() const;
  size_t getRedoSize() const;
  void executeCommand(unique_ptr<Command> c);
  void undo();
  void redo();
};
```

In the actual code listed in CommandManager.h, the interface additionally defines an enum class for selecting the undo/redo strategy during construction. I've included this option for illustrative purposes only. A production code would simply implement one undo/redo strategy and not make the underlying data structure customizable at construction.

4.4.2 Implementing Undo and Redo

To implement unlimited undo and redo, we must have a dynamically growable data structure capable of storing and revisiting commands in the order they were executed. Although one could contrive many different data structures to satisfy this requirement, we'll examine two equally good strategies. Both strategies have been implemented for the calculator and can be seen in the CommandManager.cpp file.

Consider the data structure in Figure 4-3, which I have termed *the list strategy*. After a command is executed, it is added to a list (the implementation could be a list, vector, or other suitable ordered container), and a pointer (or index) is updated to point to the last command executed. Whenever undo is called, the command currently pointed to is undone, and the pointer moves to the left (the direction of earlier commands). When redo is called, the command pointer moves to the right (the direction of later commands), and the newly-pointed-to command is executed. Boundary conditions exist when the current command pointer reaches either the far left (no more commands exist to be undone) or far right (no more commands exist to be redone). These boundary conditions can be handled either by disabling the mechanism that enables the user to call the command (e.g., grey out the undo or redo button, respectively) or by simply ignoring an undo or redo command that would cause the pointer to overrun the boundary. Of course, every time a new command is executed, the entire list to the right of the current command pointer must be flushed before the new command is added to the undo/redo list. This flushing of the list is necessary to prevent the undo/redo list from becoming a tree with multiple redo branches.

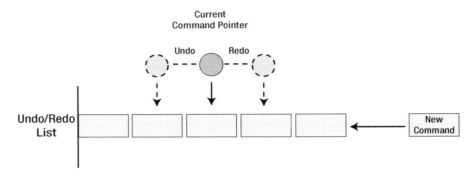

Figure 4-3. *The undo/redo list strategy*

As an alternative, consider the data structure in Figure 4-4, which I have termed the *stack strategy*. Instead of maintaining a list of commands in the order in which they were executed, we maintain two stacks, one for the undo commands and one for the redo commands. After a new command is executed, it is pushed onto the undo stack. Commands are undone by popping the top entry from the undo stack, undoing the command, and pushing the command onto the redo stack. Commands are redone by popping the top entry from the redo stack, executing the command, and pushing the command onto the undo stack. Boundary conditions exist and are trivially identified by the sizes of the stacks. Executing a new command requires flushing the redo stack.

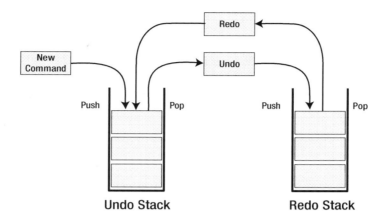

Figure 4-4. *The Undo/Redo Stack Strategy*

Practically, choosing between implementing undo and redo via either the stack or list strategy is largely a personal preference. The list strategy requires only one data container and less data movement. However, the stack strategy is slightly easier to implement because it requires no indexing or pointer shifting. That said, both strategies are fairly easy to implement and require very little code. Once you have implemented and tested either strategy, the `CommandManager` can easily be reused in future projects requiring undo and redo functionality, provided commands are implemented via the command pattern. For even more generality, the `CommandManager` could be templated on the abstract `Command` class. For simplicity, I chose to implement the included `CommandManager` specifically for the abstract `Command` class previously discussed.

4.5 The Command Dispatcher

The final component of the command dispatcher module is the `CommandDispatcher` class itself. Although this class might more aptly be named the `CommandInterpreter`, I have retained the name `CommandDispatcher` to emphasize that this class serves as the command dispatcher module's interface to the rest of the calculator. That is, as far as the other modules are concerned, the `CommandDispatcher` class is the entirety of the command dispatcher module.

As previously stated, the `CommandDispatcher` class serves two primary roles. The first role is to serve as the interface to the command dispatcher module. The second role is to interpret each command, request the appropriate command from the `CommandRepository`, and pass each command to the `CommandManager` for execution. We address these two roles sequentially.

4.5.1 The Interface

For all the complications in the implementation of the command dispatcher module, the interface to the `CommandDispatcher` class is remarkably simple (as are most good interfaces). As discussed in Chapter 2, the command dispatcher's interface consists entirely of a single function used to execute a command; the command itself is specified by a string argument. This function is, naturally, the `executeCommand()` event handler previously discussed. Thus, the `CommandDispatcher` class's interface is given by the following:

```
class CommandDispatcher
{
public:
  CommandDispatcher(UserInterface& ui);
  void executeCommand(const string& command);

private:
  unique_ptr<CommandDispatcherImpl> pimpl_;
};
```

Recall that the fundamental architecture of the calculator is based on the model-view-controller pattern and that the `CommandDispatcher` is permitted to have direct access to both the model (stack) and view (user interface). Thus, the `CommandDispatcher`'s constructor takes a reference to an abstract `UserInterface` class, the details of which are discussed in Chapter 5. A direct reference to the stack is unneeded since the stack was implemented as a singleton. As per my usual convention, the actual implementation of the `CommandDispatcher` is deferred to a private implementation class, `CommandDispatcherImpl`.

An alternative design to the one above would be to make the `CommandDispatcher` class an observer directly. As discussed in Chapter 3, I prefer designs that use intermediary event observers. In Chapter 5, I'll discuss the design and implementation of a `CommandIssuedObserver` proxy class to broker events between user interfaces and the `CommandDispatcher` class.

4.5.2 Implementation Details

Typically in this book, I do not discuss the implementation details contained in a pimpl class. In this case, though, the implementation of the `CommandDispatcherImpl` class is particularly instructive. The main function of the `CommandDispatcherImpl` class is to implement the function `executeCommand()`. This function must receive command requests, interpret these requests, retrieve commands, request execution of commands, and gracefully handle unknown commands. Had we started our decomposition of the command dispatcher module from the top down, trying to implement this function cleanly would have been exceedingly difficult. However, due to our bottom-up approach, the implementation of `executeCommand()` is largely an exercise in gluing together existing components. Consider the following implementation, where the `manager_` object is an instance of the `CommandManager` class, as shown in Listing 4-7.

Listing 4-7. The Implementation of `executeCommand()`

```
 1   void CommandDispatcher::CommandDispatcherImpl::executeCommand(const string&
 2   command)
 3   {
 4     double d;
 5     if( isNum(command, d) )
 6       manager_.executeCommand( MakeCommandPtr<EnterNumber>(d) );
 7     else if(command == "undo")
 8       manager_.undo();
 9     else if(command == "redo")
10       manager_.redo();
11     else
12     {
13       auto c = CommandRepository::Instance().allocateCommand(command);
14       if(!c)
15       {
16         ostringstream oss;
17         oss << "Command " << command << " is not a known command";
18         ui_.postMessage( oss.str() );
19       }
```

```
20        else
21        {
22          try
23          {
24              manager_.executeCommand( std::move(c) );
25          }
26          catch(Exception& e)
27          {
28              ui_.postMessage( e.what() );
29          }
30        }
31      }
32
33    return;
34    }
```

Lines 5-10 handle special commands. A special command is any command that is not entered in the command repository. In the code above, this includes entering a new number, undo, and redo. If a special command is not encountered, then it is assumed that the command can be found in the command repository. This request is made in line 13. If nullptr is returned from the command repository, the error is handled in lines 16-18. Otherwise, the command is executed by the command manager. Note that the execution of commands is handled in a try/catch block. In this manner, we are able to trap errors caused by command precondition failures and report these errors in the user interface. The CommandManager's implementation ensures that commands failing a precondition are not entered onto the undo stack (trivially, by order of execution).

The actual implementation of executeCommand() found in CommandDispatcher.cpp differs slightly from the code above. First, the actual implementation includes two additional special commands. The first of these additional special commands is help. The help command can be issued to print a brief explanatory message for all of the commands currently in the command repository. While the implementation generically prints the help information to the user interface, I only exposed the help command in the CLI (i.e., my GUI's implementation does not have a help button). The second special command deals with the handling of stored procedures. Stored procedures are explained in Chapter 8. Additionally, I placed the try/catch block in its own function. This was done simply to shorten the `executeCommand()` function and separate the logic of command interpretation from command execution.

4.6 Revisiting Earlier Decisions

At this point, we have finished two of the main modules of our calculator: the stack and the command dispatcher. Let's revisit our original design to discuss a significant subtle deviation that has arisen.

Recall from Chapter 2 that our original design handled errors by raising events in the stack and command dispatcher, and these events were to be handled by the user interface. The reason for this decision was for consistency. While the command dispatcher has a reference to the user interface, the stack does not. Therefore, we decided to simply let both modules notify the user interface of errors via events. The astute reader will notice, however, that the command dispatcher, as designed above, never raises exceptions. Instead, it directly calls the user interface when errors occur. Have we not then broken the consistency that was intentionally designed into the system? No. Actually, we implicitly redesigned the error handling mechanism of the system during the design of the command dispatcher so that no error events are ever raised by either the stack or the command dispatcher. Let's examine why.

As I just stated, it is obvious from its implementation that the command dispatcher does not raise error events, but what happened to stack events? We didn't change the `Stack` class's source code, so how did error events get eliminated? In the original design, the stack indirectly notified the user interface when errors occurred by raising events. The two possible stack error conditions were popping an empty stack and swapping the top two elements of an insufficiently sized stack. While designing the commands, I realized that if a command triggered either of these error conditions, the user interface would be notified, but the command dispatcher would not be (it is not an observer of stack events). In either error scenario, a command would have completed, albeit unsuccessfully, and been placed erroneously on the undo stack. I then realized that either the command dispatcher would have to trap stack errors and prevent erroneous placement onto the undo stack, or commands should not be permitted to make stack errors. As the final design demonstrates, I chose the easier and cleaner implementation of using preconditions before executing commands to prevent stack errors from occurring, thus implicitly suppressing stack errors.

The big question is, why didn't I change the text describing the original design and the corresponding code to reflect the change in the error reporting? Simply stated, I wanted the reader to see that mistakes do occur. Design is an iterative process, and a book trying to teach design by example should embrace that fact rather than hide it. Designs should be somewhat fluid (but maybe with a high viscosity). It is much better to change a bad design decision early than to stick with it despite encountering evidence demonstrating flaws in the original design. The later a bad design is changed, the higher the cost will be in fixing it, and the more pain the developers will incur while trying to implement a mistake. As for changing the code itself, I would have removed the superfluous code from the `Stack` class in a production system when I performed the refactor unless the `Stack` class was being designed for reuse in another program that handled errors via events. After all, as a generic design, the mechanism of reporting errors by raising events is not flawed. In hindsight, this mechanism was simply not right for pdCalc.

CHAPTER 5

The Command Line Interface

This is a very exciting chapter. While command line interfaces (CLIs) may not have the cachet of modern graphical user interfaces (GUIs), especially those of phones or tablets, the CLI is still a remarkably useful and effective user interface. This chapter details the design and implementation of the command line interface for pdCalc. By the end of this chapter, we will, for the first time, have a functioning (albeit feature incomplete) calculator, which is a significant milestone in our development.

5.1 The User Interface Abstraction

While we could design a fully functioning CLI in isolation, we know from our requirements that the feature complete calculator must have both a CLI and a GUI. Therefore, our overall design will be better served by first considering the commonality between these two interfaces and factoring this functionality into a common abstraction. Let's consider two design alternatives to constructing a user interface abstraction, a top-down approach and a bottom-up approach.

Designing an abstract interface before considering the concrete types is akin to top-down design. In terms of a user interface, you first consider the barest essentials to which any UI must conform and create an abstract interface based on this minimalist concept. Refinement to the interface becomes necessary when the abstract concept misses something required to implement a concrete type.

Designing an abstract interface after considering the concrete types is akin to bottom-up design. Again, in terms of a user interface, you first consider the needs of all the concrete types (CLI and GUI, in this case), look for the commonality between all types, and then distill the common features into an abstraction. Refinement to the

© Adam B. Singer 2017
A. B. Singer, *Practical C++ Design*, DOI 10.1007/978-1-4842-3057-2_5

interface becomes necessary when you add a new concrete type that requires additional features not considered when the abstraction was originally distilled.

Which strategy is better, in general, for creating an abstract interface: top down or bottom up? As is typical, the answer depends on the particular situation, personal comfort, and style. In this particular scenario, we are better served starting from the abstraction and working downward toward the concrete types (the top-down approach). Why? In this instance, the top-down approach is essentially free. The user interface is one of pdCalc's high-level modules, and we already defined the abstract interface for the UI in Chapter 2 when we performed our initial decomposition. Let's now turn the abstract module interface into a practical object-oriented design.

5.1.1 The Abstract Interface

The point of having an abstract interface for the UI is to enable the rest of the program to interact with the user interface without regard to whether the current interface is graphical, command line, or something else entirely. Ideally, we will be able to factor the abstract interface to the minimum number of functions required to use each concrete interface. Any functions sharing an implementation can be defined in the base class, while any functions requiring unique implementations based on the concrete type can be declared as virtual in the abstract base class and defined in the derived classes. The concept is fairly straightforward, but, as usual, the devil is in the details.

Consider the hierarchy depicted in Figure 5-1. Our goal is to design a minimal but complete interface, consistent with the Liskov Substitutability Principle, for pdCalc's UserInterface class that will work for both the CLI and the GUI. As previously discussed, we already defined a high-level interface for this UI in Chapter 2. Let's start from this predefined interface and refactor as necessary.

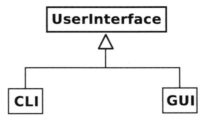

Figure 5-1. *A minimal interface hierarchy*

Referring to Table 2-2 in Chapter 2, you see that the complete interface for the `UserInterface` class consists of two event handling functions, `postMessage()` and `stackChanged()`, and one `UserInterface` raised event, `commandEntered()`. Interestingly, the `UserInterface` class is a publisher, an observer, and an abstract user interface.

The two event handling functions, `postMessage()` and `stackChanged()`, are straightforward at the interface level. As we have done with previous observers, we will simply add these two functions to the public interface of the `UserInterface` class and create proxy observer classes to broker the communication by the publisher and the actual observer. These proxies are discussed in detail in Section 5.1.2.2 below. Concrete user interfaces must handle the implementations for event handling uniquely based on how the individual UI interacts with the user. Hence, `postMessage()` and `stackChanged()` must both be pure virtual. Because there is no need for the `UserInterface` class to interject during event handling, I chose, for simplicity, to forgo the NVI pattern. However, as was discussed in Chapter 4, one could instead use the NVI pattern with trivial forwarding nonvirtual interface functions.

The `UserInterface` class's role as a publisher is slightly more complicated than its role as an observer. As you saw in Chapter 3 when designing the `Stack` class, the `Stack` implemented the publisher interface rather than substituted as a publisher. We therefore concluded that inheritance from the `Publisher` class should be private. For the `UserInterface` class, the relationship to the `Publisher` class is similar except the `UserInterface` class itself is not the publisher. The `UserInterface` class is an abstract interface for user interfaces in the system and is inheriting from the `Publisher` class only to enforce the notion that user interfaces must implement the publisher interface themselves. Both the CLI and the GUI classes will need to access public functions from `Publisher` (for example, to raise events). Thus, the protected mode of inheritance is appropriate in this instance.

Further recall from Chapter 3 that in order for the `Stack` class to implement the publisher interface, once we used private inheritance, we needed to hoist the `Publisher` class's `attach()` and `detach()` functions into the `Stack`'s public interface. The same is true here using protected inheritance. The question, however, is should the hoisting occur in the `UserInterface` class or in its derived classes? To answer this question, we need to ask how particular user interfaces will be used by pdCalc. Clearly, either a CLI or a GUI "is-a" `UserInterface`. Therefore, concrete user interfaces will publicly inherit from `UserInterface` and be expected to obey the LSP. Attaching or detaching events to or from a particular user interface must therefore be able to be accomplished without knowing the underlying UI type. Thus, the attach() and detach() functions must be visible as part of UserInterface's public interface. Interestingly, in a rather unique implementation of the observer pattern, part of the publisher interface is implemented at the UserInterface level, while another part of the publisher interface is implemented at the derived class level.

Combining all of the above points, we can finally define the UserInterface class as shown in Listing 5-1.

Listing 5-1. The UserInterface Class

```
class UserInterface : protected Publisher
{
public:
  UserInterface();
  virtual ~UserInterface();

  virtual void postMessage(const string& m) = 0;
  virtual void stackChanged() = 0;

  using Publisher::attach;
  using Publisher::detach;

  static const string CommandEntered;
};
```

The CommandEntered string is the name of the command entered event. It is needed for attaching or detaching this event and can be given any name unique to events in the UserInterface class.

For completeness, I show the final user interface hierarchy in Figure 5-2. The class diagram illustrates the relationship between the CLI, the GUI, the abstract UserInterface class, and the publisher interface. Remember that the inheritance between the UserInterface class and the Publisher class is protected, so a UserInterface (or subsequent derived class) cannot be used as a Publisher. As previously stated, however, the intent for the inheritances between the concrete CLI and GUI classes and the abstract UserInterface class are public, allowing an instantiation of either concrete type to be substituted as a UserInterface.

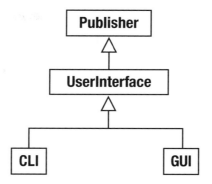

Figure 5-2. *The user interface hierarchy*

5.1.2 User Interface Events

Defining the UserInterface class does not complete the interface for the UI. Because the UserInterface class is an event publisher, we must also define the event data class that corresponds to the commandEntered() event. Additionally, defining the UserInterface class finally completes a publisher/observer pair, so we are finally ready to design and implement event proxy classes to broker events between the user interface and both the command dispatcher and the stack.

In Chapter 4, you saw that all commands are delivered to the command dispatcher via events. Specifically, the UI raises an event containing a specific command encoded as a string argument, the CommandDispatcher receives this event, and the string argument is passed to the CommandRepository, where a concrete command is retrieved for processing. As far as the command dispatcher is concerned, handling commandEntered() events is the same, irrespective of whether the encoded command string derives from the CLI or the GUI.

Likewise, when the Stack class raises a stackChanged() event, the Stack is indifferent to the particular UserInterface that handles this event. We are therefore motivated to treat the issuing of commandEntered() events and the handling of stackChanged() events uniformly at the UserInterface class level in the user interface hierarchy.

We begin by examining the common infrastructure for raising commandEntered() events. The commandEntered() event is registered for all user interfaces in the constructor of the UserInterface class. Therefore, any derived user interface class can simply raise this event by calling the raise() function defined by the Publisher interface, which, by protected inheritance, is part of any concrete UI's implementation.

101

The signature of the `raise()` function requires the name of the event and the event's data. Because the event's name is predefined in the `UserInterface`'s constructor, the only additional functionality required to raise a command entered event is a common `CommandData` class. Let's now look at its design.

5.1.2.1 Command Data

In Chapter 3, we designed our event system to use push semantics for passing event data. Recall that push semantics simply means that the publisher creates an object containing the necessary information to handle an event and pushes that object to the observers when an event is raised. The event data object must publicly inherit from the abstract `EventData` class. Observers receive the event data through the abstract interface when the event is raised, and they retrieve the data by downcasting the event data to the appropriate derived class.

For command entered events, the event data is trivially a string containing either a number to be entered on the stack or the name of a command to be issued. The `CommandData` class simply needs to accept a string command on construction, store this command, and provide a function for observers to retrieve the command. The entire implementation is given in Listing 5-2.

Listing 5-2. The Complete Implementation for the `CommandData` Class

```
class CommandData : public EventData
{
public:
  CommandData(const string& s) : command_(s) { }
  const string& command() const { return command_; }

private:
  string command_;
};
```

While the mechanics for determining how and when to raise a `CommandEntered` event is somewhat different between the CLI and the GUI, both raise events by ultimately calling `Publisher`'s `raise()` function with a `CommandData` argument encoded with the particular command being issued. That is, for some command string, cmd, the following code raises a `commandEntered()` event in the CLI, the GUI, or any other user interface that might inherit from `UserInterface`:

```
raise( UserInterface::CommandEntered, make_shared<CommandData>(cmd) );
```

Now that we can raise UI events, let's see how they're handled.

5.1.2.2 User Interface Observers

The goal for this subsection is to construct the mechanics to enable classes to listen to events. Because the abstract user interface is both a source and sink for events, the UI serves as an ideal candidate to demonstrate how publishers and observers interact with each other.

In Chapter 3, we saw that observers are classes that register for and listen to events raised by publishers. Thus far, we have encountered both the `CommandDispatcher` and `UserInterface` classes that both need to observe events. While it is possible to make the `CommandDispatcher` or `UserInterface` an observer directly, I prefer constructing a dedicated observer intermediary between the publisher and the class that needs to observe an event. I have often nebulously referred to this intermediary as a proxy. I am now ready to give a more concrete meaning to this term.

The proxy pattern [6] is a design pattern that uses a class, the proxy, to serve as the interface for something else. The something else, let's call it the target, is not strictly defined. It could be a network connection, a file, an object in memory, or, as in our case, simply another class. Often, the proxy pattern is used when the underlying target is impossible, inconvenient, or expensive to replicate. The proxy pattern uses a class buffer to allow the system to perceive the target as an object independent of its underlying composition. In our context, we are using the proxy pattern simply to buffer communication between publishers and observers.

Why are we bothering with the proxy pattern here? This strategy has several distinct advantages. First, it increases clarity in the target class's public interface by replacing a generically named `notify()` function with a descriptively named event handling function. Second, an otherwise unnecessary inheritance from the `Observer` class is removed. Eliminating this dependency reduces coupling, increases cohesion, and facilitates reuse of the target in a setting where it is not an observer. Third, using a proxy class eliminates the ambiguity that arises for a target class that needs to listen to multiple events. Without using proxy classes, an observer would be required to disambiguate events in its single notify() function. Using an individual proxy for each event enables each event to call a unique handler function in the target object. The main disadvantage of implementing the observer pattern using a proxy is the slight cost of one extra indirection for handling each event. However, in situations where using the observer pattern is appropriate, the cost of an extra indirection is negligible.

Using the proxy pattern for implementing the observer pattern leads to the following two classes for handling commandEntered() and stackChanged() events: CommandIssuedObserver and StackUpdatedObserver, respectively. The CommandIssuedObserver mediates between commandEntered() events raised by the UI and observation in the command dispatcher. The StackUpdatedObserver mediates between stackChanged() events raised by the stack and observation in the UI. The implementation for both of these classes is relatively straightforward and very similar. By way of example, let's examine the implementation for CommandIssuedObserver. See Listing 5-3.

Listing 5-3. The Declaration for CommandIssuedObserver

```
class CommandIssuedObserver : public Observer
{
public:
  CommandIssuedObserver(CommandDispatcher& ce);
  void notifyImpl(shared_ptr<EventData>) override;

private:
  CommandDispatcher& ce_;
};
```

Because it mediates events between the UI as a publisher and the CommandDispatcher as the target of the observer, the CommandIssuedObserver's constructor takes a reference to a CommandDispatcher instance, which it retains to call back to the command dispatcher when the UI raises a commandEntered() event. Recall that the CommandIssuedObserver will be stored by the UI in the Publisher's event symbol table when the observer is attached to the event. The implementation of notifyImpl() is simply a dynamic cast of the EventData parameter to a specific CommandData instance followed by a call to CommandDispatcher's commandEntered() function.

Of course, before an event is triggered, the `CommandIssuedObserver` must be registered with the UI. For completeness, the following code illustrates how to accomplish this task:

```
ui.attach( UserInterface::CommandEntered,
  make_unique<CommandIssuedObserver>(ce) );
```

where `ui` is a `UserInterface` reference. Note that since the `attach()` function was intentionally hoisted into the abstract `UserInterface` scope, attaching through a reference allows us to reuse the same call for both the CLI and the GUI. That is, registering events is accomplished through the abstract UI interface, which greatly simplifies user interface setup in pdCalc's `main()` routine. The declaration and registration of `StackUpdatedObserver` is analogous.

The complete implementation of the observer proxy classes can be found in `AppObservers.cpp`. While the usage of the observer proxies is intertwined with the event-observing classes, the proxies are not part of the interface for the target classes. Hence, they are included in their own file. The attachment of the proxies to events is performed in `main.cpp`. This code structure preserves the loose binding between publishers and observers. Specifically, publishers know which events they can raise, but not who will observe them, while observers know which events they will watch, but not who raises them. Code external to both publishers and their observers binds the two together.

5.2 The Concrete CLI Class

The remainder of this chapter is devoted to detailing the CLI concrete class. Let's start by re-examining the CLI's requirements.

5.2.1 Requirements

The requirements for pdCalc indicate that the calculator must have a command line interface, but what, precisely, is a CLI? My definition for a command line interface is any user interface to a program that responds to user commands interactively through text. Even if your definition for a command line interface is somewhat different, I believe we can certainly agree that a broad requirement simply indicating a program should have a CLI is woefully insufficient.

In a production development situation, when you encounter a requirement too vague to design a component, you should immediately seek clarification from your client. Notice I said *when* and not *if*. Regardless of how much effort you place upfront trying to refine requirements, you always have incomplete, inconsistent, or changing requirements. This usually arises for a few reasons. Sometimes, it is due to a conscious effort not to spend the upfront time refining requirements. Sometimes, it arises from an inexperienced team member not understanding how to gather requirements properly. Often, however, it simply arises because the end user doesn't know what he or she truly wants or needs until the product starts to take shape. I find this true even for small development projects for which I am my own customer! While you as the implementer always retain the expedient option of refining a requirement without engaging your customer, my experience indicates that this path invariably leads to rewriting the code repeatedly: once for what you thought the user wanted, once for what the user thought he wanted, and once for what the user actually wanted.

Obviously, for our case study, we only have a hypothetical end user, so we'll simply do the refinement ourselves. We specify the following:

1. The CLI should accept a text command for any command defined for the calculator (those that exists in the command repository plus undo, redo, help, and exit).

2. The help command should display a list of all available commands and a short explanatory message.

3. The CLI should accept space-separated commands in the order in which they should be processed. Recall that this order corresponds to Reverse Polish Notation. All commands on a line are processed after return is pressed.

4. After commands are processed, the interface should display at most the top four elements of the stack plus the stack's current size.

Surprisingly, the minimal requirements listed above are sufficient to build a simple CLI. While these requirements are somewhat arbitrary, something specific needed to be chosen in order to describe a design and implementation. If you don't like the resultant CLI, I highly encourage you to specify your own requirements and modify the design and implementation accordingly.

5.2.2 The CLI Design

The design of the CLI is remarkably simple. Because our overall architectural design placed the entire "business logic" of the calculator in the back end, the front end is merely a thin layer that does nothing more than accept and tokenize input from the user, pass that input to the controller sequentially, and display the results. Let's begin by describing the interface.

5.2.2.1 The Interface

From the analysis we performed earlier in the chapter, we know that the concrete CLI class will inherit from the abstract UserInterface class. This inheritance is public because the CLI "is a" UserInterface and must substitute as one. Hence, the CLI must implement the UserInterface's two abstract pure virtual functions, postMessage() and stackChanged(). These two methods are only called polymorphically through a UserInterface reference; therefore, both methods become part of the private interface of the CLI. Other than construction and destruction, the only functionality that the CLI needs to expose publicly is a command that starts its execution. This function drives the entire CLI and only returns (normally) when the user requests to quit the program. Combining the above, the entire interface for the CLI can be given by the code in Listing 5-4.

Listing 5-4. The Entire Interface for the CLI

```
class Cli : public UserInterface
{
  class CliImpl;
public:
  Cli(istream& in, ostream& out);
  ~Cli();

  void execute(bool suppressStartupMessage = false, bool echo = false);

private:
  void postMessage(const string& m) override;
  void stackChanged() override;

  unique_ptr<CliImpl> pimpl_;
};
```

While the interface is mostly self-explanatory, the arguments to both the constructor and the execute() function are worth explaining. To meet the requirements described above, the execute() function could be written with no arguments. The two arguments included in the interface are simply optional features that can be turned on. The first argument dictates whether or not a banner is displayed when the CLI starts. The second argument controls command echoing. If echo is set to true, then each command is repeated before displaying the result. Both of these features could be hard coded in the CLI, but I chose to add them as arguments to the execute() method for added flexibility.

The arguments to the constructor are slightly less obvious than the arguments to the execute() command. Almost by definition, a CLI takes input from cin and outputs results to cout or maybe cerr. However, hard coding these standard I/O streams arbitrarily limits the usage of this class to that of a traditional CLI. Usually, I advocate limiting functionality to exactly what you need instead of anticipating more general usage. However, using C++ stream I/O is one of my few exceptions to my rule of thumb.

Let's discuss why using references to base class C++ I/O streams is generally a good design practice. First, the desire to use different I/O modes is quite common. Specifically, redirection to or from files is a frequently requested modification to a CLI. In fact, you'll see this request in Chapter 8! Second, implementing the generic versus specific interface adds virtually no complexity. For example, instead of directly writing to cout, one simply keeps a reference to an output stream and writes to that instead. In the base case, this reference simply points to cout. Finally, using arbitrary stream input and output greatly simplifies testing. While the program may instantiate the Cli class using cin and cout, tests can instantiate the Cli class with either a file stream or a string stream. In this manner, interactive stream inputs and outputs can be simulated using strings or files. This strategy simplifies testing of the Cli class since inputs can be easily passed in and outputs easily captured as strings rather than through standard input and output.

5.2.2.2 The Implementation

The implementation of the Cli class is worth examining to observe the simplicity enabled by the modularity of pdCalc's design. The entire implementation of the Cli class is effectively contained in the execute() and postMessage() member functions. The execute() function drives the CLI. It presents a startup message to the end user, waits for commands to be entered, tokenizes these commands, and raises events to signal to the command dispatcher that a new command has been entered. The stackChanged()

function is an observer proxy callback target that writes the top of the stack to the command line after the stackChanged() event is raised. Essentially, the CLI reduces to two I/O routines where execute() handles input and stackChanged() handles output. Let's look at the implementations for these two functions starting with the execute() function shown in Listing 5-5.

Listing 5-5. The execute() Function

```
void Cli::CliImpl::execute(bool suppressStartupMessage, bool echo)
{
  if (!suppressStartupMessage) startupMessage();

  for(string line; getline(in_, line, '\n');)
  {
    Tokenizer tokenizer{line};
    for(const auto& i : tokenizer)
    {
      if(echo) out_ << i << endl;
      if(i == "exit" || i == "quit")
        return;
      else
        parent_.raise( CommandEntered, make_shared<CommandData>(i) );
    }
  }
  return;
}
```

The main algorithm for the CLI is fairly simple. First, the CLI waits for the user to input a line. Second, this input line is tokenized by the Tokenizer class. The CLI then loops over each token in the input line and raises an event with the token string as the event's data. The CLI terminates when it encounters either a quit or an exit token.

The only piece of the execute() function not previously explained is the Tokenizer class. Simply, the Tokenizer class is responsible for taking a string of text and splitting this string into individual space-separated tokens. Neither the CLI nor the Tokenizer determines the validity of tokens. Tokens are simply raised as events for the command dispatcher to process. Note that as an alternative to writing your own, many libraries (boost, for example) provide simple tokenizers.

Given the simplicity of the tokenization algorithm (see the implementation in Tokenizer.cpp), why did I design the Tokenizer as a class instead of as a function returning a vector of strings? Realistically, both designs functionally work, and both designs are equally easy to test and maintain. However, I prefer the class design because it provides a distinct type for the Tokenizer. Let's examine the advantages of creating a distinct type for tokenization.

Suppose we wanted to tokenize input in function foo() but process tokens in a separate function, bar(). Consider the following two possible pairs of functions to achieve this goal:

```
// use a Tokenizer class
Tokenizer foo(const string&);
void bar(const Tokenizer&);
```

```
// use a vector of strings
vector<string> foo(const string&);
void bar(const vector<string>&);
```

First, using a Tokenizer class, the signatures for both foo() and bar() immediately inform the programmer the intent of the functions. We know these functions involve tokenization. Using a vector of strings leaves ambiguity without further documentation (I intentionally did not provide names for the arguments). More importantly, however, typing the tokenizer enables the compiler to ensure that bar() can only be called with a Tokenizer class as an argument, thus preventing a programmer from accidentally calling bar() with an unrelated collection of strings. Another benefit of the class design is that a Tokenizer class encapsulates the data structure that represents a collection of tokens. This encapsulation shields the interface to bar() from a decision to change the underlying data structure from, for example, a vector of strings to a list of strings. Finally, a Tokenizer class can encapsulate additional state information about tokenization (e.g., the original, pre-tokenized input), if desired. A collection of strings is obviously limited to carrying only the tokens themselves.

Now let's examine a simplified implementation of the stackChanged() function, shown in Listing 5-6.

Listing 5-6. The stackChanged Function

```cpp
void Cli::CliImpl::stackChanged()
{
  unsigned int nElements{4};
  auto v = Stack::Instance().getElements(nElements);
  ostringstream oss;
  size_t size = Stack::Instance().size();

  oss << "stack\n";
  size_t j{ v. size() };
  for(auto i = v.rbegin(); i != v.rend(); ++i)
  {
    oss << j << ":\t" << *i << "\n";
    --j;
  }

  postMessage( oss. str() );
}
```

The implementation in `Cli.cpp` differs only in the fanciness of the printing. Note that whenever the stack changes, the CLI simply picks the top four (as specified in our requirements) entries of the stack (`getElements()` returns the minimum of `nElements` and the size of the stack), formats them in an `ostringstream`, and passes a string message to the `postMessage()` function. For the CLI, `postMessage()` simply writes the string to the output stream.

Before we move on, let's pause and reflect on how clean and brief the implementation for the CLI is. This simplicity is a direct result of pdCalc's overall design. Whereas many user interfaces intermix the business logic with the display code, we meticulously designed these two layers to be independent. Interpretation and processing of commands (the business logic) resides entirely in the command dispatcher. Therefore, the CLI is only responsible for accepting commands, tokenizing commands, and reporting results. Furthermore, based on the design of our event system, the CLI has no direct coupling to the command dispatcher, a decision consistent with our MVC architecture. The command dispatcher does have a direct link to the user interface, but because of our abstraction, the command dispatcher binds to an abstract `UserInterface` rather than a specific user interface implementation. In this way, the

Cli perfectly substitutes as a UserInterface (application of the LSP) and can trivially be swapped in or out as any one of many unique views to the calculator. While this flexibility may seem like overkill for the design of a calculator, the modularity of all of the components is beneficial from both a testing and separation of concerns standpoint even if the calculator were not slated to have another user interface.

5.3 Tying It Together: A Working Program

Before we conclude this chapter on the CLI, it is worthwhile to write a simple main program that ties all of the components together to demonstrate a working calculator. pdCalc's actual implementation in main.cpp is significantly more complicated because it handles multiple user interfaces and plugins. Eventually, we will build up to understanding the full implementation in main.cpp, but for now, the code in Listing 5-7 will enable us to execute a working calculator with a command line interface (of course, including the appropriate header files):

Listing 5-7. A Working Calculator

```
int main()
{
  Cli cli{cin, cout};

  CommandDispatcher ce{cli};

  RegisterCoreCommands(cli);

  cli.attach( UserInterface::CommandEntered,
    make_unique<CommandIssuedObserver>(ce) );

  Stack::Instance().attach( Stack::StackChanged,
    make_unique<StackUpdatedObserver>(cli) );

  cli.execute();

  return 0;
}
```

Due to the modularity of the design, the entire calculator can be set up, assembled, and executed in just six executable statements! The logic within the `main()` function is easy to follow. From a maintenance perspective, any new programmer to the project would easily be able trace the calculator's logic and see that the functionality for each module is clearly divided into distinct abstractions. As will be seen in future chapters, the abstraction is even more powerful as more modules are added.

To get you started quickly, a project is included in the repository source code that builds an executable, `pdCalc-simple-cli`, using the above `main()` function as the application's driver. The executable is a standalone CLI that includes all of the features discussed up to this point in the book.

In the next chapter, we'll consider the design of the graphical user interface for our calculator. As soon as the GUI is complete, many users will quickly dismiss the CLI as simply an exercise or a relic from a previous era. Before doing so, I'd like to encourage the reader not to be so quick to judge the humble CLI. CLIs are very efficient interfaces, and they are typically much easier to script for tasks requiring large deployments or automation. As for pdCalc, personally, I prefer the CLI to the GUI due to its ease of use. Of course, maybe that is just an indication that I, too, am a relic from a previous era.

CHAPTER 6

The Graphical User Interface

In this chapter, we will explore the design of the graphical user interface (GUI) for pdCalc. Whenever one designs a GUI, a widget platform needs to be selected. As previously noted, I have chosen to use Qt for the creation of the GUI. That said, this is not a how-to chapter on using Qt to design an interface. Rather, I assume that the reader has a working knowledge of Qt, and the chapter itself focuses on design aspects of the GUI. In fact, as much as possible, I will refer the reader to the source code to see detailed aspects of the widget implementations. Any discussion of the Qt implementation is either merely incidental or worthy of particular emphasis. If you have no interest in GUI design, this chapter can be skipped entirely with virtually no loss in continuity.

6.1 Requirements

In Chapter 5, we began our analysis of the command line interface (CLI) by deriving an interface abstraction that would be used by both the CLI and the GUI. Obviously, we will reuse this interface here, and we therefore already know the abstract interface to which our overall user interface must conform. We thus begin this chapter by defining the requirements for the GUI specialization.

As with the CLI, we quickly discover that the requirements from Chapter 1 are woefully inadequate for specifying a graphical user interface. The given requirements are only functional. That is, we know what buttons and operations the calculator should support, but we know nothing about the expected appearance.

© Adam B. Singer 2017
A. B. Singer, *Practical C++ Design*, DOI 10.1007/978-1-4842-3057-2_6

In a commercial project, one would (hopefully) engage the client, a graphic artist, and a human computer interactions expert to assist in designing the GUI. For our case study, it suffices to fully specify our own requirements:

1. The GUI should have a window that displays both input and output. The output is the top six entries of the current stack.

2. The GUI should have clickable buttons for entering numbers and all supported commands.

3. The GUI should have a status display area for displaying error messages.

The above requirements still do not explain what the calculator should actually look like. For that, we need a picture. Figure 6-1 shows the working calculator as it appears on my Linux desktop (Kubuntu 16.10 using Qt 5.7.1). To show the finished GUI as a prototype for designing the GUI is most certainly "cheating." Hopefully, this shortcut does not detract from the realism of the case study too much. Obviously, one would not have a finished product at this stage in the development. In a production setting, one might have mock-ups drawn either by hand or with a program such as Microsoft PowerPoint, Adobe Illustrator, Inkscape, etc. Alternatively, maybe the GUI is being modeled from a physical object, and the designer either has photographs or direct access to that object. For example, one might be designing a GUI to replace a physical control system, and the requirements specify that the interface must display identical dials and gauges (to reduce operator retraining costs).

Figure 6-1. *The GUI on Linux with no plugins*

The GUI for pdCalc was inspired by my HP48S calculator. For those familiar with any of the Hewlett-Packard calculators in this series, the interface will feel somewhat familiar. For those not familiar with this series of calculators (likely, the majority of readers), the following description explains the basic behavior of the GUI.

The top third of the GUI is a dedicated input/output (I/O) window. The I/O window displays labels for the top six stack levels on the left, with the top of the stack being at the bottom of the window. Values on the stack appear on the right side of the window on the line corresponding to the number's location on the stack. As the user enters a number, the stack reduces to showing only the top five stack elements, while the number being entered is displayed left justified on the bottom line. A number is terminated and entered onto the stack by pressing the enter button.

Assuming sufficient input, an operation takes place as soon as the button is pressed. If insufficient input is present, an error message is displayed above the I/O window. With respect to commands, a valid number in the input area is treated as the top number on the stack. That is, applying an operation while entering a number is equivalent to pressing Enter and then applying the operation.

To economize on space, some buttons have a shifted operation above and to the left of the button itself. These shifted operations can be activated by first pressing the shift button and then pressing the button below the shifted text. Pressing the shift button places the calculator in shift mode until a button with a shifted operation is pressed or until the shift button is pressed again. For clarity, a shifted operation is often the inverse of the operation on the button.

To ease input, many buttons are bound to keyboard shortcuts. Numbers are activated by pressing the corresponding number key, the enter button is activated by pressing the enter key, shift is activated by pressing the s key, backspace is activated by pressing the backspace key, the exponentiation operation is activated by pressing the e key, and the four basic arithmetic operations (+, -, *, /) are activated by pressing the corresponding keys.

Finally, a few operations are semi-hidden. When not entering numbers, the backspace button drops the top entry from the stack, while the enter button duplicates the top entry on the stack. Some of these combinations are not intuitive and therefore might not represent very good GUI design. However, they do mimic the input used on the HP48S. If you have never used an HP48 series calculator before, I highly suggest building and familiarizing yourself with the GUI from the GitHub repository before continuing.

If you're wondering what a `proc` key does, it executes stored procedures. It is one of the "new" requirements we'll encounter in Chapter 8.

One's first critique about the GUI might be that it is not very pretty. I agree. The purpose of the GUI in this chapter is not to demonstrate advanced Qt features. Rather, the purpose is to illustrate how to design a code base to be modular, robust, reliable, and extensible. Adding code to make the GUI more attractive rather than functional would distract from this message. Of course, the design permits a prettier GUI, so feel free to make your own pretty GUI on top of the provided infrastructure.

We now have sufficient detail to design and implement the calculator's GUI. However, before we begin, a short discussion on alternatives for building GUIs is warranted.

6.2 Building GUIs

Essentially, two distinct paths exist for building a GUI: construct the GUI in an integrated development environment (IDE) or construct the GUI in code. Here, I loosely use the term *code* to indicate building the GUI by text, whether it be by using a traditional programming language like C++ or a declarative markup syntax like XML. Of course, between the two extremes is the hybrid approach, which utilizes elements from both IDEs and code.

6.2.1 Building GUIs in IDEs

If all you need is a simple GUI, then, certainly, designing and building your GUI in an IDE is the easier route. Most IDEs have a graphical interface for laying out visual elements onto a canvas, which, for example, might represent a dialog box or a widget. Once a new canvas is set up, the user visually builds the GUI by dragging and dropping existing widgets onto the canvas. Existing widgets consist of the built-in graphical elements of the GUI toolkit (e.g., a push button) as well as custom widgets that have been enabled for drag-and-drop in the IDE framework. Once the layout is complete, actions can be tied together either graphically or with a little bit of code. Ultimately, the IDE creates code corresponding to the graphically laid out GUI, and this IDE-created code is compiled with the rest of your source code.

Building a GUI using an IDE has both advantages and disadvantages. Some of the advantages are as follows. First, because the process is visual, you can easily see the GUI's appearance as you perform the layout. This is in direct contrast with writing code for the GUI, where you only see the look of the GUI after compiling and executing the code. The difference is very much akin to the difference between using a WYSIWYG text editor like Microsoft Word and a markup language like LaTeX for writing a paper. Second, the IDE works by automatically generating code behind the scenes, so the graphical approach can significantly reduce the amount of coding required to write a GUI. Third, IDEs typically list the properties of a GUI element in a property sheet, making it trivial to stylize a GUI without constantly consulting the API documentation. This is especially useful for rarely used features.

Some of the disadvantages to using an IDE to build a GUI are as follows. First, you are limited to the subset of the API that the IDE chooses to expose. Sometimes the full API is exposed, and sometimes it is not. If you need functionality that the IDE's author chose not to grant you, you'll be forced into writing your own code. That is, the IDE may limit fine-tuned control of GUI elements. Second, for repetitive GUI elements, you may have to perform the same operation many times (e.g., clicking to make text red in all push buttons), while in code, it's easy to encapsulate any repeated task in a class or function call. Third, using the IDE to design a GUI limits the GUI to decisions that can be made at compile time. If you need to dynamically change the structure of a GUI, you'll need to write code for that. Fourth, designing a GUI in an IDE ties your code to a specific vendor product. In a corporate environment, this may not be a significant concern because the development environment may be uniform throughout the company. However, for an open source, distributed project, not every developer who might want to contribute to your codebase will want to be restricted to the same IDE you chose.

6.2.2 Building GUIs in Code

Building a GUI in code is exactly what the name implies. Rather than graphically placing widgets on a canvas, you instead write code to interact with the GUI toolkit. Several different options exist for how the code can be written, and often, more than one option is available to you for any given GUI toolkit. First, you can almost always write source code in the language of the toolkit. For example, in Qt, you can build your GUI entirely by writing C++ in a very imperative style (i.e., you direct the GUI's behavior explicitly). Second, some GUI toolkits permit a declarative style (i.e., you write markup code describing the style of GUI elements, but the toolkit defines the elements' behaviors). Finally, some toolkits use a script-based interface for constructing a GUI (often JavaScript or a JavaScript derivative syntax) perhaps in conjunction with a declarative markup. In the context of this chapter, building a GUI in code refers exclusively to coding in C++ against Qt's desktop widget set.

As you might expect, building a GUI in code has nearly the opposite trade-offs as building a GUI with an IDE. The advantages are as follows. First, the full API to the widgets is completely exposed. Therefore, the programmer has as much fine-tuned control as desired. If the widget library designer wanted a user to be able to do something, you can do it in code. Second, repetitive GUI elements are easily managed through the use of abstraction. For example, in designing a calculator, instead of having to customize every button manually, we can create a button class and simply instantiate it. Third, adding widgets dynamically at runtime is easy. For pdCalc, this advantage will be important in fulfilling the requirement to support dynamic plugins. Fourth, designing a GUI in code grants complete IDE independence, provided that the build system is independent of the IDE.

While building a GUI in code has many advantages, disadvantages exist as well. First, the layout is not visual. In order to see the GUI take shape, you must compile and execute the code. If it looks wrong, you have to tweak the code, try again, and repeat this process until you get it right. This can be exceedingly tedious and time consuming. Second, you must author all of the code yourself. Whereas an IDE will autogenerate a significant portion of the GUI code, particularly the parts related to the layout, when you are writing code, you must do all the work manually. Finally, when writing a GUI in code, you will not have access to all of a widget's properties succinctly on a property sheet. Typically, you'll need to consult the documentation more frequently. That said, good IDE code completion can help significantly with this task. Someone may cry foul to my last remark, claiming, "It's unfair to indicate that using an IDE can mitigate a disadvantage of not using an IDE." Remember, unless you're writing your source code in a pure text editor (unlikely), the code editor is still likely a sophisticated IDE. My comparison is between building a GUI using an IDE's graphical GUI layout tool versus writing the code manually using a modern code editor, likely itself an IDE.

6.2.3 Which GUI Building Method Is Better?

The answer to the overly general question in the section header is, of course, neither. Which technique is better for building a GUI is entirely context dependent. When you encounter this question in your own coding pursuits, consult the trade-offs above, and make the choice most sensible for your situation. Often, the best solution is a hybrid strategy where some parts of the GUI will be laid out graphically while other parts of the GUI will be built entirely from code.

A more specific question in our context is, "Which GUI building method is better for pdCalc?" For this application, the trade-offs heavily favor a code-based approach. First, the visual layout for the calculator is fairly trivial (a status window, a display widget, and a grid of buttons) and easily accomplished in code. This fact immediately removes the most significant advantage of the IDE approach: handling a complex layout visually. Second, the creation and layout of the buttons is repetitive but easily encapsulated, which is one of the advantages of a code-based approach. Finally, because the calculator must support runtime plugins, the code approach works better for dynamically adding widget elements (runtime discovered buttons).

In the remainder of this chapter, we'll explore the design of pdCalc's GUI in code. In particular, the main emphasis will be on the design of components and their interfaces. Because our focus is not on widget construction, many implementation details will be glossed over. Never fear, however. If you are interested in the details, all of the code is available for your perusal in the GitHub repository.

6.3 Modularization

From the outset of this book, we have discussed decomposition strategies for the calculator. Using the MVC architectural pattern, we split our design into a model, a view, and a controller. In Chapter 4, we saw that one of the main components, the command dispatcher, was split into subcomponents. Whereas the CLI was simple enough to not need modularization, the GUI is sufficiently complex that decomposition is useful.

In Chapter 5, we determined that any user interface for our system must inherit from the `UserInterface` abstract class. Essentially, the `UserInterface` class defines the abstract interface of the view in the MVC pattern. While the GUI module must inherit from `UserInterface` and hence present the same abstract interface to the controller, we are free to decompose the internals of the GUI however we see fit. We'll again use our guiding principles of loose coupling and strong cohesion to modularize the GUI.

When I decompose a module, I first think in terms of strong cohesion. That is, I attempt to break the module into small components that each do one thing (and do it well). Let's try that with the GUI. First, any Qt GUI must have a main window, defined by inheriting `QMainWindow`. The main window is also the entry point to the MVC view, so our main window must also inherit from `UserInterface`. The `MainWindow` is our first class. Next, visually inspecting Figure 6-1, the calculator is obviously divided into a component used for input (collection of buttons) and a component used for display. We therefore add two more classes, the `InputWidget` and the `Display`. We've already discussed that an advantage of using the code approach to building a GUI is to abstract the repeated creation of buttons, so we'll make a `CommandButton` class as well. Finally, let's add a component responsible for managing the look-and-feel of the calculator (e.g., fonts, margins, spacing, etc.), which is aptly named the `LookAndFeel` class. A component for stored procedure entry also exists, but we will delay the discussion of that component until Chapter 8.

Let's now look at the design of each class, starting with the `CommandButton`. We'll discuss any necessary refinements to this initial decomposition if and when they arise.

6.3.1 The CommandButton Abstraction

I begin the discussion by describing how buttons are abstracted. This is a sensible place to begin since buttons underlie the input mechanism for both numbers and commands to the calculator.

Qt provides a push button widget class that displays a clickable button that emits a signal when the button is clicked. This QPushButton class provides the basis for the functionality that we require for number and command input. One prospective design we could employ would be to use QPushButtons as-is. This design would require explicitly writing code to connect each QPushButton manually to its own customized slot. However, this approach is repetitive, tedious, and highly error-prone. Moreover, some buttons need additional functionality not provided by the QPushButton API (e.g., shifted input). Therefore, we instead seek a button abstraction for our program that builds upon the QPushButton, supplements this Qt class with additional functionality, but also simultaneously restricts the QPushButton's interface to meet exactly our requirements. We'll call this class the CommandButton.

In pattern parlance, we are proposing something that acts as both an adapter and a facade. We saw the adapter pattern in Chapter 3. The facade pattern is a close cousin. Whereas the adapter pattern is responsible for converting one interface into another (possibly with some adaptation), the facade pattern is responsible for providing a unified interface to a set of interfaces in a subsystem (often as a simplification). Our CommandButton is tasked with doing both. We are both simplifying the QPushButton interface to a restricted subset that pdCalc needs but simultaneously adapting QPushButton's functionality to match the requirements of our problem. So, is CommandButton a facade or an adapter? The difference is semantic; it shares characteristics of each. Remember, it is important to understand the objectives of different patterns and adapt them according to your needs. Try not to get lost in rote implementations from the Gang of Four [6] for the sake of pattern purity.

6.3.2 The CommandButton Design

Introductory remarks aside, we still must determine what exactly our CommandButton needs to do and how it will interact with the rest of the GUI. In many ways, a CommandButton looks and acts similarly to a QPushButton. For example, a CommandButton must present a visual button that can be clicked, and after the button is clicked, it should emit some kind of signal to let other GUI components know a click action has occurred. Unlike a standard QPushButton, however, our CommandButton must support both a standard and shifted state (e.g., a button that supports both sin and arcsin). This support should be both visual (both states should be shown by our CommandButton widget) and functional (click signals must describe both a standard click and a shifted click).

We therefore have two design questions to answer. First, how do we design and implement the widget to appear correctly on the screen? Second, how will the calculator, in general, handle shifted operations?

Let's first address the CommandButton appearance problem. Sure, we could implement our button from scratch, paint the screen manually, and use mouse events to trap button clicks, but that's overkill for CommandButton. Instead, we seek a solution that reuses Qt's QPushButton class. We essentially have two options for reuse: inheritance and encapsulation.

First, let's consider reusing the QPushButton class in the CommandButton class's design via inheritance. This approach is reasonable since one could logically adopt the viewpoint that a CommandButton "is-a" QPushButton. This approach, however, suffers from an immediate deficiency. An "is-a" relationship implies public inheritance, which means that the entire public interface of QPushButton would become part of the public interface for CommandButton. However, we already determined that for simplicity within pdCalc, we want CommandButton to have a restricted interface (the facade pattern). OK, let's try private inheritance and modify our viewpoint to an "implements-a" relationship between CommandButton and QPushButton. Now we encounter a second deficiency. Without public inheritance from QPushButton, CommandButton loses its indirect inheritance of the QWidget class, a prerequisite in Qt for a class to be a user interface object. Therefore, any implementation inheriting QPushButton privately would also require public inheritance from QWidget. However, because QPushButton also inherits from QWidget, the multiple inheritance of both of these classes by CommandButton would lead to ambiguities and is thus disallowed. We must seek an alternative design.

Now, consider encapsulating a QPushButton within a CommandButton (i.e., CommandButton "has-a" QPushButton). We probably should have started with this option since general practice indicates we should prefer encapsulation to inheritance whenever possible. However, many developers tend to start with inheritance, and I wanted to discuss the drawbacks of that approach without resorting merely to C++ canon. Aside from breaking the strong inheritance relationship, choosing an encapsulation approach overcomes the two drawbacks of using inheritance previously discussed. First, since the QPushButton will be encapsulated within a CommandButton, we are free to expose only those parts of the QPushButton interface (or none at all) that make sense for our application. Second, by using encapsulation, we'll avoid the multiple inheritance mess of inheriting from both the QWidget and QPushButton classes simultaneously. Note that I do not object, in principle, to designs that use multiple inheritance. Multiple inheritance is simply ambiguous in this instance.

Encapsulating relationships can either take the form of composition or aggregation. Which is right for the CommandButton class? Consider two classes, A and B, where A is encapsulating B. In a composite relationship, B is an integral part of A. In code, the relationship is expressed as follows:

```
class A
{
  // ...
private:
  B b_;
};
```

In contrast, aggregation implies that A is merely using a B object internally. In code, aggregation is expressed as follows:

```
class A
{
  // ...
private:
  B* b_; // or some suitable smart pointer or reference
};
```

For our application, I think aggregation makes more sense. That is, our CommandButton uses a QPushButton rather than is composed from a QPushButton. The difference is subtle, and an equally logical argument could be made for declaring the relationship to be composition. That said, both designs work mechanically within Qt, so your compiler really won't care how you choose to express the relationship.

Now that we have decided to aggregate the QPushButton within the CommandButton, we can proceed with the overall design of the CommandButton class. Our CommandButton must support both a primary and secondary command. Visually, I chose to display the primary command on the button and the secondary command in blue above and to the left of the button. (I'll discuss how the shifted state operates momentarily.) Therefore, the CommandButton merely instantiates a QPushButton and a QLabel and places them both in a QVBoxLayout. The QPushButton displays the text for the primary command, and the QLabel displays the text for the shifted command. The layout is depicted in Figure 6-2. To complete the design, as previously stated, in order to interact graphically with the rest of the GUI, the CommandButton must publicly inherit from the QWdiget class.

The design results in a reusable CommandButton widget class for a generic push button, declaring both a primary and secondary command. Because the push button action is achieved by using a QPushButton, the overall implementation of the CommandButton class is remarkably simple.

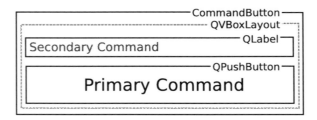

Figure 6-2. *The layout of the CommandButton*

One final, small detail for reusing the QPushButton remains. Obviously, because the QPushButton is encapsulated privately in the CommandButton, clients cannot externally connect to the QPushButton's clicked() signal, rendering it impossible for client code to know when a CommandButton is clicked. This design is actually intentional. The CommandButton will internally trap the QPushButton's clicked() signal and subsequently re-emit its own signal. The design of this public CommandButton signal is intricately linked to the handling of the shifted state.

We now return to modeling the shifted state within the calculator. We have two practical options. The first option is to have CommandButton understand when the calculator is in the shifted state and only signal the correct shifted or unshifted command. Alternatively, the second option is to have CommandButton signal with both the shifted and unshifted commands and let the receiver of the signal sort out the calculator's current state. Let's examine both options.

The first option, having CommandButton know if the calculator is in a shifted or unshifted state, is fairly easy to implement. In one implementation, the shift button notifies every button (via Qt signals and slots) when it is pressed, and the buttons toggle between the shifted and unshifted state. If desired, one could even swap the text in the shift position with the text on the button every time the shifted state is toggled. Alternatively, the shift button can be connected to one slot that sets a global shift state flag that buttons can query when they signal that a click has occurred. In either implementation scenario, when the button is clicked, only the command for the current state is signaled, and the receiver of this command eventually forwards the single command out of the GUI via a commandEntered() event.

In the second option, the CommandButton is not required to know anything about the calculator's state. Instead, when a button is clicked, it signals the click with both the shifted and unshifted states. Essentially, a button just informs its listeners when it is clicked and provides both possible commands. The receiver is then responsible for determining which of the possible commands to raise in the commandEntered() event. The receiver presumably must be responsible for tracking the shifted state (or be able to poll another class or variable holding that state).

For the CommandButton, both designs for handling the calculator's state work fairly well. However, personally, I prefer the design that does not require CommandButton to know anything about the shifted state. In my opinion, this design promotes better cohesion and looser coupling. The design is more cohesive because a CommandButton should be responsible for displaying a clickable widget and notifying the system when the button is clicked. Requiring CommandButton to understand calculator states encroaches on the independence of their abstraction. Instead of just being generic clickable buttons with two commands, the buttons become integrally tied to the concept of the calculator's global state. Additionally, by forcing CommandButton to understand the calculator's state, the coupling in the system is increased by forcing CommandButton to be unnecessarily interconnected to either the shift button or to the class they must poll. The only advantage gained by notifying every CommandButton when the shift button is pressed is the ability to swap the labels for the primary and secondary commands. Of course, label swapping could be implemented independently of the CommandButton's signal arguments.

6.3.3 The CommandButton Interface

Getting the design right is the hard part. With the design in hand, the interface practically writes itself. Let's examine a simplified version of the CommandButton class's definition, shown in Listing 6-1.

Listing 6-1. The CommandButton Class

```
class CommandButton : public QWidget
{
  Q_OBJECT // needed by all Qt objects with signals and slots
public:
  CommandButton(const string& dispPrimaryCmd, const string& primaryCmd,
    const string& dispShftCmd, const string& shftCmd,
    QWidget* parent = nullptr);
```

```
CommandButton(const string& dispPrimaryCmd, const string& primaryCmd,
  QWidget* parent = nullptr);

private slots:
  void onClicked();

signals:
  void clicked(string primCmd, string shftCmd);
};
```

The CommandButton class has two constructors: the four-argument overload and the two-argument overload. The four-argument overload permits specification of both a primary command and a secondary command, while the two-argument overload permits the specification of only a primary command. Each command requires two strings for full specification. The first string equates to the text the label will present in the GUI, either on the button or in the shifted command location. The second string equates to the text command to be raised by the commandEntered() event. One could simplify the interface by requiring these two strings to be identical. However, I chose to add the flexibility of displaying a different text than that required by the command dispatcher. Note that we require overloads instead of default arguments due to the trailing parent pointer.

The only other public part of the interface is the clicked() signal that is emitted with both the primary and shifted commands for the button. The rationale behind a two-argument versus one-argument signal was previously discussed. Despite being private, I also listed the onClicked() slot in CommandButton's interface to highlight the private slot that must be created to catch the internal QPushButton's clicked() signal. The onClicked() function's sole purpose is to trap the QPushButton's clicked() signal and instead emit the CommandButton's clicked() signal with the two function arguments.

If you look at the actual declaration of the CommandButton class in CommandButton.h, you will see a few additional functions as part of CommandButton's public interface. These are simply forwarding functions that either change the appearance (e.g., text color) or add visual elements (e.g., a tool tip) to the underlying QPushButton. While these functions are part of CommandButton's interface, they are functionally optional and are independent of CommandButton's underlying design.

6.3.4 Getting Input

The GUI is required to take two distinct types of inputs from the user: numbers and commands. Both input types are entered by the user via CommandButtons (or keyboard shortcuts mapped to these buttons) arranged in a grid. This collection of CommandButtons, their layout, and their associated signals to the rest of the GUI compose the InputWidget class.

Command entry is conceptually straightforward. A CommandButton is clicked, and a signal is emitted, reflecting the command for that particular button. Ultimately, another part of the GUI will receive this signal and raise a commandEntered() event to be handled by the command dispatcher.

Entering numbers is a bit more complicated than entering commands. In the CLI, we had the luxury of simply allowing the user to type numbers and press enter when the input was complete. In the GUI, however, we have no such built-in mechanism (assuming we want a GUI more sophisticated than a CLI in a Qt window). While the calculator does have a Command for entering numbers, remember that it assumes complete numbers, not individual digits. Therefore, the GUI must have a mechanism for constructing numbers.

Building a number consists of entering digits as well as special symbols such as the decimal point, the plus/minus operator, or the exponentiation operator. Additionally, as the user types, he might make errors, so we'll want to enable basic editing (e.g., backspace), as well. The assembly of numbers is a two-step process. The InputWidget is only responsible for emitting the button clicks required for composing and editing numbers. Another part of the GUI will receive these signals and assemble complete number input.

6.3.5 The Design of the InputWidget

Conceptually, the design of the InputWidget class is straightforward. The widget must display the buttons needed for generating and editing input, bind these buttons to keys (if desired), and signal when these buttons are clicked. As previously mentioned, the InputWidget contains buttons for both digit entry and command entry. Therefore, it is responsible for the digits 0-9, the plus/minus button, the decimal button, the exponentiation button, the enter button, the backspace button, the shift button, and a button for each command. Recall that as an economization, the CommandButton class permits two distinct commands per visual button.

For consistency throughout the GUI, we'll use the CommandButton exclusively as the representation for all of the input buttons, even for buttons that neither issue commands nor have secondary operations (e.g., the 0 button). How convenient that our design for the CommandButton is so flexible! However, that decision still leaves us with two outstanding design issues. How do we lay out the buttons visually, and what do we do when a button is clicked?

Two options exist for placing buttons in the InputWidget. First, the InputWidget itself owns a layout, it places all the buttons in this internal layout, and then the InputWidget itself can be placed somewhere on the main window. The alternative is for the InputWidget to accept an externally owned layout during construction and place its CommandButtons on that layout. In general, having the InputWidget own its own layout is the superior design. It has improved cohesion and decreased coupling over the alternative approach. The only exception where having the InputWidget accept an external layout would be preferred would be if the design called for other classes to share the same layout for the placement of additional widgets. In that special case, using a shared layout owned externally to both classes would be cleaner.

Let's now turn our attention to what happens when a button is clicked within the InputWidget. Because the InputWidget encapsulates the CommandButtons, the clicked() signal for each CommandButton is not directly accessible to consumers of the InputWidget class. Therefore, the InputWidget must catch all of its CommandButtons' clicks and re-emit them. For calculator commands like sine or tangent, re-emitting the click is a trivial forwarding command. In fact, Qt enables a shorthand notation for connecting a CommandButton's clicked() signal directly to an InputWidget commandEntered() signal, forgoing the need to pass through a private slot in the InputWidget. Digits, number editing buttons (e.g., plus/minus, backspace), and calculator state buttons (e.g., shift) are better handled by catching the particular clicked() signal from the CommandButton in a private slot in the InputWidget and subsequently emitting a InputWidget signal for each of these actions.

As just described, as each input button is pressed, the InputWidget must emit its own signal. At one extreme, the InputWidget could have individual signals for each internal CommandButton. At the other extreme, the InputWidget could emit only one signal regardless of the button pressed and differentiate the action via an argument. As expected, for our design, we'll seek some middle ground that shares elements from each extreme.

Essentially, the `InputWidget` accepts three distinct types of input: a modifier (e.g., enter, backspace, plus/minus, shift), a scientific notation character (e.g., 0-9, decimal, exponentiation), or a command (e.g., sine, cosine, etc.). Each modifier requires a unique response; therefore, each modifier binds to its own separate signal. Scientific notation characters, on the other hand, can be handled uniformly simply by displaying the input character on the screen (the role of the `Display` class). Thus, scientific notation characters are all handled by emitting a single signal that encodes the specific character as an argument. Finally, commands are handled by emitting a single signal that simply forwards the primary and secondary commands verbatim as function arguments to the signal.

In constructing the signal handling, it is important to maintain the `InputWidget` as a class for signaling raw user input to the rest of the GUI. Having the `InputWidget` interpret button presses leads to problems. For example, suppose we designed the `InputWidget` to aggregate characters and only emit complete, valid numbers. Since this strategy implies that no signal would be emitted per character entry, characters could neither be displayed nor edited until the number was completed. This situation is obviously unacceptable, as a user would definitely expect to see each character on the screen as she entered it.

Let's now turn our attention to translating our design into a minimal interface for the `InputWidget`.

6.3.6 The Interface of the InputWidget

Let's begin the discussion of the `InputWidget`'s interface by presenting the class declaration. As expected, our clear design leads to a straightforward interface. See Listing 6-2.

Listing 6-2. The InputWidget

```
class InputWidget : public QWidget
{
  Q_OBJECT
public:
  explicit InputWidget(QWidget* parent = nullptr);
```

```
signals:
  void characterEntered(char c);

  void enterPressed();
  void backspacePressed();
  void plusMinusPressed();
  void shiftPressed();

  void commandEntered(string, string);
};
```

Essentially, the entire class interface is defined by the signals corresponding to user input events. Specifically, we have one signal indicating entry of any scientific notation character, one signal to forward command button clicks, and individual signals indicating clicking of the backspace, enter, plus/minus, or shift buttons, respectively.

If you look in the GitHub repository source code in the InputWidget.cpp file, you will find a few additional public functions and signals. These extra functions are necessary to implement two features introduced in subsequent chapters. First, an addCommandButton() function and a setupFinalButtons() function are needed to accommodate the dynamic addition of plugin buttons, a feature introduced in Chapter 7. Second, a procedurePressed() signal is needed to indicate a user request to use a stored procedure. Stored procedures are introduced in Chapter 8.

6.4 The Display

Conceptually, the calculator has two displays, one for input and one for output. This abstraction can be implemented visually either as two separate displays or as one merged input/output display. Both designs are perfectly valid; each is illustrated in Figure 6-3.

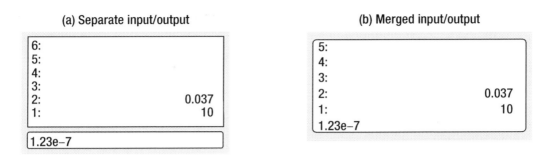

Figure 6-3. *Input and output display options*

Choosing one style of I/O versus the other ultimately reduces to the customer's preference. Having no particular affinity for either style, I chose a merged display because it looks more like the display of my HP48S calculator. With a display style chosen, let's now focus on the design implications this choice implies.

With a separate on-screen widget for input and output, as seen in Figure 6-3a, the choice to have separate input and output display classes would be obvious. The input display would have slots to receive the InputWidget's signals, and the output display would have slots to receive completed numbers (from the input display) and stack updates. The cohesion would be strong, and the separation of components would be appropriate.

Our design, however, calls for a commingled input/output display, as seen in Figure 6-3b. The commingled design significantly alters the sensibility of using independent input and output display classes. While lumping input and output display concerns into one class does decrease the cohesion of the display, trying to maintain two independent classes both pointing to the same on-screen widget would lead to an awkward implementation. For example, choosing which class should own the underlying Qt widget is arbitrary, likely resulting in a shared widget design (using a shared_ptr, perhaps?). However, in this scenario, should the input or the output display class initialize the on-screen widget? Would it make sense for the input display to signal the output display if the input display shared a pointer to the single display widget? The answer is simply that a two-class design is not tenable for a merged I/O display widget even though we might prefer to separate input and output display concerns.

The aforementioned discussion identifies a few interesting points. First, the visual presentation of the design on screen can legitimately alter the design and implementation of the underlying components. While this may seem obvious once presented with a concrete GUI example, the indirect implication is that GUI class design may need to change significantly if the on-screen widgets are changed only slightly. Second, situations exist where the result is cleaner when the design directly contradicts the elements of good design postulated in Chapter 2. Obviously, the guidelines in Chapter 2 are meant to aid the design process, not to serve as inviolable rules. That said, my general advice is to aim to preserve clarity over adherence to guidelines, but only violate best practices judiciously.

Now that we've decided to pursue a single I/O display with a single underlying `Display` class, let's look at its design.

6.4.1 The Design of the Display Class

I confess. My original design and implementation for the `Display` class was inept. Instead of using proper analysis techniques and upfront design, I grew the design organically (that is, alongside the implementation). However, as soon as my design forced the `Display` class to emit `commandEntered()` signals for the GUI to function properly, I knew the design had a "bad smell" to it. The class responsible for painting numbers on the screen should probably not be interpreting commands. That said, the implementation worked properly, so I left the code as it was and completed the calculator. However, when I finally started writing about the design, I had so much difficulty trying to formulate a rationale for my design that I finally had to admit to myself that the design was fatally flawed and desperately needed a rewrite.

Obviously, after redesigning the display, I could have simply chosen to describe only the improved product. However, I think it is instructive to study my first misguided attempt, to discuss the telltale signs that the design had some serious problems, and finally to see the design that eventually emerged after a night of refactoring. Possibly, the most interesting lesson here is that bad designs can certainly lead to working code, so never assume that working code is an indicator of a good design. Additionally, bad designs, if localized, can be refactored, and sometimes refactoring should be undertaken solely to increase clarity. Refactoring, of course, assumes your project schedule contains enough contingency time to pause periodically just to pay down technical debt. Let's briefly study my mistake before returning to a better design.

6.4.2 A Poor Design

From the analysis above, we determined that the calculator should have one unified `Display` class for handling both input and output. The fundamental mistake in my design for the display derived from incorrectly interpreting that one `Display` class implied no additional classes for orthogonal concerns. Hence, I proceeded to lump all functionality not handled by the `InputWidget` class into a single `Display` class. Let's start along that path. However, rather than completing the design and implementation as I had previously done, we'll stop and redesign the class as soon as we see the first fatal flaw emerge (which is what I should have done originally).

With a single `Display` class design, the `Display` is responsible for showing input from the user and output from the calculation engine. Showing the output is trivial. The `Display` class observes the `stackChanged()` event (indirectly, since it is not part of the GUI's external interface), and updates the screen display widget (a `QLabel`, in this case) with the new stack values. Conceptually, showing the input is trivial as well. The `Display` directly receives the signals emitted by the `InputWidget` class (e.g., `characterEntered()`) and updates the screen display widget with the current input. The simplicity of this interaction belies the fundamental problem with this design, which is that the input is not entered atomically for display. Instead, it is assembled over multiple signals by entering several characters independently and finalizing the input by pressing the enter button. This sequential construction of the input implies that the calculator must maintain an active input state, and input state has no business existing in a display widget.

So what, aside from ideological aversion, is wrong with the `Display` class maintaining an input state? Can't we just view the state as simply a display input buffer? Let's follow through with this design to see why it is flawed. Consider, for example, the backspace button, whose operation is overloaded based on the input state. If the current input buffer is nonempty, the backspace button erases one character from this buffer. However, if the current input buffer is empty, pressing the backspace button causes the issuance of the command to drop the top number from the stack. Since, under this design, the `Display` owns the input state and is the sink for the `backspacePressed()` signal, the `Display` must be the source of the dropped number from the stack command. Once the `Display` starts issuing commands, we've completely given up on cohesion, and it's time to find the pasta sauce because spaghetti code ensues. From here, instead of just abandoning the design, I doubled down, and my original design actually got worse. However, instead of proceeding further along this misguided path, let's simply move on to examining a better approach.

6.4.3 An Improved Display Design

Early in the discussion of the poor display design, I pointed out that the fatal mistake came from assuming that a unified display necessitated a single class design. However, as we've seen, this assumption was invalid. The emergence of state in the calculator implies the need for at least two classes, one for the visual display and one for the state.

Does this remind you of a pattern we've already seen? The GUI needs to maintain an internal state (a model). We're currently in the midst of designing a display (a view). We have already designed a class, the InputWidget, for accepting input and issuing commands (a controller). Obviously, the GUI itself is nothing more than an embodiment of a familiar pattern, the model-view-controller (MVC). Note that relative to the MVC archetype seen in Figure 2-2 in Chapter 2, the GUI can replace direct communication between the controller and the model with indirect communication. This minor change, which promotes decreased coupling, is facilitated by Qt's signals and slots mechanism.

We now divert our attention to the design of the newly introduced model class. Upon completion of the model, we'll return to the Display class to finish its now simpler design and interface.

6.5 The Model

The model class, which I aptly called the GuiModel, is responsible for the state of the GUI. In order to achieve this goal properly, the model must be the sink for all signals that cause the state of the system to change, and it must be the source of all signals indicating that the state of the system has changed. Naturally, the model is also the repository for the state of the system, and it should provide facilities for other components of the GUI to query the model's state. Let's look at GuiModel's interface in Listing 6-3.

Listing 6-3. The GuiModel Interface

```
class GuiModel : public QObject
{
  Q_OBJECT
public:
  enum class ShiftState { Unshifted, Shifted };
  struct State { /* discussed below */ };

  GuiModel(QObject* parent = nullptr);
  ~GuiModel();

  void stackChanged(const vector<double>& v);

  const State& getState() const;
```

```
public slots:
  // called to toggle the calculator's shift state
  void onShift();

  // paired to InputWidget's signals
  void onCharacterEntered(char c);
  void onEnter();
  void onBackspace();
  void onPlusMinus();
  void onCommandEntered(string primaryCmd, string secondaryCmd);

signals:
  void modelChanged();
  void commandEntered(string s);
  void errorDetected(string s);
};
```

The six slots in the GuiModel class all correspond to signals emitted by the InputWidget class. The GuiModel interprets these requests, changes the internal state as appropriate, and emits one or more of its own signals. Of particular note is the commandEntered() signal. Whereas the GuiModel's onCommandEntered() slot accepts two arguments, the raw primary and secondary commands corresponding to the CommandButton that was pressed, the GuiModel is responsible for interpreting the shifted state of the GUI and only re-emitting a commandEntered() signal with the active command.

The remainder of the GuiModel interface involves the GUI's state. We begin by discussing the rationale behind the nested State struct. Rather than declare each piece of the model's state as a separate member within GuiModel, I find it much cleaner to lump all of the state parameters into one struct. This design facilitates the querying of the model's state by permitting the entire system state to be returned by const reference with one function call as opposed to requiring piecemeal access to individual state members. I chose to nest the State struct because it is an intrinsic part of GuiModel that serves no standalone purpose. Therefore, the State struct naturally belongs in GuiModel's scope, but its declaration must be publicly declared in order for other components of the GUI to be able to query the state.

The constituents of the State struct define the entire state of the GUI. In particular, this State struct comprises a data structure holding a copy of the maximum number of visible numbers on the stack, the current input buffer, an enumeration defining the shift state of the system, and a Qt enumeration defining the validity of the input buffer. The declaration is shown in Listing 6-4.

Listing 6-4. The State struct for the GuiModel

```
struct State
{
  vector<double> curStack;
  string curInput;
  ShiftState shiftState;
  QValidator::State curInputValidity;
};
```

An interesting question to ask is, why does the GuiModel's State buffer the visible numbers from the top of the stack? Given that the Stack class is a singleton, the Display could access the Stack directly. However, the Display only observes changes in the GuiModel (via the modelChanged() slot). Because state changes unrelated to stack changes occur frequently in the GUI (e.g., character entry), the Display would be forced to wastefully query the Stack on every modelChanged() event since the Display is not a direct observer of the stackChanged() event. On the other hand, the GuiModel is an observer of the stackChanged() event (indirectly via a function call from the MainWindow). Therefore, the efficient solution is to have the GuiModel update a stack buffer only when the calculator's stack actually changes and give the Display class access to this buffer, which is guaranteed by construction to be current, for updating the screen.

6.6 The Display Redux

We are now ready to return our attention to the Display class. Having placed all of the state and state interactions in the GuiModel class, the Display class can be reduced simply to an object that watches for model changes and displays the current state of the calculator on the screen. Other than the constructor, the interface for the Display class consists of only two functions: the slot to be called when the model changes, and a member function to be called to show messages in the status area. The latter function call is used to display errors detected within the GUI (e.g., invalid input) as well as errors detected in the command dispatcher (as transmitted via UserInterface's postMessage()). The entire interface for the Display class is given in Listing 6-5.

Listing 6-5. The Display Class Interface

```
class Display : public QWidget
{
    Q_OBJECT
public:
  explicit Display(const GuiModel& g, QWidget* parent = nullptr,
    int nLinesStack = 6, int minCharWide = 25);

  void showMessage(const string& m);

public slots:
  void onModelChanged();
};
```

The optional arguments to the Display class's constructor simply dictate visual appearance of the stack on the screen. Specifically, a client of the Display class has flexibility over the number of stack lines to display and the minimum width (in units of fixed width font characters) of the on screen display.

6.7 Tying It Together: The Main Window

The main window is a fairly small class that serves a big purpose. To be precise, it serves three purposes in our application. First, as in most Qt-based GUIs, we need to provide a class that publicly inherits from QMainWindow that acts, naturally, as the main GUI window for the application. In particular, this is the class that is instantiated and shown in the function that launches the GUI. Following my typical creative naming style, I called this class the MainWindow. Second, the MainWindow serves as the interface class for the view module of the calculator. That is, the MainWindow also must publicly inherit from our abstract UserInterface class. Finally, the MainWindow class owns all of the previously discussed GUI components and glues these components together as necessary. For all practical purposes, gluing components together simply entails connecting signals to their corresponding slots. These straightforward implementation details can be found in the `MainWindow.cpp` source code file. We'll spend the remainder of this section discussing the `MainWindow`'s design and interface.

We've written a Qt application; it's obvious that we'll have a descendant of `QMainWindow` somewhere. That, in and of itself, is not terribly interesting. What is interesting, however, is the decision to use multiple inheritance to make the same class also serve as the `UserInterface` to the rest of pdCalc. That said, is that truly an interesting decision, or does it just seem provocative because some developers have a moral aversion to multiple inheritance?

Indeed, I could have separated the `QMainWindow` and the `UserInterface` into two separate classes. In a GUI where the main window was decorated with menus, toolbars, and multiple underlying widgets, I perhaps would have separated the two. However, in our GUI, the `QMainWindow` base serves no purpose other than to provide an entry point for our Qt application. The `MainWindow` literally does nothing else in its `QMainWindow` role. To therefore create a separate `MainWindow` class with the sole purpose of containing a concrete specialization of a `UserInterface` class serves no purpose other than to avoid multiple inheritance. While some may disagree, I think a lack of multiple inheritance, in this instance, would actually complicate the design.

The situation described above is actually an archetypical example of where multiple inheritance is an excellent choice. In particular, multiple inheritance excels in derived classes whose multiple base classes exhibit orthogonal functionality. In our case, one base class serves as the GUI entry point to Qt while the other base class serves as the `UserInterface` specialization for pdCalc's GUI view. Notice that neither base class shares functionality, state, methods, or ancestors. Multiple inheritance is especially sensible in situations where at least one of the base classes is purely abstract (a class with no state and only pure virtual functions). The scenario of using multiple inheritance of purely abstract bases is so useful that it is permitted in programming languages that do not otherwise allow multiple inheritance (e.g., interfaces in both C# and Java).

The interface for the `MainWindow` consists simply of a constructor, the overrides for the two pure virtual functions in the `UserInterface` class, and a few functions for dynamically adding commands (you'll encounter these functions in Chapter 7 when we design plugins). For completeness, the interface for `MainWindow` is shown in Listing 6-6.

Listing 6-6. The Interface for MainWindow

```cpp
class MainWindow : public QMainWindow, public UserInterface
{
  class MainWindowImpl;
public:
  MainWindow(int argc, char* argv[], QWidget* parent = nullptr);
  void postMessage(const string& m) override;
  void stackChanged() override;

  // plugin functions ...
};
```

6.8 Look-and-Feel

Before we conclude this chapter with some sample code to execute the GUI, we must return briefly to the final component of the GUI, the LookAndFeel class. The LookAndFeel class simply manages the dynamically customizable appearance of the GUI, such as font sizes and text colors. The interface is simple. For each point of customization, a function exists to return the requested setting. For example, to get the font for the display, we provide the following function:

```cpp
class LookAndFeel
{
public:
  // one function per customizable setting, e.g.,
  const QFont& getDisplayFont() const;
  // ...
};
```

Because we only need one LookAndFeel object in the calculator, the class is implemented as a singleton.

A great question to ask is, "Why do we need this class at all?" The answer is that it gives us the opportunity to dynamically modify the appearance of the calculator based on the current environment, and it centralizes in memory access to the look-and-feel of pdCalc. For example, suppose we had wanted to make our GUI DPI aware and choose font sizes accordingly (I didn't in the source code, but you might want to). With a static configuration file (or, the conceptual equivalent, registry settings), we would have to customize the settings for each platform during the installation process. Either we would have to build customization within the installer for each platform, or we would have to write code to execute during the installation to create the appropriate static configuration file dynamically. If we have to write code, why not just put it in the source where it belongs? As an implementation decision, the LookAndFeel class could be designed simply to read a configuration file and buffer the appearance attributes in memory (a look-and-feel proxy object). That's the real power of the LookAndFeel class. It centralizes the location of appearance attributes so that only one class needs to be changed to effect global appearance changes. Maybe even more importantly, a LookAndFeel class insulates individual GUI components from the implementation details defining how the GUI discovers (and possibly adapts to) the settings on a particular platform.

The full implementation for the LookAndFeel class can be found in the in LookAndFeel.cpp file. The current implementation is very simple. The LookAndFeel class provides a mechanism for standardizing the GUI's look-and-feel, but no implementation exists to allow user customization of the application. Chapter 8 briefly suggests some possible extensions one could make to the LookAndFeel class to make pdCalc user customizable.

6.9 A Working Program

We conclude this chapter with a working main() function for launching the GUI. Due to additional requirements you'll encounter in Chapter 7, the actual main() function for pdCalc is more complicated than the one listed below. However, the simplified version is worth listing to illustrate how to tie pdCalc's components together with the GUI to create a functioning, standalone executable. See Listing 6-7.

Listing 6-7. A Working main() Function

```
int main(int argc, char* argv[])
{
  QApplication app{argc, argv};
  MainWindow gui{argc, argv};

  CommandDispatcher ce{gui};
```

```
RegisterCoreCommands(gui);

gui.attach( UserInterface::CommandEntered,
  make_unique<CommandIssuedObserver>(ce) );

Stack::Instance().attach( Stack::StackChanged,
  make_unique<StackUpdatedObserver>(gui) );

gui.setupFinalButtons();
gui.show();
gui.fixSize();

return app.exec();
}
```

Note the similarities between the main() function for executing the GUI above and the main() function for executing the CLI listed at the conclusion of Chapter 5. The likenesses are not accidental and are the result of pdCalc's modular design.

As with the CLI, to get you started quickly, a project is included in the repository source code that builds an executable, pdCalc-simple-gui, using the above main() function as the application's driver. The executable is a standalone GUI that includes all of the features discussed up to this point in the book.

Before concluding this section, I'll make a few comments about the implementation above. First, the QApplication class, calling show() on the gui, and the app.exec() call are all boilerplate Qt code. As it concerns us here, those calls simply enable us to start up the GUI and show it on the screen. Second, setupFinalButtons() is called on the gui, but we never defined this function as part of MainWindow's interface. This function is needed to add the buttons correctly in the presence of plugins. With the standalone GUI designed in this chapter, the setupFinalButtons() function is unnecessary. I included this function in the code listing above so that the main() function above could be used as-is with the existing GitHub repository code. Finally, the fixSize() function is also not included in the interface built in this chapter. This function is an implementation detail and contributes nothing to the GUI's design. The function is simply used to fix the size of the GUI on screen and remove the ability to resize it. Again, the necessity of this function arises due to plugins because we can only know the final geometry of the GUI after plugins have added their buttons.

6.10 A Microsoft Windows Build Note

pdCalc is designed to be both a GUI and a CLI. In Linux, no compile time distinction exists between a console application (CLI) and a windowed application (GUI). A unified application can be compiled with the same build flags for both styles. In Microsoft Windows, however, creating an application that behaves as both a CLI and a GUI is not quite as trivial because the operating system requires an application to declare during compilation the usage of either the console or the Windows subsystem.

Why does the declaration of the subsystem matter on Windows? If an application is declared to be a windowed application, if it is launched from a command prompt, the application will simply return with no output (i.e., the application will appear as if it never executed). However, when the application's icon is double-clicked, the application launches without a background console. On the other hand, if an application is declared to be a console application, the GUI will appear when launched from a command prompt, but the GUI will launch with a background console if opened by double-clicking the application's icon.

Conventionally, Microsoft Windows applications are designed for one subsystem or the other. In the few instances where applications are developed with both a GUI and a CLI, developers have created techniques to avoid the above problem. One such technique creates two applications, a `.com` and an `.exe`, that the operating system can appropriately call depending on the option selected via command line arguments.

In order to keep pdCalc's code simple and cross platform, I ignored this problem and simply built the GUI in the console mode (`pdCalc-simple-gui`, however, having no CLI, is built in windowed mode). Indeed, this means that if the application is launched by double-clicking pdCalc's icon, an extra console window will appear in the background. If you intend to use the application primarily as a GUI, the problem can be remedied by simply removing the ability to use the console (e.g., comment out the line `win32:CONFIG += console` in the `pdCalc.pro` build file). If you need access to both the CLI and the GUI and the extraneous console drives you crazy, you have two realistic options. First, search the Internet for one of the techniques discussed above and give it a try. Personally, I've never gone that route. Second, build two separate executables (maybe called pdCalc and pdCalc-cli) instead of one executable capable of switching modes based on command line arguments. The application's flexible architecture trivially supports either decision.

CHAPTER 7

Plugins

You've probably read the chapter title, so you already know that this chapter is about plugins, specifically their design and implementation. Additionally, plugins will afford us the opportunity to explore design techniques to isolate platform-specific features. Before we dive into the details, however, let's begin by defining what a plugin is.

7.1 What Is a Plugin?

A plugin is a software component that enables new functionality to be added to a program after the program's initial compile. In this chapter, we'll concentrate exclusively on runtime plugins, that is, plugins built as shared libraries (e.g., a POSIX `.so` or Windows `.dll` file) that are discoverable and loadable at runtime.

Plugins are useful in applications for a myriad of different reasons. Here are just a few examples. First, plugins are useful for allowing end users to add features to an existing program without the need to recompile. Often, these are new features that were completely unanticipated by the original application developers. Second, architecturally, plugins enable separation of a program into multiple optional pieces that can be individually shipped with a program. For example, consider a program (e.g., a web browser) that ships with some base functionality but allows users to add specialty features (e.g., an ad blocker). Third, plugins can be used for designing an application that can be customized to a specific client. For example, consider an electronic health records system that needs different functionality depending on whether the software is deployed at a hospital or a physician's individual practice. The necessary customizations could be captured by different modules that plug into a core system. Certainly, one can think of many additional applications for plugins.

In the context of pdCalc, plugins are shared libraries that provide new calculator commands, and, optionally, new GUI buttons. How difficult could that task be? In Chapter 4, we created numerous commands and saw that adding new ones was fairly trivial.

© Adam B. Singer 2017
A. B. Singer, *Practical C++ Design*, DOI 10.1007/978-1-4842-3057-2_7

We simply inherited from the Command class (or one of its derived classes, such as UnaryCommand or BinaryCommand), instantiated the command, and registered it with the CommandRepository. For example, take the sine command, which is declared in CoreCommands.h as follows:

```
class Sine : public UnaryCommand
{
  // implement Command virtual members
};
```

and registered in CoreCommands.cpp by the line

```
registerCommand( ui, "sin", MakeCommandPtr<Sine>() );
```

It turns out that this recipe can be followed almost exactly by a plugin command except for one crucial step. Since the plugin command's class name is unknown to pdCalc at compile time, we cannot use the plugin class's name for allocation.

This seemingly simple dilemma of not knowing the class names of plugin commands leads to the first problem we'll need to solve for plugins. Specifically, we'll need to establish an abstract interface by which plugin commands become discoverable to and registered within pdCalc. Once we've agreed upon a plugin interface, we'll quickly encounter the second fundamental plugin problem, which is how do you dynamically load a plugin to even make the names in the shared library available to pdCalc. To make our lives more complicated, the solution to this second problem is platform dependent, so we'll seek a design strategy that minimizes the platform dependency pain. The final problem we'll encounter is updating our existing code to add new commands and buttons dynamically. Maybe surprisingly, this last problem is the easiest to solve. Before we get started tackling our three problems, however, we need to consider a few rules for C++ plugins.

7.1.1 Rules for C++ Plugins

Plugins are not conceptually part of the C++ language. Rather, plugins are a manifestation of how the operating system dynamically loads and links shared libraries (hence the platform-specific nature of plugins). For any nontrivially sized project, the application is typically divided into an executable and several shared libraries (traditionally, .so files in Unix, .dylib files in Mac OS X, and .dll files in MS Windows).

Ordinarily, as C++ programmers, we remain blissfully unaware of the subtleties this structure entails because the executable and libraries are built in a homogeneous build environment (i.e., same compiler and standard libraries). For a practical plugin interface, however, we have no such guarantee. Instead, we must program defensively and assume the worst case scenario, which is that plugins are built in a different, but compatible, environment to the main application. Here, we'll make the relatively weak assumption that the two environments, at minimum, share the same object model. Specifically, we require that the two environments use the same layout for handling the virtual function pointer (`vptr`). If you are unfamiliar with the concept of a virtual function pointer, all the gory details can be found in Lippman [13]. While in principle, C++ compiler writers may choose different `vptr` layouts, in practice, compilers typically use compatible layouts, especially different versions of the same compiler. Without this shared object model assumption, we would be forced to develop a C language-only plugin structure. Note that we must also assume that `sizeof(T)` is the same size for all types `T` in the main application and plugins. This eliminates, for example, having a 32-bit application and a 64-bit plugin because these two platforms have different pointer sizes.

How does programming in a heterogeneous environment affect the available programming techniques we can use? In the worst case scenario, the main application might be built with both a different compiler and a different standard library. This fact has several serious implications. First, we cannot assume that allocation and deallocation of memory between plugins and the application are compatible. This means any memory new-ed in a plugin must be `delete`-ed in the same plugin. Second, we cannot assume that code from the standard library is compatible between any plugin and the main application. Therefore, our plugin interface cannot contain any standard containers. While library incompatibility might seem odd (it's the *standard* library, right?), remember that the standard specifies the interface, not the implementation (subject to some restrictions, such as `vectors` occupying contiguous memory). For example, different standard library implementations frequently have different `string` implementations. Some prefer the small string optimization while others prefer using copy-on-write. Third, while we have assumed a compatible layout for the `vptr` in our objects, we cannot assume identical alignment. Therefore, plugin classes should not inherit from main application classes that have member variables defined in the base classes if these member variables are used in the main application. This follows since the main application's compiler may use a different memory offset to a member variable than what was defined by the plugin's compiler if each compiler uses different alignment. Fourth, due to name mangling variances across different compilers, exported interfaces must specify extern "C" linkage. The linkage requirement is bidirectional. Plugins should not call application functions without extern "C" linkage, nor should the application call plugin functions without extern "C" linkage. Note that because non-inline, non-virtual member functions require linkage across compilation units (as opposed to virtual functions, which are called via the vptr through an offset in the virtual function table), the application should only call into plugin code through virtual functions, and plugin code should not call base class non-inline, non-virtual functions compiled in the main application. Finally, exceptions are rarely portable across the binary interface between the main program and plugins, so we cannot throw exceptions in a plugin and try to catch them in the main application.

That was a mouthful. Let's recap by enumerating the rules for C++ plugins:

1. Memory allocated in a plugin must be deallocated in the same plugin.

2. Standard library components cannot be used in plugin interfaces.

3. Assume incompatible alignment. Avoid plugins inheriting from main application classes with member variables if the variables are used in the main application.

4. Functions exported from a plugin (to be called by the main application) must specify extern "C" linkage. Functions exported from the main application (to be called by plugins) must specify extern "C" linkage.

5. The main application should communicate with plugin-derived classes exclusively via virtual functions. Plugin-derived classes should not call non-inline, non-virtual main application base class functions.

6. Do not let exceptions thrown in plugins propagate to the main application.

With these rules in mind, let's return to the three fundamental problems we must solve in order to design plugins.

7.2 Problem 1: The Plugin Interface

The plugin interface is responsible for several items. First, it must enable the discovery of both new commands and new GUI buttons. We'll see that this functionality is most effectively accomplished through a class interface. Second, the plugin must support a C linkage interface for allocating and deallocating the aforementioned plugin class. Third, pdCalc should provide a `PluginCommand` class derived from `Command` to assist in correctly writing plugin commands. Technically, a `PluginCommand` class is optional, but providing such an interface helps users conform to Plugin Rules 3 and 6. Fourth, it is worthwhile for the plugin interface to provide a function for querying the API version that a plugin supports. Finally, pdCalc must provide C linkage for any of the functions it must make available for plugins to call. Specifically, plugin commands must be able to access the stack. We'll address these issues in sequence starting with the interface for discovering commands.

7.2.1 The Interface for Discovering Commands

The first problem we face is how to allocate commands from plugins when we know neither what commands the plugin provides nor the names of the classes we'll need to instantiate. We'll solve this problem by creating an abstract interface to which all plugins must conform that exports both commands and their names. First, let's address what functionality we'll need.

Recall from Chapter 4, that in order to load a new command into the calculator, we must register it with the `CommandRepository`. By design, the `CommandRepository` was specifically constructed to admit dynamic allocation of commands, precisely the functionality we need for plugin commands. For now, we'll assume that the plugin management system has access to the register command (we'll address this deficiency in Section 7.4). The `CommandRepository`'s registration function requires a `string` name for the command and a `unique_ptr` that serves as a prototype for the command. Since pdCalc knows nothing *a priori* about the command names in a plugin, the plugin interface must first make the names discoverable. Second, since C++ lacks reflection as a language feature, the plugin interface must provide a way to create a prototype command to be associated with each of the discovered names. Again, by design, the abstract `Command` interface supports the prototype pattern via the `clone()` virtual member function. Let's see how these two prior design decisions effectively enable plugins.

Based on the C++ plugin rules above, the only means we have to effect command discovery is to encapsulate it as a pure virtual interface to which all plugins must adhere. Ideally, our virtual function would return an associative container of unique_ptr<CommandPtr> values keyed by strings. However, our C++ plugin rules also stipulate that we cannot use standard containers, thus excluding string, map, unordered_map, and unique_ptr. Rather than (poorly) reimplementing custom versions of any of these containers, we'll just use a typically avoided, low-level facility available to us: arrays of pointers.

The above design is enforced by creating a Plugin class to which all plugins must conform. The purpose of this abstract class is to standardize plugin command discovery. The class declaration is given by the following:

```
class Plugin
{
public:
  Plugin();
  virtual ~Plugin();

  struct PluginDescriptor
  {
    int nCommands;
    char** commandNames;
    Command** commands;
  };

  virtual const PluginDescriptor& getPluginDescriptor() const = 0;
};
```

We now have an abstract plugin interface that, when specialized, requires a derived class to return a descriptor that provides the number of commands available, the names of these commands, and prototypes of the commands themselves. Obviously, the ordering of the command names must match the ordering of the command prototypes. Unfortunately, with raw pointers and raw arrays, the ambiguity of who owns the memory for the command names and command prototypes arises. Our inability to use standard containers forces us into an unfortunate design: contract via comment. Since our rules dictate that memory allocated in a plugin must be freed by the same plugin, the best strategy is to decree that plugins are responsible for deallocation of the `PluginDescriptor` and its constituents. As stated before, the memory contract is "enforced" by comment.

Great, our problem is solved. We create a plugin, let's call it `MyPlugin`, that inherits from `Plugin`. We'll see how to allocate and deallocate the plugin in Section 7.3 below. Inside of `MyPlugin`, we create new commands by inheriting from `Command` as usual. Since the plugin knows its own command names, unlike the main program, the plugin can allocate its command prototypes with the new operator. Then, in order to register all the plugin's commands, we simply allocate a plugin descriptor with both command names and command prototypes, return the descriptor by overriding the `getPluginDescriptor()` function, and let pdCalc register the commands. Since `Commands` must each implement a `clone()` function, pdCalc can copy the plugin command prototypes via this virtual function to register them with the `CommandRepository`. Trivially, string names for registration can be created from the `commandNames` array. For an already allocated `Plugin* p`, the following code within pdCalc could implement registration:

```
const Plugin::PluginDescriptor& d = p->getPluginDesciptor();
for(int i = 0; i < d.nCommands; ++i)
  CommandRepository::Instance().registerCommand( d.commandNames[i],
    MakeCommandPtr( d.commands[i]->clone() ) );
```

At this point, you might recognize a dilemma with our plugins. Commands are allocated in a plugin, copied upon registration with the `CommandRepository` in the main program via a `clone()` call, and then ultimately deleted by the main program when `CommandRepository`'s destructor executes. Even worse, every time a command is executed, the `CommandRepository` clones its prototype, triggering a new statement in the plugin via `Command`'s `clone()` function. The lifetime of this executed command is managed by the `CommandManager` through its undo and redo stacks. Specifically, when a command is cleared from one of these stacks, `delete` is called in the main program when the `unique_ptr` holding the command is destroyed. At least, that's how it works without some tweaking. As was alluded to in Chapter 4, `CommandPtr` is more than a simple alias for `unique_ptr<Command>`. I'll now finally describe the mechanics behind the `CommandPtr` alias and the `MakeCommandPtr()` function that allow correct plugin command memory management.

Fundamentally, we first need a function to call `delete` in the appropriate compilation unit. The easiest solution to this problem is to add a `deallocate()` virtual function to the `Command` class. The responsibility of this function is to invoke `delete` in the correct compilation unit when Commands are destroyed. For all core commands, the correct behavior is simply to delete the class in the main program. Hence, we do not make the deallocate() function pure virtual, and we give it the following default implementation:

```
void Command::deallocate()
{
  delete this;
}
```

For plugin commands, the override for the deallocate() has the same definition, only the definition appears in the plugin's compiled code (say, in a base class used by commands in a particular plugin). Therefore, when deallocate() is invoked on a Command pointer in the main application, the virtual function dispatch ensures that delete is called from the correct compilation unit. Now we just need a mechanism to ensure that we call deallocate() instead of directly calling delete when Commands are reclaimed. Fortunately, it's as if the standards committee anticipated our needs perfectly when they designed unique_ptr. Let's return to the CommandPtr alias to see how unique_ptr can be used to solve our problem.

Remarkably few lines of code are necessary to define a CommandPtr alias and to implement a MakeCommandPtr() function capable of invoking deallocate() instead of delete. The code makes use of unique_ptr's deleter object (see sidebar), which enables a custom routine to be called to reclaim the resource held by the unique_ptr when the unique_ptr's destructor is invoked. Let's look at the code:

```
inline void CommandDeleter(Command* p)
{
  p->deallocate();
  return;
}

using CommandPtr = unique_ptr<Command, decltype(&CommandDeleter)>;

inline auto MakeCommandPtr(Command* p)
{
  return CommandPtr{p, &CommandDeleter};
}
```

A brief explanation of the dense code above is warranted. A CommandPtr is simply an alias for a unique_ptr that contains a Command pointer that is reclaimed by calling the CommandDeleter() function at destruction. The CommandDeleter() function invoked by the unique_ptr is a simple inline function that calls the virtual deallocate() function previously defined. To ease the syntactic burden of creating CommandPtrs, we introduce an inlined MakeCommandPtr() helper function that constructs a CommandPtr from a Command pointer. That's it. Now, just as before, unique_ptrs automatically manage the memory for Commands. However, instead of directly calling delete on the underlying Command, the unique_ptr's destructor invokes the CommandDeleter function, which calls deallocate(), which issues a delete on the underlying Command in the correct compilation unit.

If you look at the source code for MakeCommandPtr(), in addition to the version of the function seen above that takes a Command pointer argument, you will see a very different overload that uses a variadic template and perfect forwarding. This overloaded function must exist due to a different semantic usage of MakeCommandPtr() in the construction of stored procedures. We'll revisit the reasoning behind the two forms of the function in Chapter 8. If the suspense is overwhelming, feel free to skip ahead to Section 8.1.2.

MODERN C++ DESIGN NOTE: UNIQUE_PTR DESTRUCTION SEMANTICS

The unique_ptr<T,D> class template is a smart pointer that models unique ownership of a resource. The most common usage specifies only the first template parameter, T, which declares the type of pointer to be owned. The second parameter, D, specifies a custom delete callable object that is invoked during the destruction of a unique_ptr. Let's look at a conceptual model for the destructor for unique_ptr:

```cpp
template<typename T, typename D = default_delete<T>>
class unique_ptr
{
  T* p_;
  D d_;

public:
  ~unique_ptr()
  {
    d_(p_);
  }
};
```

Rather than directly calling delete, unique_ptr's destructor passes the owned pointer to the deleter using function call semantics. Conceptually, default_delete is implemented as follows:

```
template<typename T>
struct default_delete
{
  void operator()(T* p)
  {
    delete p;
  }
};
```

That is, the default_delete simply deletes the underlying pointer contained by the unique_ptr. However, by specifying a custom deleter callable object during construction (the D template argument), unique_ptr can be used to free resources requiring customized deallocation semantics. As a trivial example, combined with a lambda expression, unique_ptr's delete semantics allow us to create a simple RAII (resource acquisition is initialization) container class, MyObj, allocated by malloc():

```
MyObj* m = static_cast<MyObj*>( malloc(sizeof(MyObj) ) );
auto d = [](MyObj* p){ free(p); };
auto p = unique_ptr<MyObj, decltype(d)>{m, d};
```

Of course, our design for pdCalc shows another instance of the usefulness of the custom delete semantics of unique_ptr. It should be noted that shared_ptr also accepts a custom deleter in an analogous fashion.

7.2.2 The Interface for Adding New GUI Buttons

Conceptually, dynamically adding buttons is not much different than dynamically adding commands. The main application does not know what buttons need to be imported from the plugin, so the Plugin interface must provide a virtual function providing a button descriptor. Unlike commands, however, the plugin does not actually need to allocate the button itself. Recall from Chapter 6 that the GUI CommandButton widget only requires text for construction. In particular, it needs the push button's display text (optionally, the shifted state text) and the command text issued with the clicked() signal. Therefore, even for plugin commands, the corresponding GUI button itself resides entirely in the main application; the plugin must only provide text. This leads to the following trivial interface in the Plugin class:

```
class Plugin
{
public:
  struct PluginButtonDescriptor
  {
    int nButtons;
    char** dispPrimaryCmd; // primary command label
    char** primaryCmd;     // primary command
    char** dispShftCmd;    // shifted command label
    char** shftCmd;        // shifted command
  };

  virtual const PluginButtonDescriptor* getPluginButtonDescriptor() const = 0;
};
```

Again, due to the rules we must follow for plugins, the interface must be comprised of low-level arrays of characters rather than a higher level STL construct.

One interesting facet of the getPluginButtonDescriptor() function relative to the getPluginDescriptor() is the decision to return a pointer rather than a reference. The rationale behind this choice is that a plugin writer might wish to write a plugin that exports commands that do not have corresponding GUI buttons (i.e., CLI-only commands). The converse, of course, is nonsensical. That is, I cannot envision why someone would write a plugin that exported buttons for nonexistent commands. This practicality is captured in the return type for the two descriptor functions. Since both functions are pure virtual, Plugin specializations must implement them. Because getPluginDescriptor() returns a reference, it must export a non-null descriptor. However, by returning a pointer to the descriptor, getPluginButtonDescriptor() is permitted to return a nullptr indicating that the plugin exports no buttons. One might argue that the getPluginButtonDescriptor() function should not be pure virtual and instead provide a default implementation that returns a nullptr. This decision is technically viable. However, by insisting a plugin author manually implement getPluginButtonDescriptor(), the interface forces the decision to be made explicitly.

7.2.3 Plugin Allocation and Deallocation

Our original problem was that the main program did not know the class name of plugin commands and therefore could not allocate them via a call to new. We solved this problem by creating an abstract Plugin interface responsible for exporting command prototypes, command names, and sufficient information for the GUI to create buttons. Of course, to implement this interface, plugins must derive from the Plugin class, thereby creating a specialization, the name of which the main application cannot know in advance. Seemingly, we have made no progress and have returned to our original problem.

Our new problem, similar as it may be to the original problem, is actually much easier to solve. The problem is solved by creating a single extern "C" allocation/deallocation function pair in each plugin with prespecified names that allocate/deallocate the Plugin specialization class via the base class pointer. To satisfy these requirements, we add the following two functions to the plugin interface:

```
extern "C" void* AllocPlugin();
extern "C" void DeallocPlugin(void*);
```

Obviously, the AllocPlugin() function allocates the Plugin specialization and returns it to the main application, while the DeallocPlugin() function deallocates the plugin once the main application is finished using it. Curiously, the AllocPlugin() and DeallocPlugin() functions use void pointers instead of Plugin pointers. This interface is necessary to preserve C linkage since an extern "C" interface must conform to C types. An unfortunate consequence of maintaining C linkage is the necessity of casting. The main application must cast the void* to a Plugin* before using it, and the shared library must cast the void* back to a Plugin* before calling delete. Note, however, that we do not need the concrete Plugin's class name. Thus, the AllocPlugin()/DeallocPlugin() function pair solves our problem.

7.2.4 The Plugin Command Interface

Technically, a special plugin command interface is not necessary. However, providing such an interface facilitates writing plugin commands that obey the C++ Plugin Rules. Specifically, by creating a PluginCommand interface, we assure plugin developers of two key features. First, we provide an interface that guarantees that plugin commands do not inherit from a command class that has any state (to avoid alignment problems).

This property is obvious by construction. Second, we adapt the
checkPreconditionsImpl() function to create an exception-free interface across the
plugin boundary. With this guidance in mind, here is the PluginCommand interface:

```
class PluginCommand : public Command
{
public:
  virtual ~PluginCommand();

private:
  virtual const char* checkPluginPreconditions() const noexcept = 0;
  virtual PluginCommand* clonePluginImpl() const noexcept = 0;

  void checkPreconditionsImpl() const override final;
  PluginCommand* cloneImpl() const override final;
};
```

While only mentioned briefly in Chapter 4, all of the pure virtual functions in
the Command class are marked noexcept except for checkPreconditionsImpl()
and cloneImpl() (see the sidebar on keyword noexcept). Therefore, to ensure
that plugin commands do not originate exceptions, we simply implement the
checkPreconditionsImpl() and cloneImpl() functions at the PluginCommand
level of the hierarchy and create new, exception-free, pure virtual functions for
its derived classes to implement. checkPreconditionsImpl() and cloneImpl()
are both marked final in the PluginCommand class to prevent specializations
from inadvertently overriding either of these functions. The implementation for
checkPreconditionsImpl() can trivially be written as follows:

```
void PluginCommand::checkPreconditionsImpl() const
{
  const char* p = checkPluginPreconditions();
  if(p) throw Exception(p);

  return;
}
```

Note that the key idea behind the implementation above is that the PluginCommand
class's implementation resides in the main application's compilation unit, while
any specializations of this class reside in the plugin's compilation unit. Therefore,

via virtual dispatch, a call to checkPreconditionsImpl() executes in the main application's compilation unit, and this function in turn calls the exception-free checkPluginPreconditions() function that resides in the plugin's compilation unit. If an error occurs, the checkPreconditionsImpl() function receives the error via a nullptr return value and subsequently originates an exception from the main application's compilation unit rather than from the plugin's compilation unit.

A similar trivial implementation for cloneImpl() can be found in Command.cpp. Plugin commands that inherit from PluginCommand instead of Command, UnaryCommand, or BinaryCommand are much more likely to avoid violating any of the C++ Plugin Rules and are therefore much less likely to generate difficult-to-diagnose, plugin-specific runtime errors.

MODERN C++ DESIGN NOTE: NOEXCEPT

The C++98 standard admits using exception specifications. For example, the following specification indicates that the function foo() does not throw any exceptions (the throw specification is empty):

```
void foo() throw();
```

Unfortunately, many problems existed with C++98 exception specifications. While they were a noble attempt at specifying the exceptions a function could throw, they often did not behave as expected. For example, the compiler never guaranteed exception specifications at compile time but instead enforced this constraint through runtime checks. Even worse, declaring a no throw exception specification could impact code performance. For these reasons and more, many coding standards were written declaring that one should simply avoid exception specifications (see, for example, Standard 75 in [27]).

While specifying which specifications a function can throw has proven not to be terribly useful, specifying that a function cannot throw any exceptions can be an important interface consideration. Fortunately, the C++11 standard remedied the exception specification mess by introducing the noexcept keyword. For an in-depth discussion of the uses of the noexcept specifier, see Item 14 in [19]. For our discussion, we'll concentrate on the keyword's usefulness in design.

Performance optimization aside, the choice to use `noexcept` in a function's specification is largely a matter of preference. For most functions, no exception specification is the norm. Even if a function's code does not itself emit exceptions, it is difficult to ensure statically that nested function calls within a function do not emit any exceptions. Therefore, `noexcept` is enforced at runtime rather than guaranteed at compile time. Thus, my personal recommendation is to reserve the usage of the `noexcept` specifier for particular instances where making a strong statement about the intent of a function is necessary. pdCalc's `Command` hierarchy illustrates several situations where not throwing an exception is important for correct operation. This requirement is codified in the interface to inform developers that throwing exceptions will lead to runtime faults.

7.2.5 API Versioning

Invariably, over the lifetime of a long-lived application, the specification for plugins may change. This implies that a plugin written at one point in time may no longer function with an updated API version. For an application shipped as a single unit, the components composing the whole (i.e., the multiple shared libraries) are synchronized by the development schedule. For a complete application, versioning is used to express to the external world that the overall application has changed. However, because plugins are designed to be standalone from the main application's development, synchronizing plugin releases with application releases may be impossible. Furthermore, the plugin API may or may not change with each application release. Therefore, to ensure compatibility, we must version the plugin API separately from the main application. While you may not anticipate changing the plugin API in the future, if you don't add the ability to query plugins for their supported API version upfront as part of the API itself, you'll have to introduce a breaking change to add this feature later. Depending on your requirements, such a breaking change may not be feasible, and you'll never be able to add API versioning. Therefore, even if it's not used initially, adding a function to query a plugin's supported API version in the plugin interface should be considered an implicit requirement. As is hopefully apparent, the API version is distinct from the application's version.

The actual API version numbering scheme can be as simple or as complicated as is deemed appropriate. On the simple side, it can be a single integer. On the more complicated side, it can be a structure containing several integers for major version, minor version, etc. For pdCalc, I chose a simple structure utilizing only a major version and a minor version number. The interface code is given by the following:

```
class Plugin
{
public:
  struct ApiVersion
  {
    int major;
    int minor;
  };

  virtual ApiVersion apiVersion() const = 0;
};
```

Because pdCalc is at its first release, the main application requires no algorithm more sophisticated than checking that a plugin is using API version 1.0. If this constraint is violated, the offending plugin is not loaded.

7.2.6 Making the Stack Available

Part of the plugin interface consists of making plugins and their commands discoverable to pdCalc. The other part of pdCalc's plugin interface consists of making necessary parts of pdCalc's functionality available to plugins. Specifically, the implementation of new commands requires access to pdCalc's stack.

As we saw when we developed the core commands, commands require only very basic access to the stack. Specifically, they need the ability to push elements onto the stack, to pop elements off of the stack, and potentially to inspect elements from the stack (to implement preconditions). Our strategy for making this functionality available to the core commands was to implement the Stack class as a singleton with a public interface that included push, pop, and inspection member functions. However, this design fails to extend to plugin commands because it violates two of the C++ Plugin Rules. Namely, our current interface does not conform to C linkage (the stack provides a C++ class interface) and the current inspection function returns stack elements via an STL vector.

The solution to this problem is quite trivial. We simply add a new interface to the stack (preferably in a specially designated header file) consisting of a collection of global (outside the pdCalc namespace) extern "C" functions that translate between C linkage and C++ class linkage (the adapter pattern again). Recall that since the Stack class was implemented as a singleton, neither the plugins nor the global helper functions need to own a Stack reference or pointer. The helper functions directly access the Stack through its Instance() function. I chose to implement the following five functions in a separate StackPluginInterface.h header file:

```
extern "C" void StackPush(double d, bool suppressChangeEvent);
extern "C" double StackPop(bool suppressChangeEvent);
extern "C" size_t StackSize();
extern "C" double StackFirstElement();
extern "C" double StackSecondElement();
```

For simplicity, since my example plugin did not need deeper access to the stack than the top two elements, I created only two inspection functions, StackFirstElement() and StackSecondElement(), for getting the top two elements of the stack. If desired, a function returning the elements of the stack to any depth could have been implemented. To maintain extern "C" linkage, the implementer of such a function would need to remember to use a raw array of doubles rather than an STL vector.

The complete, straightforward implementations for the above five functions appear in the StackPluginInterface.cpp file. As an example, the implementation of the StackSize() function is given by the following:

```
size_t StackSize()
{
  return pdCalc::Stack::Instance().size();
}
```

7.3 Problem 2: Loading Plugins

As previously stated, plugins are platform specific, and, inherently, the loading of plugins requires platform-specific code. In this section, we will consider two topics. First, we'll address the platform-specific code necessary for loading libraries and their respective symbols. Here, we'll look at two platform interfaces: POSIX (Linux, UNIX, Mac OS X) and win32 (MS Windows). Second, we'll explore a design strategy to mitigate the source code clutter often arising from the use of platform-specific code.

7.3.1 Platform-Specific Plugin Loading

In order to work with plugins, we only need three platform-specific functions: a function to open a shared library, a function to close a shared library, and a function to extract symbols from an opened shared library. Table 7-1 lists these functions and their associated header file by platform. Let's look at how these functions are used.

Table 7-1. *Plugin functions for different platforms*

	POSIX	win32
header	dlfcn.h	windows.h
load library	dlopen()	LoadLibrary()
close library	dlclose()	FreeLibrary()
get library symbol	dlsym()	GetProcAddress()

7.3.2 Loading, Using, and Closing a Shared Library

The first step in using a plugin is asking the runtime system to open the library and make its exportable symbols available to the current working program. The open command on each platform requires the name of the shared library to be opened (POSIX also requires a flag specifying the desired symbol binding, either lazy or immediate), and it returns an opaque handle to the library, which is used to refer to the library in subsequent function calls. On a POSIX system, the handle type is a void*, while on a win32 system, the handle type is an HINSTANCE (which, after some unraveling, is a typedef for a void*). As an example, the following code opens a plugin library, libPlugin.so, on a POSIX system:

```
void* handle = dlopen("libPlugin.so", RTLD_LAZY);
```

where the RTLD_LAZY option simply tells the runtime system to perform lazy binding, which resolves symbols as the code that references them is executed. The alternative option is RTLD_NOW, which resolves all undefined symbols in the library before dlopen() returns. The null pointer is returned if the open fails. A simple error handling scheme skips loading any functionality from a null plugin, warning the user that opening the plugin failed.

Aside from the different function names, the main platform-specific difference for opening a plugin is the canonical naming convention employed by the different platforms. For example, on Linux, shared libraries begin with `lib` and have a `.so` file extension. On Windows, shared libraries (usually called dynamically linked libraries, or simply DLLs) have no particular prefix and a `.dll` file extension. On Mac OS X, shared libraries conventionally are prefaced with `lib` and have the `.dylib` extension. Essentially, this naming convention matters only in two places. First, the build system should create plugins with an appropriate name for the respective platform. Second, the call to open a plugin should specify the name using the correct format. Since plugin names are specified at runtime, we need to ensure that plugin names are correctly specified by the user supplying the plugin.

Once a plugin has been opened, we'll need to export symbols from the shared library in order to call the functions contained within the plugin. This export is accomplished by calling either `dlopen()` or `LoadLibrary()` (depending on the platform), either of which uses a plugin function's string name to bind the plugin function to a function pointer. The bound plugin function is then called in the main application indirectly via this obtained function pointer.

In order to bind to a symbol in the shared library, we need to have a plugin handle (the return value from opening a plugin), to know the name of the function in the plugin we want to call, and to know the signature of the function we want to call. For pdCalc, the first plugin function we need to call is `AllocPlugin()` to allocate the embedded `Plugin` class (see Section 7.2.3 above). Because this function is declared as part of the plugin interface, we know both its name and its signature. As an example, on Windows, for an already loaded plugin pointed to by `HINSTANCE handle`, we bind the plugin's `AllocPlugin()` function to a function pointer with the following code:

```
// function pointer of AllocPlugin 's type:
extern "C" { typedef void* (*PluginAllocator)(void); }
// bind the symbol from the plugin
auto alloc = GetProcAddress(handle, "AllocPlugin");
// cast the symbol from void* (return of GetProcAddress)
// to the function pointer type of AllocPlugin
PluginAllocator allocator{ reinterpret_cast<PluginAllocator>(alloc) };
```

Subsequently, the plugin's Plugin specialization is allocated by the following:

```
// only dereference if the function was bound properly
if(allocator)
{
  // dereference the allocator, call the function,
  // cast the void* return to a Plugin*
  auto p = static_cast<Plugin*>((*allocator)());
}
```

The concrete Plugin is now available for use (e.g., loading plugin commands, querying the supported plugin API) through the abstract Plugin interface.

An analogous sequence of code is required to bind and execute the plugin's DeallocPlugin() function upon plugin deallocation. The interested reader is referred to the platform-specific code in the GitHub repository for the details. Remember that before deallocating a plugin, since commands allocated by the plugin are resident in memory in the main application (but must be reclaimed in the plugin), a plugin must not be closed until all of its commands are freed. Examples of plugin commands resident in the main application's memory space are command prototypes in the CommandRepository and commands on the undo/redo stack in the CommandManager.

Since a plugin is an acquired resource, we should release it when we are finished using it. This action is performed on a POSIX platform by calling dlclose() and on a win32 platform by calling FreeLibrary(). For example, the following code for a POSIX system closes a shared library (the handle) that was opened with dlopen():

```
// only try to close a non-null library
if(handle) dlclose(handle);
```

Now that we have discussed the platform-specific mechanics of opening, using, and closing plugins, let's turn our attention to a design strategy that mitigates the inherent complications of working with multi-platform source code.

7.3.3 A Design for Multi-Platform Code

Portability across platforms is a laudable goal for any software project. However, achieving this goal while maintaining a readable codebase requires significant forethought. In this section, we'll examine some design techniques for achieving platform portability while maintaining readability.

7.3.3.1 The Obvious Solution: Libraries

The obvious (and preferred) solution to the portability problem is to use a library that abstracts platform dependencies for you. Using a high quality library for any development scenario always saves you the effort of having to design, implement, test, and maintain functionality required for your project. Using a library for cross-platform development has the additional benefit of hiding platform-specific code behind a platform-independent API. Such an API, of course, allows you to maintain a single codebase that works seamlessly across multiple platforms without littering the source code with preprocessor directives. Although I did not explicitly discuss these merits in Chapter 6, Qt's toolkit abstraction provides a platform-independent API for building a GUI, an otherwise platform-dependent task. In pdCalc, we used Qt to build a GUI that compiles and executes on Windows and Linux (and, presumably OS X, although I have not verified that fact) without changing a single line of the source code between platforms.

Alas, the obvious solution is not always available. Many reasons exist for not incorporating libraries in a project. First, many libraries are not free, and the cost of a library may be prohibitive, especially if the license has usage fees in addition to development fees. Second, a library's license may be incompatible with a project's license. For example, maybe you are building a closed source code, but the only available library has an incompatible open source license (or vice versa). Third, libraries are frequently shipped without source code. Lacking source code makes extending a library's functionality impossible. Fourth, you might require support for a library, but the vendor might not supply any. Fifth, a library may ship with an upgrade cycle incompatible with your own. Sixth, a library might be incompatible with your toolchain. Finally, a library may not exist at all for the functionality you are seeking. Therefore, while using a library typically is the first choice to achieve portability, enough counterexamples to using a library exist to merit discussing how to achieve portability without one.

7.3.3.2 Raw Preprocessor Directives

Using raw preprocessor directives is undoubtedly the first method tried when attempting to achieve cross-platform code. Nearly everyone who has written portable code probably started this way. Simply, everywhere platform dependent code appears, the platform-specific pieces are surrounded by preprocessor #ifdef directives. Let's take, for example, the runtime loading of a shared library in both Linux and Windows:

```
#ifdef POSIX
  void* handle = dlopen("libPlugin.so", RTLD_LAZY);
#elif WIN32
  HINSTANCE handle = LoadLibrary("Plugin.dll");
#endif
```

Don't forget the preprocessor directives surrounding the header files too:

```
#ifdef POSIX
  #include <dlfcn.h>
#elif WIN32
  #include <windows.h>
#endif
```

For a small number of platforms or for a very few instances, using raw preprocessor directives can be tolerable. However, this technique scales poorly. As soon as either the number of platforms or the number of code locations requiring platform-dependent code increases, using raw preprocessor directives quickly becomes a mess. The code becomes difficult to read, and finding all the platform-dependent locations when adding a new platform becomes a nightmare. In even a medium sized project, sprinkling the code with #ifdefs quickly becomes untenable.

7.3.3.3 (Slightly) More Clever Preprocessor Directives

Where platform APIs are different in name but identical in function call arguments (more common than you might expect since similar functionality, unsurprisingly enough, requires similar customizations), we can be a little more clever in our usage of the preprocessor. Instead of placing the preprocessor directives at the site of every platform-dependent function call and type declaration, we can instead create platform-dependent macro names and define them in a centralized location. This idea is better explained with an example. Let's look at closing a shared library on Linux and Windows:

```
// some common header defining all platform dependent analogous symbols
#ifdef POSIX
  #define HANDLE void*
  #define CLOSE_LIBRARY dlclose
```

```
#elif WIN32
  #define CLOSE_LIBRARY FreeLibrary
  #define HANDLE HINSTANCE
#endif

// in the code, for some shared library HANDLE handle
CLOSE_LIBRARY(handle);
```

This technique is significantly cleaner than the naive approach of sprinkling #ifdefs at every function call invocation. However, it is severely limited by only working for function calls with identical arguments. Obviously, we would still need an #ifdef at the call site for opening a shared library because the POSIX call requires two arguments, while the Windows call requires only one. Certainly, with the abstraction capabilities of C++, we can do better.

7.3.3.4 A Build System Solution

An interesting idea that seems appealing at first is to separate platform-specific code into platform-specific source files and then use the build system to choose the correct file based on the platform. Let's consider an example. Place all of the Unix-specific code in a file called UnixImpl.cpp, and place all of the Windows-specific code in a file called WindowsImpl.cpp. On each respective platform, code your build scripts to only compile the appropriate platform-specific file. Using this technique, no platform preprocessor directives are required since any given source file only contains source for one platform.

The above scheme suffers from two distinct drawbacks. First, the method only works if you maintain identical interfaces (e.g., function names, class names, argument lists) to your own source code across all platform-specific files on all platforms. This feat is easier said than done, especially if you have independent teams working and testing on each platform. Compounding the problem, because the compiler only sees the code for a single platform at any given time, there is no language mechanism (e.g., type system) to enforce these cross-platform interface constraints. Second, the mechanics of achieving cross-platform compatibility are completely opaque to any developer examining the source code on a single platform. On any one platform, only one of the many platform-dependent source files effectively exists, and this source file supplies no hint of the others' existence. Of course, this latter problem exacerbates the former because the lack of cross-platform source transparency coupled with the lack of language support for the technique makes it nearly impossible to maintain interface consistency. For these reasons, a pure build system solution is intractable.

With the downsides of this technique noted, we must be careful not to throw out the baby with the bathwater, for the kernel of our final solution lies in a language supported mechanism at the juxtaposition of both the preprocessor and the build system solutions. This design technique is examined in the following section.

7.3.3.5 A Platform Factory Function

Scattering preprocessor macros throughout a code everywhere platform-specific functionality is required is analogous to using integer flags and `switch` statements to execute type-specific code. Not coincidentally, both problems have the same solution, which is to build an abstract class hierarchy and execute specific functionality via polymorphism.

We'll build our solution of designing a general cross-platform architecture in two steps. First, we'll design a platform hierarchy for handling dynamic loading. Second, we'll extend this specific solution into a framework for abstracting platform dependence into a platform-independent interface. In both steps, we will employ a hybrid solution that utilizes the build system in a type-safe manner through a minimum use of platform-specific preprocessor directives. Along the way, we'll encounter two additional, important design patterns: the factory method and the abstract factory. Let's start by examining the platform-independent dynamic loading of plugins.

To address our specific problem, we start by first defining a platform-independent abstract interface for a `DynamicLoader` base class. Our `DynamicLoader` only needs to do two things: allocate and deallocate plugins. The base class is therefore trivially defined as follows:

```
class DynamicLoader
{
public:
  virtual ~DynamicLoader();

  virtual Plugin* allocatePlugin(const string& pluginName) = 0;
  virtual void deallocatePlugin(Plugin*) = 0;
};
```

The design intent of the above base class is that the hierarchy will be specialized by platform.

Notice that the interface itself is platform independent. The platform-dependent allocation and deallocation is an implementation detail handled by the platform-specific derived classes of this interface through the virtual functions. Furthermore, because each platform-specific implementation is wholly contained in a derived class, by placing each derived class in a separate file, we can use the build system to selectively compile only the file relevant for each platform, obviating the need for platform preprocessor directives anywhere within the hierarchy. Even better, once a `DynamicLoader` has been allocated, the interface abstracts away the platform-specific details of plugin loading, and the consumer of a plugin need not be concerned with plugin loading details. Loading just works. For the implementer of the derived classes of the `DynamicLoader`, the compiler can use type information to enforce interface consistency across platforms since each derived class must conform to the interface specified by the abstract base class, which is common to all platforms. The design is summarized pictorially in Figure 7-1. The included source code for pdCalc implements platform-specific loaders for a POSIX compliant system and for Windows.

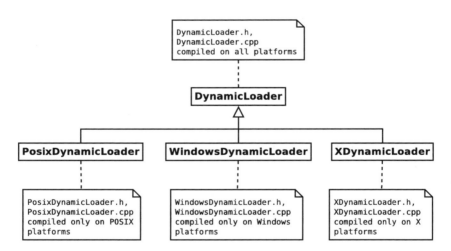

Figure 7-1. *The dynamic loader hierarchy for platform-independent plugin allocation and deallocation*

The above design hides platform-specific details behind an abstract interface, alleviating the need for a plugin consumer to understand how a plugin is loaded. That is, of course, assuming that the plugin consumer instantiates the correct platform-specific derived class, something that cannot be handled automatically by the `DynamicLoader` hierarchy. Here, we introduce a new design pattern, the factory function, to solve the problem of instantiating the correct derived class. Simply, the factory function is a pattern that separates type creation from the logical point of instantiation.

Before progressing, I should point out the semantic difference between a factory function and the factory method pattern, as defined by the Gang of Four [6]. Simply, the factory method pattern implements a factory via a separate class hierarchy. A factory, more generally, is any mechanism of separating the selection of the specific derived class in a hierarchy from the point of logical instantiation. A factory function is a factory composed of a single function rather than a separate creational hierarchy.

Typically, a factory is implemented by calling a function that takes a flag (an integer, an enumeration, a string, etc.) to delimit the specialization of a hierarchy and returns a base class pointer. Let's examine an artificial example. Suppose we have a hierarchy of Shapes with the derived classes Circle, Triangle, and Rectangle. Furthermore, suppose we have defined the following enumerated class:

```
enum class ShapeType {Circle, Triangle, Rectangle};
```

The following factory function could be used to create shapes:

```
unique_ptr<Shape> shapeFactory(ShapeType t)
{
  switch(t)
  {
    case ShapeType::Circle:
      return make_unique<Circle>();
    case ShapeType::Triangle:
      return make_unique<Triangle>();
    case ShapeType::Rectangle:
      return make_unique<Rectangle>();
  }
}
```

A Circle could be created by the following function call:

```
auto s = shapeFactory(ShapeType::Circle);
```

Why is the above construction anymore useful than typing

```
auto s = make_unique<Circle >();
```

Truthfully, it's not. Instead, however, consider a factory function that accepts a `string` argument instead of an enumerated type (replacing the `switch` statement with a series of `if` statements). We can now construct a `Circle` with the following statement:

```
auto s = shapeFactory("circle");
```

The above is a much more useful construct than direct instantiation using a class name because discovery of the value of the `string` argument to `shapeFactory()` can be deferred to runtime. A typical usage of the simple factory method as described above is to enable the condition defining which specialization is instantiated to appear in a configuration file or an input file.

In our case, the factory is even simpler. Since our hierarchy is specialized by platform, rather than passing in a flag to choose the appropriate derived class, we simply make the selection by using preprocessor directives, as shown in Listing 7-1.

Listing 7-1. A Dynamic Loader Factory Function

```
unique_ptr<DynamicLoader> dynamicLoaderFactory()
{
#ifdef POSIX
  return make_unique<PosixDynamicLoader>();
#elif WIN32
  return make_unique<WindowsDynamicLoader>();
#else
  return nullptr;
}
```

By compiling the `dynamicLoaderFactory()` function into its own source file, we can achieve platform-independent plugin creation by isolating one set of preprocessor directives in one source file. The factory function is then called to return the correct type of `DynamicLoader` at the site where plugin allocation or deallocation is needed. By having the factory return a `unique_ptr`, we need not worry about memory leaks. The following code snippet illustrates the platform-independent usage of the `DynamicLoader`:

```
// Question: What plaform?
auto loader = dynamicLoaderFactory();
// Answer: Who cares?
auto plugin = (loader ? loader->allocatePlugin(pluginName) : nullptr);
```

For the purposes of pdCalc, we could stop with the `DynamicLoader` hierarchy and our simple factory function. We only have the need to abstract one platform-dependent feature (the allocation and deallocation of plugins), and the code above is sufficient for this purpose. However, we've come this far, and it's worth taking one extra step to see a generalized implementation of platform independence applicable to situations calling for a number of different platform-dependent features, even if it is not specifically needed for our case study.

7.3.3.6 An Abstract Factory for Generalized Platform Independent Code

As software developers, we are constantly faced with design challenges caused by platform dependence. The following is an incomplete list of common platform-specific programming tasks for a C++ developer: plugin loading, interprocess communication, navigation of the file system (standardized in C++17), graphics, threading (standardized in C++11), persistent settings, binary serialization, `sizeof()` built-in data types, timers (standardized in C++11), and network communication. Most, if not all, of the functionality on this list can be obtained through platform-independent APIs in libraries such as boost or Qt. For me personally, the platform-specific feature that has caused the most aggravation has been the humble directory separator (/ on a Posix system and \ on a Windows system).

Suppose our calculator required the ability to read, write, and save persistent custom settings (see Chapter 8 for some reasons why this might be necessary for a calculator). Typically, Linux systems save settings in text files (for example, on Ubuntu, user settings are saved in files in the `.config` directory in home), while on Windows systems, persistent settings are saved in the system registry. In practice, the best solution would be to use an existing library that has already implemented this abstraction (e.g., Qt's `QSettings` class). For instructional purposes, we'll assume that no external libraries are available, and we'll examine a design that adds persistent settings (or any number of platform-dependent functionality) alongside our existing dynamic loader. Our focus will be on the abstraction rather than the specifics of the settings implementation on each platform.

The easy solution is to piggyback on our dynamic loader and simply add the necessary settings interface directly into the `DynamicLoader` class. Of course, we would need to rename the class to something more generic, such as `OsSpecificFunctionality`, with derived classes such as `LinuxFuntionality` and `WindowsFunctionality`. This method is simple, fast, and quickly intractable; it is antithetical to cohesion. For any sizable code, this technique eventually leads to uncontrollable bloat and thus a complete lack of maintainability of the interface. Despite time pressures on projects, I recommend always avoiding this quick solution because it merely increases your technical debt and causes longer delays in the future than would be experienced in the present with a proper solution.

Instead of bloating our existing `DynamicLoader` class, we instead take inspiration from its design and create a separate, analogous settings hierarchy as depicted in Figure 7-2. Again, we have the problem of instantiating a platform-specific derived class on each unique platform. However, instead of adding an additional `settingsLoaderFactory()` function to mirror the existing `dynamicLoaderFactory()` function, we instead seek a generalized solution that enables indefinite functional extension while preserving the single code point for platform selection. As expected, we are not the first programmers to encounter this particular problem and a solution already exists: the abstract factory pattern.

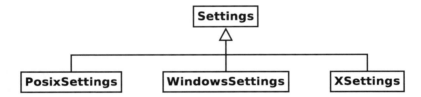

Figure 7-2. *The settings hierarchy for platform-independent persistent settings*

According to Gamma *et al* [6], an abstract factory "provides an interface for creating families of related or dependent objects without specifying their concrete classes." Essentially, the pattern can be constructed in two steps:

1. Create independent hierarchies (families) for each of the related objects (e.g., a dynamic loader hierarchy and a settings hierarchy, related by their platform dependence).

2. Create a hierarchy, specializing on the dependent relationship (e.g., the platform), that provides factory functions for each of the families.

I find the above abstraction very difficult to comprehend without a concrete example; therefore, let's consider the problem we are trying to solve in pdCalc. As you walk through this example, refer to the (overly complex) class diagram in Figure 7-3.

Recall that the overall goal of this abstraction is to create a single source location capable of providing a platform-independent mechanism for creating any number of platform-specific specializations.

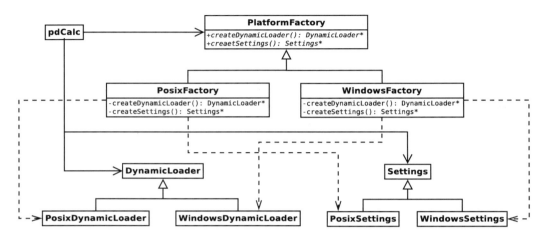

Figure 7-3. *The abstract factory pattern applied to pdCalc*

As we've already seen, the platform-dependent functionality can be abstracted into parallel, independent hierarchies. These hierarchies enable platform-dependent implementations to be accessed through platform-independent base class interfaces via polymorphism. For pdCalc, this pattern translates into providing platform-agnostic Settings and DynamicLoader hierarchies to abstract persistent settings and dynamic loading, respectively. For example, we can allocate and deallocate a plugin polymorphically through the abstract DynamicLoader interface, provided the system instantiates the correct underlying derived class (PosixDynamicLoader or WindowsDynamicLoader) based on the platform. This part of the abstract factory is represented by the DynamicLoader hierarchy in Figure 7-3.

The problem now reduces to instantiating the correct derived class based on the current platform. Instead of providing separate factory functions to instantiate the DynamicLoader and Settings objects (a decentralized approach requiring separate platform #ifdefs in each factory), we instead create a hierarchy that provides an abstract interface for providing the factory functions necessary to create the DynamicLoader and Settings objects. This abstract factory hierarchy (the PlatformFactory hierarchy in Figure 7-3) is then specialized on the platform so that we have platform-specific derived classes of the factory hierarchy that create platform-specific derived classes of the functional hierarchies. This scheme centralizes the platform dependence into a single factory function that instantiates the correct `PlatformFactory` specialization. In pdCalc's implementation, I chose to make the `PlatformFactory` a singleton and thereby "hide" the `PlatformFactory`'s factory function in the `Instance()` function.

The abstract factory pattern might still not make a lot of sense, so let's look at some sample code, viewing the abstraction in a top-down fashion. Ultimately, the abstract factory pattern enables us to write the following platform-independent, high-level code in pdCalc:

```
// PlatformFactory Instance returns either a PosixFactory or a
// WindowsFactory instance (based on the platform), which in turn
// creates the correct derived DynamicLoader
auto loader = PlatformFactory::Intance().createDynamicLoader();

// The correctly instantiated loader provides platform specific
// dynamic loading functionality polymorphically through a platform
// independent interface
auto plugin = loader->allocatePlugin(pName);
// ...
loader->deallocatePlugin(plugin);

// Same principle for settings ...
auto settings = PlatformFactory::Instance().createSettings();
settings->readSettingsFromDisk();
// ...
settings->commitSettingsToDisk();
```

Drilling down, the first function we'll examine is the `PlatformFactory`'s `Instance()` function, which returns either a `PosixFactory` or a `WindowsFactory`, depending on the platform.

```
PlatformFactory& PlatformFactory::Instance()
{
#ifdef POSIX
  static PosixFactory instance;
#elif WIN32
  static WindowsFactory instance;
#endif
  return instance;
}
```

The above function is doing something subtle but clever, and it's a trick worth knowing. From the client's perspective, `PlatformFactory` looks like an ordinary singleton class. One calls the `Instance()` function, and a `PlatformFactory` reference is returned. Clients then use the `PlatformFactory`'s public interface as they would any other singleton class. However, because the `Instance()` member function returns a reference, we are free to use the instance polymorphically. Since `PosixFactory` and `WindowsFactory` both derive from `PlatformFactory`, the `instance` variable instantiated is the specialization that matches the platform as defined by the `#ifdef` in the implementation. We have cleverly disguised an implementation detail, the mechanics of the abstract factory pattern, from the user of the class. Unless the client noticed that the factory functions in the `PlatformFactory` are pure virtual, he would probably not realize he was consuming an object-oriented hierarchy. Of course, the goal is not to hide anything from the user in a nefarious plot to obscure the implementation. Rather, this information hiding is utilized to reduce the complexity burden on the client of the `PlatformFactory`.

We next examine the trivial implementations of the `createDynamicLoader()` functions in the `PosixFactory` and `WindowsFactory` classes (note the covariant return type of the functions):

```
unique_ptr<DynamicLoader> PosixFactory::createDynamicLoader()
{
  return make_unique<PosixDynamicLoader>();
}

unique_ptr<DynamicLoader> WindowsFactory::createDynamicLoader()
{
  return make_unique<WindowsDynamicLoader>();
}
```

Above, we've simply replaced the dynamic loader factory function (see Listing 7-1) by a class hierarchy, replacing the platform `#ifdef`s with polymorphism. With only one piece of functionality dependent on the platform, the replacement of a factory function with an abstract factory is certainly overkill. However, for our example, we have the independent `DynamicLoader` and `Settings` families both dependent on the same platform criterion (in principle, we could have any number of such hierarchies), and the abstract factory pattern allows us to centralize the platform dependency in one location (here, in the `PlatformFactory`'s `Instance()` function) instead of scattering it through multiple independent factory functions. From a maintenance standpoint, the value proposition is similar to preferring polymorphism to switch statements.

The final pieces of the puzzle are the implementations of both the `DynamicLoader` and `Settings` hierarchies. Fortunately, these implementations are identical to the ideas outlined in Section 7.3.3, and I need not repeat their implementations here. Using the abstract factory pattern indeed adds no inherent complication to the implementation of platform-dependent functions. The pattern only adds mechanics around the instantiation of these classes via a single factory hierarchy instead of a sequence of factory functions.

In the source code in pdCalc's repository, no `Settings` hierarchy (or its associated `readSettingsFromDisk()` and `commitSettingsToDisk()` functions in `PlatformFactory`) implementation exists because pdCalc, as written, has no need for a persistent settings abstraction. The `Settings` hierarchy was merely manufactured as a plausible example to demonstrate concretely the mechanics and relevance of the abstract factory pattern. That said, I did opt to include a full abstract platform factory implementation in pdCalc's code for the `DynamicLoader` alone just to illustrate a practical implementation of the abstract factory pattern even though a simpler single factory function would have sufficed and been preferred for production code.

7.4 Problem 3: Retrofitting pdCalc

We now turn to the final plugin problem, which is retrofitting the already developed classes and interfaces to accommodate adding calculator functionality dynamically. This problem is not about plugin management. Rather, the problem we are addressing here is extending pdCalc's module interfaces to accept plugin features. Essentially, where Section 7.2 defined how to discover commands and buttons in a plugin, this section describes how to incorporate these newly discovered commands into pdCalc.

Let's begin by creating an interface to enable the injection of newly discovered plugin commands. Recall from Chapter 4 how core commands are loaded into the `CommandRepository` when the application starts. First, the main application calls the `RegisterCoreCommands()` function. Second, within this function, the `registerCommand()` function of the `CommandRepository` class is called for each core command, registering the command's name and a command prototype with the `CommandRepository`. In Section 7.2, we developed an interface for exporting command names and command prototypes from plugins. Obviously, to register these plugin commands, we simply need to extend the command dispatcher module's interface to include the `registerCommand()` function. This interface extension, however, raises an interesting question. What does it mean to extend a module interface in C++, a language with no formal module definition?

7.4.1 Module Interfaces

Until now, we have not rigorously defined a mechanism for implementing or describing modules. We have only loosely declared certain classes to be parts of certain modules (e.g., the `CommandRepository` being part of the command dispatcher module). But what does that really mean? The C++ language, as it currently stands, does not implement a module concept. Therefore, the module is essentially a meta-language concept, and the language itself gives very little help in the enforcement of a module interface. We do, however, have a few basic options for defining modules and their interfaces. First, encapsulate all classes not directly part of the interface in one source file and only expose a limited module interface in a single header file. Second, build each module into a separate DLL and use the DLL symbol export mechanism to selectively export interface functions. Third, implicitly define module boundaries via declarations in documentation and comments. Let's explore each of these options.

7.4.1.1 Source Code Hiding

Let's begin by discussing the encapsulation model that has always been available to C programmers: hide non-public interface classes and functions in source files and do not expose their interfaces in headers. This is the only mechanism that C++ provides for truly hiding symbols (remember, access modifiers, such as `private`, cannot be used for classes themselves, as would be possible in Java or C#). You've already seen this mechanism employed in hiding class details behind the pimpl pattern.

At the module level, this encapsulation scheme implies that all of the source for a module would have to reside in a single source file, and only the public parts of the module's interface would appear in a single module header file. For example, for pdCalc's command dispatcher module, only the `CommandDispatcher` and the `Command` interface would appear in a single header, and the definitions of the `CommandDispatcher` class as well as the declarations and definitions of all the concrete commands, the `CommandRepository`, and the `CommandManager` would reside in a single source file. The biggest disadvantage of source hiding is that it can lead to very large single files for complicated modules. Large files create the dual dilemmas of being difficult to read due to sheer size and having long compile times for minimal changes since all of the code must be recompiled for any change in the module. The advantages of this technique are that it can be natively implemented in the C++ language and it does not require each module to reside in a separate dynamically linked library.

I have personally seen this strategy employed in at least one open source package. While it does accomplish module interface hiding from a technical perspective, the result is an entire library distributed as a single header file and a single source file. The header file is over 3,000 lines long and the source file is nearly 20,000 lines long. I cannot imagine this solution being optimally designed for readability or maintainability. This open source package, to the best of my knowledge, has a single author. Readability and maintainability for a team of developers were, therefore, unlikely to have been his primary objectives.

7.4.1.2 DLL Hiding

If you are using C++, have a large code base, and want true hiding of a module's interface, using DLL hiding is the most reasonable option. Employing this option is, of course, outside the scope of the C++ language itself. DLL hiding is based on the operating system's library format and implemented via compiler directives. Essentially, the programmer decorates classes or functions with special compiler directives to indicate whether a function is to be imported or exported from a DLL. The compiler then creates a DLL that only publicly exports the appropriately marked symbols, and code linking to the DLL must specify which symbols it intends to import. Since the same header must be marked as an export while compiling the DLL and as an import while compiling code using the DLL, the implementation is typically accomplished by using compiler/OS-specific preprocessor directives. For example, in Windows, the following code (or a similar variant) would be employed:

```
// Declspec .h
#ifdef BUILDING_DLL
  #define DECLSPEC __declspec(export)
#else
  #define DECLSPEC __declspec(import)
#endif
```

The declaration of a function foo() that we want to export from our DLL would be written as

```
#include "Declspec.h"
DECLSPEC void foo();
```

When the DLL is built, the preprocessor macro BUILDING_DLL is defined; therefore, the DECLSPEC macro expands to __declspec(export). When the DLL is used, the BUILDING_DLL macro is left undefined, and the DECLSPEC macro expands to __declspec(import). Any function or class not decorated with the DECLSPEC macro remains private to the DLL. GCC implements a similar mechanism using a slightly different syntax.

Most Windows programmers are very familiar with the DLL hiding mechanism for controlling module interfaces because globally hiding symbols in DLLs is the default paradigm for Visual Studio. If a symbol is not decorated, it will not be exported from the DLL. Therefore, to make a DLL that can be called from externally (is there any other kind?), Windows programmers must manually export symbols using the __declspec directive. Many UNIX programmers, however, are unfamiliar with DLL hiding because the default shared library implementation publicly exports all symbols. That is, in a typical UNIX or Linux system, no need exists to decorate symbols as an export or an import in shared library code because all symbols in a shared library are made publicly available to the calling program by the linker when the shared library is loaded. Compiler command line options can reverse the default visibility from public to private, if so desired, and symbols can be marked manually for either import or export analogously to a Windows build.

I started this section by stating that if you want true hiding of a module's interface for a large C++ code base, using DLL hiding is the most reasonable option. It enables a very fine level of granularity for module access control provided you are content to devote a separate DLL to each module. The main disadvantages to this technique are in readability, maintainability, and portability. Using the technique does require using compiler and operating system-specific decorators that are not part of the C++ language for each exportable function. While the extra DECLSPEC macro is not too unbearable for each function or class, the definition of the macro can get unwieldy quickly when accounting for multiple operating systems or multiple compilers. Additionally, diagnosing problems caused by forgetting to define the correct preprocessor macro when building or using a DLL can confound novice programmers. Finally, correctly implementing DLL imports and exports in the presence of template code can be nontrivial.

7.4.1.3 Implicit or Documentation Hiding

The technique that I have termed implicit hiding is nothing more than hiding the interface by not documenting it. What does this mean in practice? Since the C++ language does not directly support modules, implicit hiding simply draws a logical construct around a group of classes and functions, and declares those classes to compose a module. The language allows any public function of any class to be called from code external to the module. Therefore, the module's public interface is "declared" by only documenting those functions that should be called from the outside. From a purely technical perspective, implicit hiding is no hiding at all!

Why would anyone choose implicit hiding over either source code hiding or DLL hiding? Quite simply, the choice is made for expedience. Using implicit hiding allows developers to organize classes and source code in a logical, readable, and maintainable style. Each class (or group of closely related classes) can be grouped into its own header and source file pair. This enables minimal inclusion of only necessary code, which leads to faster compile times. Implicit hiding also does not force the boundary definitions for inclusion into a particular shared library, which could be important if there is a design goal of minimizing the number of individual shared libraries shipped with a package.

The problem with implicit hiding is, of course, that no language mechanism exists to prevent the misuse of functions and classes not intended by the designer to be used outside of a logical module. Is this a serious problem or not? Why might we want to forcibly prevent users from calling part of the interface not deemed public? The main design reason is that we do not want users to rely upon undocumented features since the nonpublic interface is subject to change. Unsurprisingly, this reason is identical to why we prize encapsulation in class design. That is, implementations should be allowed to change independently of interfaces. So, how important is it to forcibly hide the nonpublic interface? Ultimately, it depends on how much you trust the users of your code to either not call undocumented interfaces or at least accept ownership of the unplanned maintenance forced upon them by changes to undocumented interfaces.

7.4.1.4 Module Design for pdCalc

I chose to use implicit hiding in the design of pdCalc. For this project, I felt that the benefits of simplicity outweighed the complications necessary to use one of the other modes of module interface hiding. Which technique you choose for your own projects will naturally reduce to your personal preferences. Given the relatively small code base of pdCalc, the choice to use implicit hiding enables grouping classes by logic rather than along module boundaries. Furthermore, implicit hiding allows lumping several of the modules (e.g., command dispatcher, stack, and plugin management) into one shared, back-end library.

My choice to use implicit hiding has a direct implication for solving the original problem of extending the command dispatcher module's interface to include the `registerCommand()` function from the `CommandRepository` class. This extension can simply be accomplished by decree, or, more precisely, by a documentation change. Essentially, this function can be added to the interface by updating Table 2-2 in Chapter 2.

Implicit hiding does not have a specific language supported feature, so you cannot point to one specific class and say, "This header defines the module's interface." Instead, documentation is used to draw an implicit line around selected pieces of the public classes and functions that define a module's interface. Therefore, once the documentation has been changed, the `main()` function can inject plugin commands during plugin loading by calling `CommandRepository`'s existing `registerCommand()` function. No code change is needed to retrofit pdCalc for plugin command injection.

7.4.2 Adding Plugin Buttons to the GUI

Recall at the outset of this section that we outlined two problems to be solved in retrofitting pdCalc for plugins. The first problem, which we just solved, was how to add plugin commands to the `CommandRepository` after a plugin is loaded. The solution turned out to be quite trivial since we had already written the necessary function and needed only to extend the module's defined public interface. The second problem involves retrofitting pdCalc to be able to add buttons to the GUI that correspond to plugin commands.

By the design of our command dispatcher, once a command is registered, it can be executed by any user interface raising a `commandEntered()` event with the command's name as the event's argument. Hence, for the CLI, a plugin command can be executed by the user by typing in its name. That is, plugin commands become immediately accessible to the CLI as soon as they are registered. Making a plugin command accessible in the GUI, of course, is slightly more complicated because a button that can raise a `commandEntered()` event must be created for each discovered plugin command.

In Section 7.2, we defined an interface for labeling `CommandButtons`. Each plugin provides a `PluginButtonDescriptor` that defines the primary command label, the secondary command label, and the underlying commands associated with the labels. Therefore, in order to add a new GUI button corresponding to a plugin command, we must simply extend the interface of the GUI's `MainWindow` class to include a function for adding buttons based on their labels:

```
class MainWindow : public QMainWindow, public UserInterface
{
public:
  // Existing interface plus the following:
  void addCommandButton(const string& dispPrimaryCmd,
    const string& primaryCmd, const string& dispShftCmd,
    const string& shftCmd);
};
```

Of course, this function will also need to lay out the buttons based on some suitable algorithm. My trivial algorithm simply places buttons left to right with four buttons in a row.

As was briefly mentioned in Chapter 6, the `MainWindow` class also includes a `setupFinalButtons()` function and a `fixSize()` function. The `setupFinalButtons()` function adds the `undo`, `redo`, and `proc` (see Chapter 8) buttons as the top row in the GUI. The `fixSize()` function forces the GUI's geometry to stay fixed at its current dimensions. These operations can only logically be called after all plugin buttons have been added.

Unlike the `registerCommand()` function of the `CommandRegistry`, the `addCommandButton()` was not a preexisting public function of the `MainWindow` class. Therefore, we must add and implement this new function. In all likelihood, a modular implementation of the GUI would have already had a similar function somewhere in the GUI module, as this functionality was already required to create buttons for core commands. Therefore, implementation of the `addCommandButton()` function might be as trivial as forwarding this call from the `MainWindow` to the appropriate internal GUI class, where the function may have already existed.

7.5 Incorporating Plugins

Thus far, we have discussed guidelines for C++ plugins, the plugin interface, plugin command memory management, loading and unloading plugins, design patterns for abstracting platform-dependent code behind interfaces, and retrofitting pdCalc to enable plugin command and GUI injection. However, we have yet to discuss any mechanism for finding plugins, actually loading and unloading plugins from disk, managing the lifetime of plugins, or injecting plugin functionality into pdCalc. These operations are performed by a `PluginLoader` class and the `main()` function of the application, both of which are now described.

7.5.1 Loading Plugins

Loading plugins is accomplished by a `PluginLoader` class. The `PluginLoader` is responsible for finding plugin dynamic library files, loading the plugins into memory, and serving the concrete `Plugin` specializations to pdCalc, on demand. The `PluginLoader` is also responsible for deallocating plugin resources at the appropriate times. As we've seen previously, a good design will implement automatic deallocation via RAII.

The first step in loading plugins is determining which plugins should be loaded and when. Really, only two practical options exist to answer this question. Either plugins are loaded automatically by pdCalc when the program starts (e.g., files specified in a configuration file or all DLLs in a specific directory), or plugins are loaded on demand by direct user requests. Of course, these options are not mutually exclusive, and a `PluginLoader` class could be designed that incorporates both options, possibly with the ability for the user to direct which manually loaded plugins should be automatically loaded in the future. There is no right or wrong answer to how plugins are loaded. The decision must be addressed by the program's requirements.

For simplicity, I chose to implement a plugin loader that automatically loads plugins during pdCalc's startup. The `PluginLoader` finds these plugins by reading an ASCII configuration file comprised of lines of text each individually listing the file name of a plugin. The configuration file is arbitrarily named `plugins.pdp`, and this file must be located in the current executable path. Plugin files listed in `plugins.pdp` can be specified using either a relative or absolute path. A more sophisticated plugin loader implementation would probably store the location of the plugins file in an operating system-specific configuration location (e.g., the Windows registry) and use a better file format, such as XML. A good library, like Qt, can help you parse XML and find system-specific configuration files using a platform-independent abstraction.

With the above plugin loader design constraints in mind, the `PluginLoader` interface is quite trivial:

```
class PluginLoader
{
public:
  void loadPlugins(UserInterface& ui, const string& pluginFileName);
  const vector<const Plugin*> getPlugins();
};
```

The `loadPlugins()` function takes the name of the configuration file as input, loads each library into memory, and allocates an instance of each library's `Plugin` class. The `UserInterface` reference is solely for error reporting. When the `main()` function is ready to inject the plugins' commands, the `getPlugins()` function is called to return a collection of loaded `Plugins`. Of course, the `loadPlugins()` and `getPlugins()` functions could be combined, but I prefer a design that enables the programmer to retain finer tuned control over the timing of plugin loading versus plugin usage. My implementation of the `PluginLoader` makes use of a few clever techniques for using RAII to manage the automatic deallocation of the plugins. As the implementation here is orthogonal to the design, the interested reader is referred to the `PluginLoader.cpp` source file for details.

7.5.2 Injecting Functionality

Having decided that plugins should be loaded automatically from a configuration file, the most logical placement for plugin loading is somewhere in the `main()` function call tree. Essentially, this `loadPlugins()` function simply puts together all of the pieces we have previously discussed: loading plugin libraries, loading plugins, extracting commands and buttons from the plugin descriptors, and injecting these commands and buttons into pdCalc. Of course, a proper implementation will also perform error checking on the plugins. For example, error checking might include checking the plugin API version, ensuring the commands have not already been registered, and ensuring the GUI buttons correspond to commands in the command repository. Listing 7-2 is a skeleton of a function for loading plugins. Its inputs are a `UserInterface` reference for reporting errors and a `PluginLoader` reference.

Listing 7-2. A Fuction for Loading Plugins

```
void setupPlugins(UserInterface& ui, PluginLoader& loader)
{
  loader.loadPlugins(ui, "plugins.pdp");
  auto plugins = loader.getPlugins();

  for(auto p : plugins)
  {
    auto apiVersion = p->apiVersion();
    // verify plugin API at correct level

    // inject plugin commands into CommandRepository - recall
    // the cloned command will auto release in the plugin
    auto descriptor = p->getPluginDescriptor();
    for(int i = 0; i < descriptor.nCommands; ++i)
    {
      registerCommand( ui, descriptor.commandNames[i],
        MakeCommandPtr( descriptor.commands[i]->clone() ) );
    }

    // if gui, setup buttons
    auto mw = dynamic_cast<MainWindow*>(&ui);
    if(mw)
    {
      auto buttonDescriptor = p->getPluginButtonDescriptor();
      if(buttonDescriptor)
      {
        for(int i = 0; i <buttonDescriptor->nButtons; ++i)
        {
          auto b = *buttonDescriptor;
          // check validity of button commands
          mw->addCommandButton(b.dispPrimaryCmd[i], b.primaryCmd[i],
            b.dispShftCmd [i], b.shftCmd[i]);
        }
      }
    }
  }
```

```
  }
  return;
}
```

After a long chapter describing how to implement C++ plugins, the denouement is somewhat anticlimactic, as most of the mechanics are handled at deeper layers of the abstraction. Of course, this "boringness," as you've learned in this book, is only achieved through meticulous design. Simplicity is always more difficult to achieve than the code itself indicates. Had any complications leaked through at this high-level abstraction, it would surely have implied an inferior design.

7.6 A Concrete Plugin

After a long discussion explaining how to incorporate native C++ plugins into pdCalc, we've finally reached the point where we can implement a concrete plugin. Based on our requirements from Chapter 1, we need to write a plugin that adds commands for the natural logarithm, its inverse exponentiation algorithm, and the hyperbolic trigonometric functions. Of course, you should feel free to add plugins encompassing any functionality you might like. For example, two interesting plugins might be a probability plugin and a statistics plugin. The probability plugin could compute permutations, combinations, factorials, and random numbers, while the statistics plugin could compute mean, median, mode, and standard deviation. For now, however, we'll simply consider the design and implementation of our hyperbolic, natural log plugin.

7.6.1 Plugin Interface

The implementation of the `HyperbolicLnPlugin` is actually quite straightforward. We'll begin with the interface for the class and then, uncharacteristically, examine a few implementation details. The code chosen for further examination highlights particular details relevant to native C++ plugins.

The interface for `HyperbolicLnPlugin` is given by the class definition specializing the `Plugin` class and the required plugin allocation and deallocation functions; see Listing 7-3.

Listing 7-3. The Interface for HyperbolicLnPlugin

```
class HyperbolicLnPlugin : public pdCalc::Plugin
{
  class HyperbolicLnPluginImpl;
public:
  HyperbolicLnPlugin();
  ~HyperbolicLnPlugin();

  const PluginDescriptor& getPluginDescriptor() const override;
  const PluginButtonDescriptor* getPluginButtonDescriptor()
    const override;
  pdCalc::Plugin::ApiVersion apiVersion() const;

private:
  unique_ptr<HyperbolicLnPluginImpl> pimpl_;
};

extern "C" void* AllocPlugin();
extern "C" void DeallocPlugin(void*);
```

As expected, the class implements the three pure virtual functions in the Plugin class and defers the bulk of its implementation to a private implementation class. The AllocPlugin() and DeallocPlugin() functions have their obvious implementations. The AllocPlugin() simply returns a new HyperbolicLnPlugin instance, while the DeallocPlugin() function casts its void* argument to a Plugin* and subsequently calls delete on this pointer. Note that plugins are, by definition, not part of the main program and should therefore not be part of the pdCalc namespace. Hence, the explicit namespace qualification in a few locations.

The responsibility of the HyperbolicLnPluginImpl class is simply to serve plugin descriptors on demand and manage the lifetime of the objects needed by the descriptors. The PluginDescriptor provides command names and the corresponding Commands implemented by the plugin. These Commands are described in Section 7.6.3 below. The PluginButtonDescriptor for the plugin simply lists the names of the Commands as defined by the PluginDescriptor and the corresponding labels to appear on the GUI buttons. Because the commands in the HyperbolicLnPlugin all have natural inverses, we simply label each button with a forward command and attach the secondary (shifted) command to the inverse. I used the obvious labels for the commands provided by the plugin: `sinh`, `asinh`, `cosh`, `acosh`, `tanh`, `atanh`, `ln`, and `exp`. Whether you choose ln for the primary and exp as the secondary or vice versa is simply a matter of preference.

For reasons already discussed, plugin descriptors transfer content without using STL containers. Where we would normally prefer to use `vectors` and `unique_ptrs` in the interface to manage resources, we are forced instead to use raw arrays. Of course, the encapsulation provided by the pimpl enables the implementation of whatever memory management scheme we desire. For the `HyperbolicLnPlugin`, I chose a complicated scheme of automatic memory management using `strings`, `unique_ptrs`, and `vectors`. The advantage of using an RAII memory management scheme is that we can be assured that the plugin will not leak memory in the presence of exceptions (namely, an out-of-memory exception thrown during construction). Realistically, I would not expect the calculator to be executed in a low memory environment, and even if it were, it's unclear that leaking memory during plugin allocation would matter much since the user's likely next action in this situation would be to reboot his computer. Therefore, in retrospect, a simpler memory management scheme with naked `news` in the constructor and `deletes` in the destructor would probably have been more pragmatic.

7.6.2 Source Code Dependency Inversion

Surprisingly, the above class declaration for `HyperbolicLnPlugin` is indeed the complete interface to the plugin. I say surprisingly because, at first glance, one might be surprised that the plugin's interface bears no relationship on the functionality the plugin provides. Of course, this situation is exactly as it should be. The calculator functionality that the plugin provides is indeed merely an implementation detail and can be contained entirely within the plugin's implementation file.

The above subtlety, namely that pdCalc knows only the interface to a plugin and nothing about the functionality itself, should not be overlooked. As a matter of fact, this source code dependency inversion is the entire point of plugin design. What exactly is source code dependency inversion and why is it important? To answer this question, we must first embark on a short history lesson.

Traditionally (think 1970s Fortran), code was extended by simply writing new functions and subroutines. The primary design problem with this approach was that requiring the main program to call new functions bound the main program to the concrete interface of any extension. Thus, the main program became dependent on interface changes defined by the whims of extension authors. That is, every new extension defined a new interface to which the main program had to conform. This setup was extremely brittle because the main program required constant modification to keep pace with the changes to its extensions' interfaces. Since each new extension required unique modifications to the main program's source code, the complexity of the main program's code for handling extensions grew linearly with the number of extensions. If that wasn't bad enough, adding new functionality always required recompiling and relinking the main program. In concrete terms, imagine a design for pdCalc that would require modifying, recompiling, and relinking pdCalc's source code every time a new plugin command was added.

The above problem can be solved without object-oriented programming via function pointers and callbacks, albeit in a somewhat inelegant and cumbersome fashion. However, with the rise of object-oriented programming, specifically inheritance and polymorphism, the solution to the dependency problem was solved in a type-safe manner with language support. These techniques enabled the popularization of source code dependency inversion. Specifically, source code dependency inversion states that the main program defines an interface (e.g., the plugin interface we've studied in this chapter) to which all extensions must conform. Under this strategy, the extensions become subservient to the main program's interface rather than the reverse. Hence, the main program can be extended via plugins without modifying, recompiling, or relinking the main program's source code. More importantly, however, the interface for extensibility is dictated by the application rather than its plugins. In concrete terms, pdCalc provides the `Plugin` interface class to define the addition of new functionality, but pdCalc is never aware of the implementation details of its extensions. A plugin that does not conform to pdCalc's interface is simply unable to inject new Commands.

7.6.3 Implementing HyperbolicLnPlugin's Functionality

By this stage in the game, we know that the `HyperbolicLnPlugin` will provide its functionality by implementing a command class for each operation. After implementing a few of these classes, one would quickly notice that all of the commands in the plugin are unary commands. Unfortunately, based on the third rule of C++ plugins (assume incompatible alignment), we cannot inherit from the `UnaryCommand` class and instead must inherit from the `PluginCommand` class. Note that our alignment assumption even precludes using the UnaryCommand class via multiple inheritance, and we must reimplement the unary command functionality in our HyperbolicLnPluginCommand base class. While this does feel a bit duplicative, the rules for C++ plugins leave us with no alternatives (although we could provide source code for a UnaryPluginCommand and a UnaryBinaryCommand, but these would have to be separately compiled with each plugin).

We, therefore, finally arrive at the interface class from which all commands within the HyperbolicLnPlugin derive; see Listing 7-4.

Listing 7-4. The HyperbolicLnPluginCommand Class

```
class HyperbolicLnPluginCommand : public pdCalc::PluginCommand
{
public:
  HyperbolicLnPluginCommand() {}
  explicit HyperbolicLnPluginCommand(const HyperbolicLnPluginCommand& rhs);
  virtual ~HyperbolicLnPluginCommand() {}
  void deallocate() override;

protected:
  const char* checkPluginPreconditions() const noexcept override;

private:
  void executeImpl() noexcept override;
  void undoImpl() noexcept override;
  HyperbolicLnPluginCommand* clonePluginImpl() const noexcept override;

  virtual HyperbolicLnPluginCommand* doClone() const = 0;
  virtual double unaryOperation(double top) const = 0;

  double top_;
};
```

As with the UnaryCommand class, the HyperbolicLnPluginCommand class implements the pure virtual executeImpl() and undoImpl() commands, delegating the command operation to the pure virtual unaryOperation() function. Additionally, the HyperbolicLnPluginCommand class implements the checkPluginPreconditions() function to ensure at least one number is on the stack before the command is called. The function is protected so that a subclass can directly override the precondition function if it must implement any additional preconditions yet still call the base class's checkPluginPreconditions() to make the unary command precondition check.

The deallocate() and clonePluginImpl() functions have obvious implementations but play critical roles in the plugin. The deallocate() function is simply implemented as

```
void HyperbolicLnPluginCommand::deallocate()
{
  delete this;
}
```

Recall that the point of the deallocate() function is to force memory deallocation of the plugin's commands in the plugin's compilation unit. It is called via the CommandDeleter() function when the unique_ptr holding a command is destroyed.

The clonePluginImpl() function is given by

```
HyperbolicLnPluginCommand*
HyperbolicLnPluginCommand::clonePluginImpl() const noexcept
{
  HyperbolicLnPluginCommand* p;
  try
  {
    p = doClone();
  }
  catch(...)
  {
    return nullptr;
  }

  return p;
}
```

The sole purpose of this function is to adapt the cloning of a plugin command to ensure that exceptions do not cross the memory boundary between the plugin and the main application.

All that remains to complete the HyperbolicLnPlugin is to subclass HyperbolicLnPluginCommand for each mathematical operation required in the plugin and implement the few remaining pure virtual functions (unaryOperation(), doClone(), and helpMessageImpl()). At this point, the implementation of these functions is no different than the implementation of the unary functions of Chapter 4. The interested reader is referred to the source code in HyperbolicLnPlugin.cpp for details.

7.7 Next Steps

After a rather long discussion about C++ plugins, and with the implementation of
the hyperbolic trigonometric and natural logarithm plugin, we have completed the
requirements for pdCalc set forth in Chapter 1. The calculator, as originally described,
is complete! Well, version 1.0 is complete, anyway. However, as experienced software
developers, we know that any "finished" product is just a temporary milestone before
the customer requests new features. The next chapter handles this exact situation, where
we'll modify our design to incorporate unplanned extensions.

CHAPTER 8

New Requirements

It's a beautiful Monday morning, and you just stepped into work after a relaxing weekend. After all, you just finished pdCalc on Friday, and now you are ready to ship. Before you can sit down and have your morning cup of coffee, your project manager steps into your office and says, "We're not done. The client requested some new features."

The above scenario is all too common in software development. While new features probably won't be requested on the go live date, new features will almost inevitably be requested well after you have completed large parts of both your design and your implementation. Therefore, one should develop as defensively as practical to anticipate extensibility. I say as *defensively as practical* rather than as *defensively as possible* because overly abstract code can be as much of a detriment to development as overly concrete code. Often, it is easier to simply rewrite inflexible code if the need arises than it is to maintain highly flexible code for no reason. In practice, we seek to strike a balance for code to be both simple and maintainable yet somewhat extensible.

In this chapter, we'll explore modifying our code to implement features beyond the design of the original requirements. The discussion of the new features introduced in this chapter ranges from full design and implementation to design only to suggestions merely for self-exploration. Let's begin with two extensions that we'll take from requirements all the way through implementation.

8.1 Fully Designed New Features

In this section, we'll examine two new features: batch operation of the calculator and execution of stored procedures. Let's begin with batch operation.

© Adam B. Singer 2017
A. B. Singer, *Practical C++ Design*, DOI 10.1007/978-1-4842-3057-2_8

8.1.1 Batch Operation

For those few unfamiliar with the term, *batch operation* of any program is simply the execution of the program, from beginning to end, without interaction from the user once the program is launched. Most desktop programs do not run in batch mode. However, batch operation is still very important in many branches of programming, such as scientific computing. Perhaps of greater interest, for those of you employed by large corporations, your payroll is probably run by a program operating in batch mode.

Let's be honest. Batch operation for pdCalc, other than maybe for testing, is not a very useful extension. I've included it mainly because it demonstrates how trivially a well-designed CLI can be extended to add a batch mode.

Recall from Chapter 5 that pdCalc's CLI has the following public interface:

```
class Cli : public UserInterface
{
  class CliImpl;
public:
  Cli(istream& in, ostream& out);
  ~Cli();

  void execute(bool suppressStartupMessage = false, bool echo = false);
};
```

To use the CLI, the class is constructed with cin and cout as the arguments, and execute() is called with empty arguments:

```
Cli cli{cin, cout};
// setup other parts of the calculator
cli.execute();
```

How do we modify the Cli class to enable batch operation? Amazingly, we do not need to modify the class's code at all! By design, the CLI is essentially a parser that simply takes space-separated character input from an input stream, processes the data through the calculator, and generates character output to an output stream. Because we had the forethought not to hard code these input and output streams as cin and cout, we can convert the CLI to a batch processor by making the input and output streams to be file streams as follows:

```
ifstream fin{inputFile};
ofstream fout{outputFile};
Cli cli{fin, fout};
// setup other parts of the calculator
cli.execute(true, true);
```

where `inputFile` and `outputFile` are file names that could be acquired through command line arguments to pdCalc. Recall that the arguments to the `execute()` function simply suppress the startup banner and echo commands to the output.

Yes, that really is it (but see `main.cpp` for a few implementation tricks). Our CLI was built originally so that it could be converted to a batch processor simply by changing its constructor arguments. You could, of course, argue that I, as the author, intentionally designed the `Cli` class this way because I knew the calculator would be extended in this manner. The reality is, however, that I simply construct all of my CLI interfaces with stream inputs rather than hard coded inputs because this design makes the CLI more flexible with nearly no additional cognitive burden.

Before leaving this section, I'll quickly note that the reality is that pdCalc's CLI, with an assist from the operating system, already had a batch mode. By redirecting input and output at the command line, we can achieve the same results:

```
my_prompt> cat inputFile | pdCalc --cli > outputFile
```

For Windows, simply replace the Linux `cat` command with the Windows `type` command.

8.1.2 Stored Procedures

Adding a batch mode to pdCalc was, admittedly, a somewhat contrived example. The added functionality was not terribly useful, and the code changes were trivial. In this section, we'll examine a more interesting feature extension: stored procedures.

What is a stored procedure? In pdCalc, a stored procedure is a stored, repeatable sequence of operations that operate on the current stack. Stored procedures provide a technique to expand the calculator's functionality by creating user-defined functions from existing calculator primitives. You can think of executing a stored procedure as being analogous to running a very simple program for the calculator. The easiest way to understand the concept is to consider an example.

Suppose you need to frequently calculate the hypotenuse of a triangle. For the right triangle depicted in Figure 8-1, we can compute the length of the hypotenuse, c, using the Pythagorean formula: $c = \sqrt{a^2 + b^2}$.

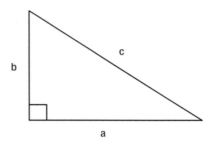

Figure 8-1. *A right triangle*

Suppose we had a triangle with sides $a = 4$, $b = 3$, and these values were entered onto pdCalc's stack. In the CLI, you would see the following:

```
Top 2 elements of stack (size = 2):
2:      3
1:      4
```

In order to compute c for this triangle, we would implement the following sequence of instructions: dup * swap dup * + 2 root. After pressing enter, the final result would be

```
Top element of stack (size = 1):
1:      5
```

If the commands were entered one at a time, we would see the intermediate resultant stack every time we pressed enter. Had we entered all of the commands on a single line and then pressed enter, pdCalc would display each intermediate stack before showing the final result. Note, of course, that this command sequence is not unique. The same result could have been achieved using, for example, the command sequence 2 pow swap 2 pow + 2 root.

If you are anything like me, if you had to compute hypotenuses with pdCalc repeatedly, you would probably want to automate the operation after the first manual computation. That is precisely what stored procedures allow. Not only does automation save time, but it is also less error-prone since stored procedures that encapsulate many consecutive commands can be written, tested, and subsequently reused. Provided the operation can be assembled from pdCalc primitives (including plugin functions), stored procedures enable extending the calculator's functionality to compute simple formulas without needing to write any C++ code. Now we just need to design and implement this new feature.

8.1.2.1 The User Interface

pdCalc has both a GUI and a CLI, so adding any user-facing feature will require some modification to both user interface components. For stored procedures, the modifications to the user interfaces are remarkably minor. First, a stored procedure is simply a text file containing an ordered sequence of pdCalc instructions. Therefore, a user can create a stored procedure using any plain text editor. Thus, unless you want to provide a stored procedure text editor with syntax highlighting, the user interface for stored procedures reduces to enabling their execution from the CLI and the GUI.

Let's first address incorporating stored procedures in the CLI. As previously stated, stored procedures are simply text files in the file system. Recall that the CLI works by tokenizing space-separated input and then passing each token individually to the command dispatcher by raising an event. Therefore, a trivial method for accessing a stored procedure is simply to pass the name of the stored procedure file to the CLI. This file name will then be tokenized like any other command or number and passed to the command dispatcher for processing. To ensure that the file name is interpreted by the command dispatcher as a stored procedure rather than a command, we simply prepend the symbol `proc:` to the file name and change the command dispatcher's parser. For example, for a stored procedure named `hypotenuse.psp`, we would issue the command `proc:hypotenuse.psp` to the CLI. I adopted the file extension `psp` as a shorthand for pdCalc stored procedure. Naturally, the file itself is an ordinary ASCII text file containing a sequence of commands for calculating the hypotenuse of a right triangle, and you can use the `.txt` extension if you prefer.

Recall that the GUI is designed to pass commands to the command dispatcher identically to the CLI. Therefore, to use a stored procedure, we add a button that opens a dialog to navigate the file system to find stored procedures. Once a stored procedure is selected, we prepend `proc:` to the file name and raise a `CommandEntered` event. Obviously, you can make your stored procedure selection dialog as fancy as you would like. I opted for a simplistic design that permits typing the name of the file into an editable combo box. For ease of use, the combo box is prepopulated with any files in the current directory with a `.psp` extension.

8.1.2.2 Changes to the Command Dispatcher

Listing 8-1 is an abbreviated listing of CommandDispatcher's executeCommand() function including the logic necessary for parsing stored procedures. The omitted portions of the code appear in Section 4.5.2.

Listing 8-1. CommandDispatcher's executeCommand() Function

```
void CommandDispatcher::CommandDispatcherImpl::executeCommand(const string&
command)
{
  // handle numbers, undo, redo, help in nested if
  // ...
  else if(command.size() > 6 && command.substr(0, 5) == "proc:")
  {
    auto filename = command.substr(5, command.size() - 5);
    handleCommand( MakeCommandPtr<StoredProcedure>(ui_, filename) );
  }
  // else statement to handle Commands from CommandRepository
  // ...

  return;
}
```

From the code above, we see that the implementation simply peels off the proc: from the string command argument to create the stored procedure filename, creates a new StoredProcedure Command subclass, and executes this class. For now, we'll assume that making the StoredProcedure class a subclass of the Command class is the optimal design. I'll discuss why this strategy is preferred and examine its implementation in the following sections. However, before we get there, let's discuss this new overload of the MakeCommandPtr() function.

In Section 7.2.1, we first saw a version of MakeCommandPtr given by the following implementation:

```
inline void CommandDeleter(Command* p)
{
  p->deallocate();
  return;
}
```

```
using CommandPtr = std::unique_ptr<Command, decltype(&CommandDeleter)>;

inline auto MakeCommandPtr(Command* p)
{
  return CommandPtr{p, &CommandDeleter};
}
```

The above function is a helper function used to create CommandPtrs from raw Command pointers. This form of the function is used to create a CommandPtr from the cloning of an existing Command (e.g., as in CommandRepository::allocateCommand()):

```
auto p = MakeCommandPtr( command->clone() );
```

Semantically, however, in CommandDispatcherImpl::executeCommand(), we see a completely different usage, which is to construct an instance of a class derived from Command. Certainly, we can meet this use case with the existing MakeCommandPtr prototype. For example, we could create a StoredProcedure as follows:

```
auto c = MakeCommandPtr(new StoredProcedure{ui, filename});
```

However, whenever possible, it's best not to pollute high-level code with naked news. We therefore seek to implement an overloaded helper function that can perform this construction for us. Its implementation is given by the following:

```
template<typename T, typename... Args>
auto MakeCommandPtr(Args&&... args)
{
  return CommandPtr{new T{std::forward<Args>(args)...}, &CommandDeleter};
}
```

Prior to C++11, no simple and efficient technique existed for constructing generic types with variable numbers of constructor arguments, as is necessary to create any one of the possible classes derived from the Command class, each having different constructor arguments. Modern C++, however, provides an elegant solution to this problem using variadic templates and perfect forwarding. This construct is the subject of the sidebar below.

MODERN C++ DESIGN NOTE: VARIADIC TEMPLATES AND PERFECT FORWARDING

Variadic templates and perfect forwarding each solve different problems in C++. Variadic templates enable type-safe generic function calls with unknown numbers of typed arguments. Perfect forwarding enables correct type forwarding of arguments to underlying functions inside of template functions. The mechanics of each of these techniques can be studied in your favorite C++11 reference text (e.g., [23]). This sidebar shows a type-safe, generic design technique for constructing concrete objects that require different numbers of constructor arguments. This technique is enabled by the combination of variadic templates and perfect forwarding. Due to a lack of naming creativity, I named this pattern the generic perfect forwarding constructor (GPFC). Let's begin by presenting the underlying problem that GPFC solves.

Let's consider every author's favorite overly simplified object-oriented programming example, the shapes hierarchy:

```cpp
class Shape
{
public:
  virtual double area() const = 0;
};

class Circle : public Shape
{
public:
  Circle(double r) : r_{r} {}
  double area() const override { return 3.14159 * r_ * r_; }

private:
  double r_;
};

class Rectangle : public Shape
{
public:
  Rectangle(double l, double w) : l_{l}, w_{w} {}
  double area() const override { return l_ * w_; }
```

```
private:
  double l_, w_;
};
```

In C++, substitutability, implemented as virtual dispatch, solves the problem of needing to call a derived type's specific implementation via a base class pointer using an interface guaranteed by the base class. In the shapes example, substitutability implies the ability to compute the area as follows:

```
double area(const Shape& s)
{
  return s.area();
}
```

for any class derived from Shape. The exact interface for the virtual function is fully prescribed, including the number and type of any function arguments (even in the vacuous case as in the area() function in this example). The problem, however, is that object construction can never be "virtualized" in this manner, and even if it could, it wouldn't work since the information necessary to construct an object (its arguments) is very frequently different from one derived class to the next.

Enter the generic perfect forwarding constructor pattern. In this pattern, we use variadic templates to provide a type-safe interface that can take any number of constructor arguments with different types. The first template argument is always the type we want to construct. Then, perfect forwarding is used to guarantee the arguments are passed to the constructor with the correct types. Precisely why perfect forwarding is necessary in this situation derives from how types are deduced in templates and is beyond the scope of this discussion (see [19] for details). For our shapes example, applying the GPFC pattern results in the following implementation:

```
template<typename T, typename... Args>
auto MakeShape(Args&&... args)
{
  return make_unique<T>(forward<Args>(args)...);
}
```

The following code illustrates how the MakeShape() function can be used to create different types with different numbers of constructor arguments:

```
auto c = MakeShape<Circle>(4.0);
auto r = MakeShape<Rectangle>(3.0, 5.0);
```

Note that the GPFC pattern also works for creating classes not related to each other in an inheritance hierarchy. The GPFC pattern, in fact, is used by the make_unique() function in the standard library for making unique_ptrs in an efficient, generic manner without requiring a naked new. While they are, strictly speaking, distinct, I like to think of the GPFC pattern as the generic analogue of the factory method.

8.1.2.3 Designing the StoredProcedure Class

We now return to the thorny problem of designing the StoredProcedure class. The first question we ask is do we need a class at all. We already have a design for parsing individual commands, executing them, and placing them on an undo/redo stack. Maybe the correct answer is to treat a stored procedure in a manner similar to the treatment of batch input. That is, during an interactive session (either GUI or CLI), handle stored procedures by reading the stored procedure file, parsing it, and executing the commands in batch (as we would a long line with multiple commands in the CLI) without introducing a new StoredProcedure class.

The aforementioned design can be dismissed almost immediately after considering the following very simple example. Suppose you implemented a stored procedure for computing the area of a triangle. The stored procedure's input would be the base and height of the triangle on the stack. triangleArea.psp is given by the following:

```
*

0.5
*
```

If we did not have a StoredProcedure class, then each of the commands in triangleArea.psp would be executed and entered, in order, on the undo/redo stack. For the values 4 and 5 on the I/O stack, forward execution of the stored procedure would yield the correct result of 10 and an undo stack, as depicted in Figure 8-2. Based on this undo stack, if the user tried to undo, rather than undoing the triangle area stored procedure, the user would undo only the top operation on the stack, the final multiply. The I/O stack would read

4
5
0.5

(and the undo stack would have a * between the 5 and 0.5) instead of

4
5

Figure 8-2. *The undo stack without a StoredProcedure class*

To fully undo a stored procedure, the user needs to press undo *n* times, where *n* is equal to the number of commands in the stored procedure. The same deficiency is present for the redo operation. In my opinion, the expected behavior for undoing a stored procedure should be to undo the entire procedure and leave the I/O stack in its state prior to executing the stored procedure. Hence, the design for handling stored procedures not employing a StoredProcedure class fails to implement undo and redo properly and must therefore be discarded.

8.1.2.4 The Composite Pattern

Essentially, in order to solve the undo/redo problem with stored procedures, we need a special command that encapsulates multiple commands but behaves as a single command. Fortunately, the composite pattern solves this dilemma. According to Gamma *et al* [6], the composite pattern "lets clients treat individual objects and compositions of objects uniformly." Typically, the composite pattern refers to treed data structures. I prefer a looser definition where the pattern may be applied to any data structure admitting uniform treatment of composite objects.

Figure 8-3 illustrates the composite pattern in its general form. The Component class is an abstract class that requires some action to be performed. This action can be performed individually by a Leaf node or by a collection of Components known as a Composite. Clients interact with objects in the component hierarchy polymorphically through the Component interface. Both Leaf nodes and Composite nodes handle doSomething() requests indistinguishably from the client's point of view. Usually, Composites implement doSomething() by simply calling the doSomething() command for Components (either Leafs or nested Composites) it holds.

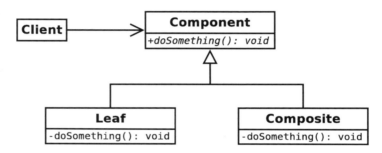

Figure 8-3. *General form of the composite pattern*

In our particular concrete case, the Command class takes the role of the Component, concrete commands such as Add or Sine take the role of Leaf nodes, and the StoredProcedure class is the composite. The doSomething() command is replaced by the executeImpl() and undoImpl() pair of pure virtual functions. I suspect combining the command and composite patterns in this fashion is rather common.

Previously, we learned that in order to properly implement the undo/redo strategy for stored procedures, a class design was necessary. Application of the composite pattern, as described above, motivates subclassing the StoredProcedure class from the Command class.

Let's now design a StoredProcedure class and examine its implementation as a concrete application of the composite pattern.

8.1.2.5 A First Attempt

A common approach to implementing the composite pattern is via recursion. The Composite class holds a collection of Components, often either via a simple vector or perhaps something more complex such as nodes in a binary tree. The Composite's doSomething() function simply iterates over this collection calling doSomething() for each Component in the collection. The Leaf nodes' doSomething() functions actually *do something* and terminate the recursion. Although not required, the doSomething() function in the Component class is often pure virtual.

Let's consider the above approach for implementing the composite pattern for StoredProcedures in pdCalc. We have already established that pdCalc's Command class is the Component and that the concrete command classes, such as Add, are the Leaf classes. Therefore, we need only to consider the implementation of the StoredProcedure class itself. Note that since the current implementation of the Component and Leaf classes can be used as is, the composite pattern can be trivially applied to extend the functionality of an existing code base.

Consider the following skeletal design for the StoredProcedure class:

```
class StoredProcedure : public Command
{
private:
  void executeImpl() noexcept override;
  void undoImpl() noexcept override;

  vector<unique_ptr<CommandPtr>> components_;
};
```

The executeImpl() command would be implemented as follows:

```
void StoredProcedure::executeImpl()
{
  for(auto& i : components_)
    i->execute();

  return;
}
```

undoImpl() would be implemented analogously but with a reverse iteration over the component_ collection.

Does the above design solve the undo/redo problem previously encountered when entering stored procedure commands directly onto the undo/redo stack without a StoredProcedure class? Consider the undo stack shown in Figure 8-4 for the triangleArea.psp example that we previously examined. The stored procedure, shown as SP in the figure, appears as a single object in the undo stack rather than as individual

207

objects representing its constituent commands. Hence, when a user issues an undo command, the `CommandManager` will undo the stored procedure as a single command by calling the stored procedure's `undoImpl()` function. This stored procedure's `undoImpl()` function, in turn, undoes the individual commands via iteration over its container of `Commands`. This behavior is precisely what was desired, and this application of the composite pattern indeed solves the problem at hand.

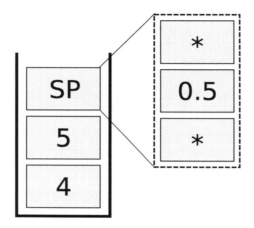

Figure 8-4. *The undo stack using a StoredProcedure class*

To complete the implementation of the `StoredProcedure` class, we need to parse the stored procedure file's string commands (with error checking) and use them to populate the `StoredProcedure`'s `components_` vector. This operation could be written in the `StoredProcedure`'s constructor, and the implementation would be both valid and complete. We would now have a `StoredProcedure` class that could transform string commands into `Commands`, store them in a container, and be able to execute and undo these stored `Commands` on demand. In other words, we would have essentially rewritten the command dispatcher! Instead, let's consider an alternative design that implements the `StoredProcedure` class by reusing the `CommandDispatcher` class.

8.1.2.6 A Final Design for the StoredProcedure Class

The goal in this design is to reuse the `CommandDispatcher` class as-is. Relaxing this constraint and modifying the `CommandDispatcher`'s code can clean up the implementation slightly, but the essence of the design is the same either way. Consider the following modified skeletal design of the `StoredProcedure` class:

```
class StoredProcedure : public Command
{
private:
  void executeImpl() noexcept override;
  void undoImpl() noexcept override;

  std::unique_ptr<Tokenizer> tokenizer_;
  std::unique_ptr<CommandDispatcher> ce_;
  bool first_ = first;
};
```

The present design is almost identical to our previous design except the components_ vector has been replaced by a CommandDispatcher, and the need for a tokenizer has been made explicit. Good thing we wrote our tokenizer to be reusable in Chapter 5!

We are now prepared to see the complete implementations of executeImpl() and undoImpl(). Note that while the below implementation does not use the canonical version of the pattern seen above, this implementation of the StoredProcedure class is still simply an application of the composite pattern. First, let's examine executeImpl():

```
void StoredProcedure::executeImpl() noexcept
{
  if(first_)
  {
    for(auto c : *tokenizer_)
    {
      ce_->commandEntered(c);
    }
    first_ = false;
  }
  else
  {
    for(unsigned int i = 0; i < tokenizer_->nTokens(); ++i)
      ce_->commandEntered("redo");
  }

  return;
}
```

The first time that executeImpl() is called, the tokens must be extracted from the tokenizer and executed by the StoredProcedure's own CommandDispatcher. Subsequent calls to executeImpl() merely request the StoredProcedure's CommandDispatcher to redo the forward execution of each of the StoredProcedure's commands. Remember, StoredProcedure's executeImpl() function will itself be called by pdCalc's CommandDispatcher; hence, our design calls for nested CommandDispatchers. Figure 8-5 shows this design for the triangle area stored procedure example, where CD represents the CommandDispatcher.

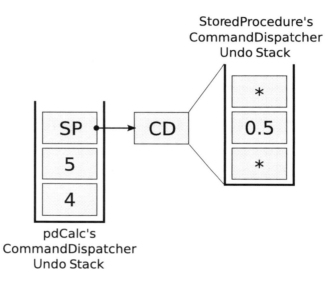

Figure 8-5. *The undo stack using nested CommandDispatchers*

The implementation of StoredProcedure's undoImpl() is trivial:

```
void StoredProcedure::undoImpl () noexcept
{
  for(unsigned int i = 0; i < tokenizer_->nTokens(); ++i)
    ce_->commandEntered("undo");
  return;
}
```

Undo is implemented by requesting the underlying CommandDispatcher to undo the number of commands in the stored procedure.

Before concluding our discussion of the final StoredProcedure class, we should consider tokenization of the commands within the StoredProcedure class. The tokenization process for a `StoredProcedure` involves two steps. The stored procedure file must be opened and read, followed by the actual tokenization of the text stream. This process needs to be performed only once per `StoredProcedure` instantiation, at initialization. Therefore, the natural placement for tokenization is in the `StoredProcedure`'s constructor. However, placement of tokenization in the `StoredProcedure`'s constructor creates an inconsistency with pdCalc's error handling procedure for commands. In particular, pdCalc assumes that commands can be constructed, but not necessarily executed, without failure. If a command cannot be executed, the expectation is that this error is handled by checking a command's preconditions. Can tokenization fail? Certainly. For example, tokenization would fail if the stored procedure file could not be opened. Therefore, in order to maintain consistency in error handling, we implement tokenization in `StoredProcedure`'s `checkPreconditionsImpl()` function, which will be called when pdCalc's `CommandDispatcher` first attempts to execute the stored procedure. Since tokenization needs to be performed once, we only perform the operation on the first execution of the `checkPreconditionsImpl()` function. The complete implementation can be found in the `StoredProcedure.cpp` file.

8.2 Designs Toward a More Useful Calculator

Up until now, all of the discussion about pdCalc has focused on the design and implementation of a completed code available for download from GitHub. The remainder of this chapter, however, marks a departure from this style. Henceforth, we will discuss only ideas for extensions and suggestions for how pdCalc might be modified to accommodate these new features. Not only is working code not provided, but working code was not created before writing these sections. Therefore, the designs I'm about to discuss have not been tested, and the adventurous reader choosing to complete these extensions may discover the ideas to be discussed are suboptimal, or, dare I say, wrong. Welcome to the wild west of designing features from a blank slate! Experimentation and iteration will be required.

8.2.1 Complex Numbers

The original design specification for the calculator called for double precision numbers, and we designed and implemented the calculator explicitly to handle only double precision numbers. However, requirements change. Suppose your colleague, an electrical engineer, drops by your office, falls in love with your calculator, but requires a calculator that handles complex (imaginary) numbers. That's a reasonable request, so let's look at how we might refactor our calculator to satisfy this new feature.

Adding complex numbers requires four main modifications to pdCalc: using a complex number representation internally instead of representing numbers as `doubles`, changing input and output (and, by extension, parsing) to accommodate complex numbers, modifying pdCalc's stack to store complex numbers instead of `doubles`, and modifying commands to perform their calculations on complex numbers instead of real valued inputs. The first change, finding a C++ representation for complex numbers is trivial; we'll use `std::complex<double>`. A number with only a real part will simply be stored as a `complex<double>` with its imaginary part set to 0. The other three changes are less trivial. Let's now look in more depth at some design options capable of accommodating these changes.

8.2.1.1 Modifying Input and Output

Of all the required changes, modifying the I/O routines is actually the easiest. The first item to be addressed is how will complex numbers be interpreted and presented. For example, do we want a complex number, c, to be represented as `c = re + im * i` (maybe the imaginary number should be `j` since the feature request came from an electrical engineer). Perhaps we prefer using `c = (re, im)` or a variant that uses angle brackets or square brackets instead. There is no correct answer to this question. Although some choices might be easier to implement than others, since this choice is merely a convention, in practice, we would defer resolution to our customer. For our case study, we'll simply adopt the convention `c = (re, im)`.

I'll only discuss modifying the command line version of the I/O. Once the infrastructure to handle complex numbers is in place for the CLI, adapting the GUI should be reasonably straightforward. The first problem that we encounter is the `Tokenizer` class. The original design for this class simply tokenized by splitting input on whitespace. However, for complex numbers, this scheme is insufficient. For example, complex numbers would be tokenized differently based on whether or not a space was inserted after the comma.

At some point, input becomes sufficiently complex that you'll need to employ a language grammar and migrate the simple input routines to a "real" scanner and parser (possibly using libraries such as lex and yacc). Some might argue that by adding complex numbers, we have reached this level of complexity. However, I think that we can probably scrape by with our existing simple input tokenizer if we modify the `tokenize()` routine to scan for the (token and create one "number" token for anything between and including the opening and closing parenthesis. Obviously, we would need to perform some basic error checking to ensure correct formatting. Another alternative would be to decompose the input stream based on regular expression matching. This is essentially how lex operates, and I would investigate using lex or a similar library before writing a sophisticated scanner from scratch.

The next input problem we encounter is parsing of numbers in `CommandDispatcherImpl`'s `executeCommand()` function. Currently, a string argument (the token) is passed to this function, and the string is parsed to determine if it is a number or a command. Upon inspection, we can see that `executeCommand()` will work for complex numbers if we modify `isNum()` to identify and return complex numbers instead of floating point numbers. Finally, the `EnterNumber` command will need to be updated to accept and store a `complex<double>`.

That takes care of modifying the input routines, but how do we modify the output routines? Recall that the `Cli` class is an (indirect) observer of the `Stack`'s `stackChanged()` event. Whenever the `Stack` raises this event, `Cli`'s `stackChanged()` function will be called to output the current stack to the command line. Let's examine how `Cli::stackChanged()` is implemented. Essentially, the CLI calls back to the stack to fill a container with the top `nElements` using the following function call:

```
auto v = Stack::Instance().getElements(nElements);
```

An `ostringstream`, `oss`, is then created and filled first with some stack metadata and then with the stack elements using the following code:

```
size_t j{ v.size() };
for(auto i = v.rbegin(); i != v.rend(); ++i)
{
  oss << j << ":\t" << *i << "\n";
  --j;
}
```

Finally, the `oss`'s underlying string is posted to the CLI. Amazingly enough, once `Stack`'s `getElements()` function is modified to return a `vector<complex<double>>`, `Cli`'s `stackChanged()` function will work as expected just by recompiling. Because of our use of `auto`, and because `operator<<()` is overloaded for `std::complex`, as long as we are happy with the standard formatting of complex numbers, our output modifications were completed without doing anything! That's the beauty of well-designed and well-implemented code.

8.2.1.2 Modifying the Stack

In Chapter 3, we originally designed the calculator's stack to operate only on double precision variables. Clearly, this limitation means the Stack class must now be refactored in order to handle complex numbers. At the time, we questioned the logic of hard coding the target data type for the stack, and I recommended not designing a generic Stack class. My suggestion was, in general, to not design generic interfaces until the first reuse case is clearly established.

Designing good generic interfaces is generally harder than designing specific types, and, from my personal experience, I've found that serendipitous reuse of code infrequently comes to fruition. However, for our Stack class, the time to reuse this data structure for another data type has come, and it is prudent, at this point, to convert the Stack's interface into a generic interface rather than merely refactor the class to be hard coded for complex numbers.

Making the Stack class generic is almost as easy as you might expect. The first step is to make the interface itself generic by replacing explicit uses of double with our generic type T. The interface becomes

```cpp
template<typename T>
class Stack : private Publisher
{
public:
  static Stack& Instance();
  void push(T, bool suppressChangeEvent = false);
  double pop(bool suppressChangeEvent = false);
  void swapTop();

  std::vector<T> getElements(size_t n) const;
  void getElements(size_t n, std::vector<T>&) const;

  using Publisher::attach;
  using Publisher::detach;
};
```

With a generic interface, using the pimpl pattern is no longer necessary. Recall that use of the pimpl pattern enables us to hide the implementation of a class by referring to its implementation indirectly via a pointer to an implementation class defined only in a source file. However, in order to make the Stack generic, its implementation must also be generic (since it must store any type, T, rather than the single known type, double). This implies that StackImpl would also need to be templated. C++ rules insist that this StackImpl<T>'s definition would need to be visible when Stack<T> is instantiated for a particular T, hence dictating that StackImpl<T>'s definition appear in the header file before Stack<T>. Once we've lost the ability to make StackImpl<T> private, we no longer have a reason to use the pimpl pattern and instead just define the stack's implementation directly in the Stack<T>'s class.

In general, the required implementation changes are straightforward. Uses of double are replaced with T, and the implementation itself is moved to the header file. Uses of the Stack class within pdCalc obviously must be refactored to use the generic rather than the non-templated interface.

The last part of the interface that requires modification is the five global extern "C" helper functions added in Chapter 7 for exporting stack commands to plugins. Because these functions must have C linkage, we cannot make them templates nor can they return the C++ complex type in place of a double. The first problem is not quite as dire as it may appear at first glance. While our goal is to make the Stack class generic and reusable, the stack's plugin interface does not need to be generic. For any particular version of pdCalc, either one that operates on real numbers or one that operates on complex numbers, only one particular instantiation of Stack<T> will exist in the system, and this one instantiation will have a particular realization for T. Therefore, the C linkage interface to the stack for pdCalc needs to only reflect the choice of T used in the calculator. That is, the container is designed to be generic and reusable, but the interface for plugins does not require this flexibility since it is not reused once a data format for the calculator has been chosen.

Replacing the complex<double> representation in the C linkage interface to the stack is straightforward. We have several options. First, we could replace each double with a sequence of two doubles, one representing the real part and one representing the complex part. Of course, since a function cannot return two doubles, we would have to modify the functions returning a stack value to use pointer parameters in their argument lists to "return" complex values. A second option would be to return complex numbers through an array. Given my preference to eliminate raw pointers in interfaces when possible, I consider this option suboptimal. A final solution, and my preferred choice, would be to simply define a `struct` as in

```
struct Complex
{
  double re;
  double im;
};
```

to complement the interface functions, replacing the current use of `double` with `Complex`. While this new `Complex struct` does duplicate the storage of the standard `complex` class, we cannot use the standard `complex` class in a pure C interface.

8.2.1.3 Modifying Commands

Modifying commands to work with complex numbers is really quite easy since the C++ library provides overloads for all of the mathematical operations required by our calculator. Minus the syntactic changes of replacing `Stack` with `Stack<complex<double>>` (hopefully we've aliased that somewhere) and swapping `complex<double>` for `double` in `BinaryCommand` and `UnaryCommand`, most of the commands remain unchanged. For example, clearing a stack of real numbers versus clearing a stack of complex numbers is identical. Adding two complex numbers versus adding two real numbers is identical, given operator overloading. Of course, we might want to add additional commands such as complex conjugate, but even that functionality is provided by the C++ `complex` class. In the event that a command you've created uses an algorithm not supported natively by the `complex` class, you are likely to encounter more mathematical difficulties than programmatic ones in modifying commands to support complex numbers.

8.2.2 Variables

Earlier in this chapter, we implemented stored procedures as a method for storing a simple instruction sequence. While stored procedures work fine for trivial operations that only use each input once (e.g., the Pythagorean theorem), you'll very quickly run into problems trying to implement more complicated formulas that use each input more than once (e.g., the quadratic formula). To overcome this difficulty, you'll need to implement the ability to store arguments in named variables.

Implementing variables in pdCalc will require several modifications to existing components, including the addition of one prominent new component, a symbol table. For simplicity in the example code, I have reverted to using a real number representation for pdCalc. However, using complex numbers would add no additional design complexity. Let's now explore some possible design ideas for implementing variables.

8.2.2.1 Input and New Commands

Obviously, using variables will require some means of providing symbolic names. Currently, our calculator only accepts numbers and commands as input. Inputting any string that cannot be found in the CommandRepository results in an error. Recall, however, that this error is generated in the CommandDispatcher, not in the tokenizer. Therefore, we need to modify the CommandDispatcher to not reject strings but instead to somehow place them on the stack. For now, we'll assume that the stack can accept strings in addition to numbers. I'll discuss the necessary modifications to the Stack class in the upcoming sections. Again, I'll restrict our discussion to the command line interface. The only additional complication posed by the graphical user interface is providing a mechanism to input character strings in addition to numbers (perhaps a virtual keyboard to accompany the virtual numeric keypad).

Technically, we could allow any string to represent a variable. However, we are probably better served by restricting the allowable syntax to some subset of strings, possibly delimited by a symbol to differentiate variable names from commands. Because this choice is merely convention, you are free to choose whatever rules suit yours or your users' tastes. Personally, I would probably choose something like *variable names must begin with a letter and can contain any combination of letters, numbers, and possibly a few special symbols such as the underscore*. To eliminate confusion between variable names and commands, I would enclose variables in either single or double quotation marks.

Now that we've established the syntax for variables, we'll still need a mechanism for taking a number from the stack and storing it into a variable. The simplest method for accomplishing this task is to provide a new binary command, store, that removes a number and a string from the stack and creates a symbol table entry linking this variable name to this number. For example, consider the stack

```
4.5
2.9
"x"
```

Issuing the `store` command should result in an entry of $x \to 2.9$ in the symbol table and a resultant stack of

```
4.5
```

Implicitly, variables should be converted to numbers for use during calculations but appear as names on the stack. We should also provide an explicit command, `eval`, to convert a symbolic name into a number. For example, given the stack

```
"x"
```

issuing the `eval` command should result in the stack

```
2.9
```

Such a command should have a fairly obvious implementation: replace the variable on the top of the stack with its value from the symbol table. Obviously, requesting the evaluation of a variable not in the symbol table should result in an error. Evaluating a number can either result in an error or, preferably, just return the number. You can probably think of any number of fancy commands for working with variables (e.g., list the symbol table). However, `store` and `eval` commands comprise the minimum necessary command set to use variables.

8.2.2.2 Number Representation and the Stack

Until now, our stack has only needed to represent a single, unique type, either a real or complex number. However, since variables and numbers can both be stored on the stack, we need the ability for the stack to store both types simultaneously. We dismiss immediately the notion of a stack that could handle two distinct types simultaneously because this would lead quickly to chaos. Instead, we seek a uniform representation capable of handling both number and variable types through a single interface. Naturally, we turn to a hierarchy.

Consider the design expressed in the class diagram in Figure 8-6. This hierarchy enables both `Variables` and `Numbers` to be used interchangeably as `Values`. This polymorphic design solves three problems that we've already encountered. First, `Variables` and `Numbers` can both be stored uniformly in a `Stack<Value*>` (likely using a more appropriate smart pointer storage scheme). Second, when commands such as `Add` or `Sine` need a number to perform an operation, they can pop `Values` from the stack and request `doubles` through the virtual `evaluate()` function. Obviously, a `Number` directly stores the double that it represents, while a Variable stores the variable's name, which can be converted to a numeric value via lookup in the variable symbol table. Finally, subclasses of Value can return a string representation of their underlying value (either a Number's numeric value or a Variable's name). This string conversion is necessary for display on the I/O stack.

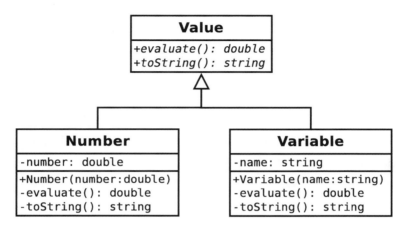

Figure 8-6. *A hierarchy capable of representing both numbers and variables uniformly*

8.2.2.3 The Symbol Table

At its core, a symbol table is merely a data structure that allows symbolic lookup by pairing a key to a value (an associative array). In this case, the name of the variable serves as the key and the numeric value serves as the value. The C++ standard library provides this service directly through either a map or an unordered_map, depending on the desired underlying data structure. However, as in Chapter 3, I highly recommend against directly using a standard library container as an external facing interface within a program. Instead, one should employee the adapter pattern to encapsulate the library container behind an interface defined by the application itself. This pattern adds no restrictions to the users of a class, but it does permit the designer to restrict, expand, or later modify the component's interface independently of the interface of the underlying library container.

Therefore, the recommended design for a symbol table is to create a SymbolTable class to wrap an unordered_map<string, double>. This underlying hash table provides a storage type to map between the variable name as a string and the underlying numeric value. The public interface for the SymbolTable class provides member functions for adding and, optionally (we did not specify a command for clearing variables), removing variables from the symbol table. The SymbolTable should probably be implemented as a singleton since we only need one symbol table in the calculator.

8.2.2.4 A Trivial Extension: Numeric Constants

Once we've established the mechanics for storing user-defined variables, we can make a trivial extension to provide user-defined constants. Constants are simply variables that cannot be altered once set. Constants could be hard coded in pdCalc, added at program launch through reading a constants file, or added dynamically during calculator execution.

Obviously, in order to store a constant, we will need to add a new command; let's call it cstore. cstore works identically to store except that the command informs the symbol table that the variable being stored cannot be changed. We have two obvious options for implementation. First, inside the SymbolTable class, we add a second map that indicates whether a given name represents a variable or a constant. The advantage of this approach is that adding an additional map will require minimal implementation changes to the existing code. The disadvantage is that this approach requires two independent lookups for each call to the symbol table. The better approach is to modify the original map to store the value type as an Entry instead of a double, where an Entry is defined as

```
struct Entry
{
  double val;
  bool isConst;
};
```

Of course, to avoid hard coding the double type, we could, of course, template both SymbolTable and Entry.

8.2.2.5 Functionality Enabled by Variables

Let's examine what variables enable us to do. Consider the quadratic equation $ax^2+bx+c = 0$ with roots given by

$$r = \frac{-b \pm \sqrt{b^2 - 4ac}}{2a}$$

Where we formerly could not write a stored procedure for computing both roots, we can now write the stored procedure

```
"c" store "b" store "a" store "b" 2 pow 4 "a" "c" * * - sqrt "root" store
"b" - "root" + 2 a * / "b" - "root" 2 a * /
```

which will take three entries from the stack representing the coefficients *a, b, c* and return two entries representing the roots of the quadratic equation. Now our calculator is getting somewhere!

8.3 Some Interesting Extensions for Self-Exploration

This chapter concludes with a section listing a few interesting extensions to pdCalc that you might consider trying on your own. In contrast to the previous section, I offer no design ideas to get you started. I have provided merely a brief description of each challenge.

8.3.1 High DPI Scaling

Monitors with extremely high pixel resolutions are becoming increasingly the norm. Consider how you would modify the GUI for pdCalc to properly handle scaling for such displays. Is this feature operating system independent or do we have another use for the PlatformFactory from Chapter 7? Since version 5.6, Qt helps you out with this task via an interface for high DPI scaling.

8.3.2 Dynamic Skinning

In Chapter 6, a class was introduced to manage the look-and-feel of the GUI. However, the provided implementation only centralized the look-and-feel. It did not permit user customization.

Users often want to customize the look-and-feel of their applications. Applications that permit such changes are considered "skinable," and each different look-and-feel is a called a skin. Consider an interface and the appropriate implementation changes necessary to the LookAndFeel class to enable skinning of pdCalc. Some possible options include a dialog for customizing individual widgets or a mechanism to choose skins from skin configuration files. Having a centralized class to handle the look-and-feel for the application should make this change straightforward. Don't forget to add a signal to LookAndFeel so the other GUI elements will know when they need to repaint themselves with a new appearance!

8.3.3 Flow Control

With variables, we greatly enhanced the flexibility of stored procedures. For computing most formulas, this framework should prove sufficient. However, what if we wanted to implement a recursive formula such as computing the factorial of a number? While we have the ability to perform such complex computations via plugins, it would be nice to extend this functionality to users of the calculator who are not also experienced C++ programmers. To accomplish this task, we would need to devise a syntax for flow control. The simplest design would at least be able to handle looping and conditional operations. Adding flow control to pdCalc would be a fairly significant enhancement in terms of both added capability and implementation effort. It might be time to move to a real scanner and parser!

8.3.4 An Alternative GUI Layout

The pdCalc GUI currently has a vertical orientation inspired by the HP48S calculator. However, modern screen resolutions tend to be wider than they are tall, making the vertical orientation suboptimal. Hard coding a horizontal orientation is no more challenging than the original vertical orientation. Consider instead how to redesign pdCalc to be able to switch between orientations at runtime. Maybe vertical orientation is simply a different skin option?

8.3.5 A Graphing Calculator

The HP48 series of calculators were not merely scientific calculators, they were graphing calculators. Although it might not be practical to implement a graphing calculator for a computer when sophisticated standalone graphing programs exist, the exercise might prove to be a lot of fun. Starting with version 5.7, Qt now includes a graphing module to make this task significantly easier than it would have been previously. Given this graphing widget set, the biggest challenge might simply be devising a method for graphical input. If you're in the mood for a silly throwback to the 1970s, consider implementing an ASCII graphing calculator for the CLI!

8.3.6 A Plugin Management System

Currently, plugins are loaded during pdCalc's startup, and which plugins to load are determined by reading shared library names from a text file. Plugins, once loaded, cannot be unloaded. Consider implementing a dynamic plugin management system so that plugins can be selected, loaded, and unloaded at runtime. You could even extend the plugin interface to enable dynamic querying of plugin descriptions. I think the real gotcha here will be in figuring out how to handle the unloading of a plugin that has one of its commands currently on the undo/redo stack.

8.3.7 A Mobile Device Interface

In my original machinations for creating this book, I envisioned a chapter describing how to extend pdCalc to an iOS or Android tablet. The Qt library can once again help you with this task. The reason I did not include such a chapter in this book is that I do not have any practical experience with tablet programming. I felt it would be disingenuous to try to teach others how to design a tablet interface from my first-ever foray into that design space. Well, it might have been an excellent example of a bad design! Nonetheless, extending pdCalc to a tablet or smartphone interface is a worthy challenge, and the last one I leave you with.

APPENDIX A

Acquiring, Building, and Executing pdCalc

This appendix explains how to acquire and build pdCalc, the program described in this book.

A.1 Getting the Source Code

The source code for pdCalc is hosted on Apress's GitHub repository. The easiest way to find the correct repository is through this book's Apress website:

`http://www.apress.com/us/book/9781484230565`

Clicking the Download source code button will take you directly to the GitHub-hosted site. Once there, you have two options for downloading the source code. The first option is to use a git client (`https://git-scm.com/`) and clone the repository to your local computer. For those familiar with managing source code with git, this is the preferred source code acquisition method. Using git to clone the repository will enable you to pull periodic bug updates from the online repository. Maybe you'll even decide to contribute a bug fix to pdCalc yourself! The second option for acquiring the source code is to download a single zip file of pdCalc from GitHub. Obviously, downloading a single zip file makes updating the source code significantly more challenging than using git if you have made any local changes.

A.2 Dependencies

Now that you have the source code, you'll probably want to build and execute pdCalc and its unit test suite. Before that can be accomplished, however, you'll need to ensure that you have an appropriate tool chain. Intentionally, pdCalc requires very few external

© Adam B. Singer 2017
A. B. Singer, *Practical C++ Design*, DOI 10.1007/978-1-4842-3057-2

dependencies, in fact, only two, both of which can be obtained for Linux, Windows, or Mac OS X at no cost. In order to build pdCalc, you will need a modern C++ compiler (C++14 compliant) and Qt (version 4 or 5).

As someone willing to have read this book, you probably already have or know how to get a C++ compiler. That said, for simplicity, the build system I provided for pdCalc assumes use of the gcc compiler (mingw in Windows). If you do not have gcc on your Linux system, it should be available through your system's package manager. If that fails, it can be downloaded from the Free Software Foundation's website (`https://gcc.gnu.org/`). On Windows, mingw is bundled with Qt as an optional component. I highly recommend obtaining it through Qt's installer.

On Linux, Qt, including its native integrated development environment (IDE) named Qt Creator, can usually be obtained through the system's package manager. If you go this route, ensure that you install the development packages for Qt and not just the runtime libraries. For both Linux and Windows, Qt can also be downloaded from `http://www.qt.io/download/`. Once you are on the website, select the Desktop and Mobile edition, and then choose the version that is licensed appropriately for your use. pdCalc is distributed under the GPL version 3, so the open source edition of Qt is compatible. From Qt's download page, you can select a fully downloadable binary installer, a network-based binary installer, or the complete source code. Unless you are experienced in building complex libraries from source, I recommend one of the binary installers. On Windows, be sure to install the mingw compiled version of Qt as well as the mingw tool chain. On all operating systems, while not strictly necessary, I highly recommend also installing Qt Creator. Please be patient with the download. Qt, with its many modules, is a powerful, but very sizable package.

A.3 Building pdCalc

To avoid additional dependencies, pdCalc uses qmake for its build system and Qt Test for its unit test framework. Other good alternatives for these tasks are cmake for the build system and any of boost test, cppunit, or Google Test for unit testing. To build pdCalc, you can either configure and compile at the command line or use Qt Creator. Both build methods rely on qmake. Therefore, before discussing how to build pdCalc, a brief explanation of how qmake operates is warranted.

Using qmake to build a solution is a two-step process involving both qmake and your tool chain's native make tool. qmake itself does not directly call the compiler and linker. Rather, qmake is simply a cross-platform makefile generator. Therefore, in the first step of the build process, qmake reads project files and produces makefiles native to the tool chain you're using. This step needs to be performed before the first buiid and subsequently only after changes requiring modification to project files (e.g., the addition of a new source file). In the second step, the object code is built using your tool chain's native make tool, which, in turn, calls the compiler and linker. For pdCalc, on a Linux system, you'll use make, which will, in turn, use gcc for compiling and linking. On a Windows system, you'll use mingw32-make, which will, in turn, use the mingw compiler and linker.

Now that you understand how qmake works, let's examine how to build pdCalc using either Qt Creator or the command line.

A.3.1 Using Qt Creator

If your preference is to use Qt Creator, most of the complexity of using qmake will be hidden from you. To begin, simply launch the IDE, and open the pdCalc.pro project. This file is located at the top level of the source tree.

The first time you open a qmake project file with Qt Creator, you will be presented with a configuration list asking you which version of Qt to target. If you only have one version of Qt on your computer, you may only have one option. If you expand the Details button for your selected Qt version, you will be given the option to configure pdCalc for debug, release, and profile and the option to select a folder as your out-of-source build directory. Once you have selected your configuration options, click the Configure Project button. If you need to change your configuration options later, Qt Creator has a tool for that.

After Qt Creator configures your project, you will be presented with the edit mode for the project. The edit mode of Qt Creator is a good tool for exploring the source code. The complete source tree will appear in an expandable tree control on the left side of the display, and individual files can be opened by clicking them. The source tree for pdCalc is described in Appendix B.

Qt Creator works similarly to any other fully featured IDE you have probably used, and a complete description of its usage is beyond the scope of this Appendix (see http://doc.qt.io/qtcreator/ for the full manual). However, I will highlight a few quick features to help get you started.

The first shortcut to learn is choosing which configuration of your project you want to build and run. These options are selected by the monitor icon in the lower left corner of the display. It will currently be labeled with the active project (pdCalc if it's the only project loaded) and the current configuration (e.g., Debug or Release). If you click this monitor icon, a pane will open allowing you to select which configuration you wish to build and which executable you wish to run. For pdCalc, you'll have four executable options: pdCalc, pdCalc-simple-cli, pdCalc-simple-gui, and testDriver. pdCalc runs the full version of pdCalc (the GUI by default), pdCalc-simple-cli runs the simple CLI constructed at the end of Chapter 5, pdCalc-simple-gui runs the simple GUI constructed at the end of Chapter 6, and testDriver runs the unit test suite. If you want to change the build or run configuration options, you can click the Projects button (folder icon) on the left side of the display to open the configuration panel. Clicking the Edit button will bring you back to edit mode.

pdCalc can be built either through the Build menu or by clicking the hammer icon (at least that's what it looks like to me) on the lower left side of the display. If you want to watch the compiler output as it builds, press the Compile Output button on the bottom of your screen. If you have any build issues, they can be found on the Issues tab of the same information panel. Clicking one of these issues should take you to the offending line of source code. Hopefully, pdCalc will build for you with no issues, no warnings, and no errors. If you have build problems, see the "Troubleshooting" section below.

A.3.2 Using the Command Line

If Qt Creator is not for you, pdCalc can be built directly at the command line. qmake supports out-of-source builds, which is the recommended strategy. Simply create a build directory for each configuration of pdCalc that you wish to build, change your path to the build directory, and issue the following command:

```
qmake -recursive CONFIG+=$CONFIG $PATH_TO_PDCALC
```

where $CONFIG can be replaced by either debug or release (default is debug if the CONFIG option is not specified) and $PATH_TO_PDCALC should be replaced by the path to pdCalc's pdCalc.pro file.

The command above triggers qmake to descend the pdCalc directory tree recursively reading each project file and writing a corresponding makefile. If everything executes normally, the output from the above command should be a sequence of lines informing you which project files qmake read. After the makefiles are written, pdCalc can be built by issuing the make command for your system (make on Linux, mingw32-make on Windows) in the same top-level directory from which the qmake command was issued. The code should build cleanly with no warnings or errors.

A.4 Executing pdCalc

pdCalc, pdCalc-simple-cli, and pdCalc-simple-gui, and the unit test suite can be executed from Qt Creator, the command line, or by double-clicking the executable (if all of your library paths are correctly set). Let's look at the details for the first two options. Hopefully, double-clicking is self-explanatory.

A.4.1 Using Qt Creator

Using Qt Creator, the currently selected executable can be started by pressing the green triangular run button in the lower left corner. The green triangle with the magnifying glass will start the executable in Qt Creator's interactive debugger. If the source code is out of date, the project will be built before execution begins. If you currently have the testDriver executable selected, the unit test suite will execute, and its output will appear in the Application Output information panel. Hopefully, you will see details of individual tests passing with a final message of "All tests passed." If you currently have either the pdCalc or pdCalc-simple-gui executable selected, the GUI should launch. If you have the pdCalc-simple-cli executable selected, the CLI will launch in the Application Output information panel. However, you cannot interact with the CLI using this panel, making this mode of executing the CLI rather useless.

A.4.2 Using the Command Line

Due to slight differences in how shared libraries are handled, the Unix (including Linux) and Windows builds target different directories for binaries. On a Unix system, all executables are built in the bin directory and all shared libraries are built in the lib directory. Therefore, pdCalc's lib directory must be added to the library path before the executables are launched. For example, for a command line execution of pdCalc on Linux, one must first issue the following command:

```
export LD_LIBRARY_PATH=$PATH_TO_PDCALC_LIB
```

where $PATH_TO_PDCALC_LIB is the relative or absolute path to the pdCalc lib directory. As an example, $PATH_TO_PDCALC_LIB can be set to ../lib for the relative path if executing pdCalc from the bin directory.

Windows does not separate the shared library path from the executable path. This lack of distinction implies that either the lib directory must be added to the main path or that pdCalc's libraries must reside in the bin directory. I selected the latter option for pdCalc's build on Windows. That is, both executables and dynamically linked libraries are built directly into the bin directory.

A build of pdCalc creates four executables: pdCalc, pdCalc-simple-cli, pdCalc-simple-gui, and testPdCalc (all have an .exe extension in Windows). testPdCalc runs the unit test suite; it is a command line-only program. As each unit test runs, you will see the names of the individual tests, the passage or failure of each test, and some statistics for each unit test suite. If all of the tests pass, an "All tests passed" message will be issued as the final output.

The pdCalc executable launches the complete calculator. It can be launched with the --gui option to run the graphical user interface, the --cli option to run the command line interface, or the --batch option to run the calculator in batch mode. Batch operation requires an input file and, optionally, an output file. pdCalc can also be given the --help option to see a listing of the various modes of operation. If no command line option is given, pdCalc defaults to launching the GUI.

The pdCalc-simple-cli executable launches the simple CLI built at the end of Chapter 5. The pdCalc-simple-gui executable launches the simple GUI built at the end of Chapter 6. Strictly speaking, both of these executables are unnecessary. They are provided merely as a convenience to the reader to be able to run pdCalc before it reaches feature complete status. In agile terms, these feature-incomplete executables provide stages of a minimum viable product.

A.5 Troubleshooting

For simplicity, the default qmake project files assume usage of a gcc-based compiler (mingw in Windows). Theoretically, the source code should build without modification on any platform using any C++14-compliant compiler compatible with Qt. Life in the real world never seems to match this ideal. Therefore, some changes to the flags for compiling and linking may be necessary if you choose to use a different compiler. In particular, pdCalc cannot be built by the MSVC compiler provided with Microsoft's

Visual Studio using the default configuration. Additional modifications may also be needed to support exporting names from DLLs using MSVC. If I receive enough reader requests, I may extend the build system to include MSVC in a future update.

The above caveat stated, and despite considerable effort to ensure trouble-free building of pdCalc, I still find that every different combination of Qt, gcc, environment variables, operating system, and probably the weather manages to create some new, wonderful build error. If you encounter build or runtime errors, I encourage you to make an effort to diagnose and correct them yourself. Diagnosing and correcting build errors are skills worth acquiring. This will also give you a greater appreciation for the thankless soul on your team tasked with maintaining your cross-platform build system. Often the problem is as trivial as conflicting compiler versions or incorrect/missing paths.

In building on Windows, I have found two confounding problems that I will detail now to prevent anyone else from spending inordinate amounts of time debugging them. First, I discovered an obscure qmake Windows-only bug. If you see "Fatal error: MainWindow.moc: No such file or directory" in a Windows release build, congratulations, you found it too. Try changing versions of Qt. The bug appears to be fixed by version 5.9.1.

If you see the error "The system cannot find the file specified" during the building of the `hyperbolicLnPlugin`, the build has failed to copy the `plugins.pdp.win` file to the bin directory. This error indicates that `mingw32-make` has found `sh.exe` in your path and is building using the `sh.exe` shell, but qmake has configured your project to use the standard Windows shell, `cmd.exe`. If you cannot figure out why you have `sh.exe` in your path, often the culprit is the installation of git. This problem can be fixed by any of the following three different workarounds:

1. Remove `sh.exe` from your path and rebuild. This will cause `mingw32-make` to correctly build using `cmd.exe`.

2. Manually copy the `plugins.pdp.win` file to the bin directory, rename it `plugins.pdp`, delete line 16 (line beginning `win32:QMAKE_PRE_LINK+=`) from `hyperbolicLnPlugin.pro`, rerun qmake, and then rerun `mingw32-make`.

3. Modify line 16 of `hyperbolicLnPlugin.pro` to use the Unix `cp` instead of the Windows `copy` command. To do this, simply replace the line with

    ```
    win32:QMAKE_PRE_LINK+=cp $$PWD /../plugins.pdp.win
    $$HOME/bin/plugins.pdp
    ```

    rerun `qmake`, and rerun `mingw32-make`.

Finally, I do understand that it can be extremely frustrating to invest time (and possibly money) on a new book and find that you cannot build the accompanying source code per the author's instructions. If you've tried unsuccessfully to fix a build or runtime error yourself and find yourself ready to throw your computer (or this book!) out of the nearest window, just send me an email (`PracticalDesignBook@gmail.com`). I'll do my best to get you up and running as quickly and as painlessly as possible.

APPENDIX B

Organization of the Source Code

The easiest way to observe the source code is through an IDE such as Qt Creator. However, this appendix is provided as a navigational guide to the source code tree. In addition to the source code files listed in the tables below, the source tree also contains qmake project files, a few assorted configuration files, and a few baseline files for regression tests.

The root level in the source code tree contains two directories, src and test, which contain the source code for pdCalc and the unit tests, respectively. Let's look at these directories separately.

B.1 The src Directory

The src directory subdivides into five directories: app, utilities, backend, ui, and plugins. The app directory is a folder for containing the pdCalc, pdCalc-simple-cli, and pdCalc-simple-gui directories. The ui directory is a folder for containing a cli directory and a gui directory. Each directory contains the files necessary for building the respective module defined by the directory's name. Each module compiles into a distinct shared library encapsulating the module's functionality. The exceptions are the three subdirectories of the app directory, which contain source code for compiling executables. Let's now look at the files contained in each directory.

B.1.1 The pdCalc Directory

The pdCalc directory contains the source code that compiles into the pdCalc executable. Notably, this directory contains the main() function located in main.cpp, which is the entry point into the application.

© Adam B. Singer 2017
A. B. Singer, *Practical C++ Design*, DOI 10.1007/978-1-4842-3057-2

B.1.2 The pdCalc-simple-cli Directory

The pdCalc-simple-cli directory contains the source code that compiles into the simple CLI-only executable defined at the end of Chapter 5. This directory contains a single file, main.cpp.

B.1.3 The pdCalc-simple-gui Directory

The pdCalc-simple-gui directory contains the source code that compiles into the simple GUI-only executable defined at the end of Chapter 6. This directory contains a single file, main.cpp.

B.1.4 The utilities Directory

The utilities directory contains generic, reusable components, none of which are specifically associated with the calculator's logic. Table B-1 lists the files contained in the utilities directory.

Table B-1. *Source Files in the utilities Directory*

Header Files	Source Files
Exception.h	
Observer.h	Observer.cpp
Publisher.h	Publisher.cpp
Tokenizer.h	Tokenizer.cpp
UserInterface.h	UserInterface.cpp

B.1.5 The backend Directory

The backend directory contains all of the "business logic" for the calculator. From the model-view-controller perspective, this director contains the model and the controller. The backend directory also contains all of the logic for loading and managing plugins as well as the observer intermediary classes. Table B-2 lists the files contained in the backend directory.

Table B-2. *Source Files in the backend Directory*

Header Files	Source Files
AppObservers.h	AppObservers.cpp
Command.h	Command.cpp
CommandDispatcher.h	CommandDispatcher.cpp
CommandManager.h	CommandManager.cpp
CommandRepository.h	CommandRepository.cpp
CoreCommands.h	CoreCommands.cpp
DynamicLoader.h	DynamicLoader.cpp
PlatformFactory.h	PlatformFactory.cpp
Plugin.h	
PluginLoader.h	PluginLoader.cpp
PosixDynamicLoader.h	PosixDynamicLoader.cpp
PosixFactory.h	PosixFactory.cpp
Stack.h	Stack.cpp
StackPluginInterface.h	StackPluginInterface.cpp
StoredProcedure.h	StoredProcedure.cpp
WindowsDynamicLoader.h	WindowsDynamicLoader.cpp
WindowsFactory.h	WindowsFactory.cpp

B.1.6 The cli Directory

The cli directory contains the source code for the command line interface module. This module is one of the simplest modules in pdCalc and only contains two files, Cli.h and Cli.cpp.

B.1.7 The gui Directory

The gui directory contains the source code for the graphical user interface. The files in this directory encompass the main GUI window, the GUI's input and output classes, and the class governing the look-and-feel of the GUI. Table B-3 lists the source files found in the gui directory.

Table B-3. *Source Files in the gui Directory*

Header Files	Source Files
CommandButton.h	CommandButton.cpp
Display.h	Display.cpp
GuiModel.h	GuiModel.cpp
InputWidget.h	InputWidget.cpp
LookAndFeel.h	LookAndFeel.cpp
MainWindow.h	MainWindow.cpp
StoredProcedureDialog.h	StoredProcedureDialog.cpp

B.1.8 The plugins Directory

The plugins directory is a placeholder directory for the source code for plugins to pdCalc. It only includes one subdirectory, hyperbolicLnPlugin, which contains the source code for the hyperbolic functions and natural logarithm plugin developed in this book. The two source files in the hyperbolicPlugin directory are HyperbolicLnPlugin.h and HyperbolicLnPlugin.cpp. The source code implementing plugin loading and plugin management is all contained in the backend directory.

B.2 The test Directory

The test directory is the home directory for all of the unit tests for pdCalc. This directory is simply a container for the following subdirectories, each of which tests the module corresponding to its name: testDriver, utilitiesTest, backendTest, cliTest, guiTest, pluginsTest. While I like to believe that I have been diligent in testing pdCalc thoroughly, I am certain of two things: I could have tested the code more, and bugs will be found after publication. I now detail the contents of each of the directories under test.

B.2.1 The testDriver Directory

The testDriver directory contains a single source file, main.cpp. This file sets up the Qt Test environment and registers all of the individual test modules. main.cpp compiles into the testPdCalc executable (testPdCale.exe in Windows), which is responsible for running all of the unit tests.

B.2.2 The utilitiesTest Directory

The utilitiesTest directory contains the files necessary for testing the utilities module. The files contained in this directory are listed in Table B-4.

Table B-4. *Source Files in the utilitiesTest Directory*

Header Files	Source Files
PublisherObserverTest.h	PublisherObserverTest.cpp
TokenizerTest.h	TokenizerTest.cpp

B.2.3 The backendTest Directory

The backendTest directory contains the source code for testing the backend module of pdCalc. The files contained in this directory can be found in Table B-5. In addition to the source code files, the directory also contains a hypotenuse file containing a test stored procedure and the files plugins.unix.pdp and plugins.unix.win, which are plugin loader files for the two respective operating systems.

Table B-5. *Source Files in the backendTest Directory*

Header Files	Source Files
CommandDispatcherTest.h	CommandDispatcherTest.cpp
CommandManagerTest.h	CommandManagerTest.cpp
CommandRepositoryTest.h	CommandRepositoryTest.cpp
CoreCommandsTest.h	CoreCommandsTest.cpp
PluginLoaderTest.h	PluginLoaderTest.cpp
StackTest.h	StackTest.cpp
StoredProcedureTest.h	StoredProcedureTest.cpp

B.2.4 The cliTest Directory

The cliTest directory contains the source code files necessary for testing the command line interface. The two source files in this directory are CliTest.h and CliTest.cpp. In addition to the source files, the cliTest directory contains a subdirectory, testCases. The testCases directory contains input files and output baselines used in testing the command line interface.

B.2.5 The guiTest Directory

It is difficult, in general, to test graphical user interfaces automatically. Only the Display class within the GUI is automatically tested in pdCalc's unit tests. The two source files for testing the Display class, DisplayTest.h and DisplayTest.cpp, are found in the guiTest directory.

B.2.6 The pluginsTest Directory

The pluginsTest directory contains the source files for testing the single plugin included with pdCalc, the hyperbolic functions and natural logarithm plugin. These tests are contained in the following two source files: HyperbolicLnPluginTest.h and HyperbolicLnPluginTest.cpp.

References

[1] Aho, Alfred V., and Moica S. Lam, Ravi Sethi, and Jeffrey D. Ullman. *Compilers: Principles, Techniques, and Tools*, second edition. Boston, Massachusetts: Addison-Wesley, 2007.

[2] Alexandrescu, Andrei. *Modern C++ Design: Generic Programming and Design Patterns Applied*. Boston, Massachusetts: Addison-Wesley, 2001.

[3] Booch, Grady, and Robert A. Maksimchuk, Michael W. Engel, Bobbi J. Young, Jim Conallen, and Kelli A. Houston. *Object-Oriented Analysis and Design with Applications*, third edition. Boston, Massachusetts: Addison-Wesley, 2007.

[4] Booch, Grady, and James Rumbaugh and Ivar Jacobson. *The Unified Modeling Language User Guide*. Boston, Massachusetts: Addison-Wesley, 1999.

[5] Cormen, Thomas H., and Charles E. Leiserson, Ronald L. Rivest, and Clifford Stein. *Introduction to Algorithms*, third edition. Cambridge, Massachusetts: The MIT Press, 2009.

[6] Gamma, Erich, and Richard Helm, Ralph Johnson, and John Vlissides. *Design Patterns: Elements of Reusable Object-Oriented Software*. Boston, Massachusetts: Addison-Wesley, 1995.

[7] Free Software Foundation, Inc. GNU Public Licence version 3, June 2007. `http://www.gnu.org/licenses/gpl.html`.

[8] Josuttis, Nicolai M. *The C++ Standard Library: A Tutorial and Reference*, second edition. Upper Saddle River, New Jersey: Addison-Wesley, 2012.

[9] Kernighan, Brian W., and Rob Pike. *The Practice of Programming*. Reading, Massachusetts: Addison-Wesley, 1999.

© Adam B. Singer 2017
A. B. Singer, *Practical C++ Design*, DOI 10.1007/978-1-4842-3057-2

[10] Knuth, Donald E. *The Art of Computer Programming: Volume 1, Fundamental Algorithms*, third edition. Boston, Massachusetts: Addison-Wesley, 1997.

[11] Knuth, Donald E. *The Art of Computer Programming: Volume 2, Seminumerical Algorithms*, third edition. Boston, Massachusetts; Addison-Wesley, 1998.

[12] Knuth, Donald E. *The Art of Computer Programming: Volume 3, Sorting and Searching*, third edition. Boston, Massachusetts: Addison-Wesley, 1998.

[13] Lippman, Stanley B. *Inside The C++ Object Model*. Reading, Massachusetts: Addison-Wesley, 1996.

[14] Lippman, Stanley B., and Josée Lajoie. *C++ Primer*, third edition. Reading, Massachusetts: Addison-Wesley, 1998.

[15] McConnell, Steve. *Code Complete*, second edition. Redmond, Washington: Microsoft Press, 2004.

[16] Meyers, Scott. *More Effective C++*. Boston, Massachusetts: Addison-Wesley, 1996.

[17] Meyers, Scott. *Effective STL*. Boston, Massachusetts: Addison-Wesley, 2001.

[18] Meyers, Scott. *Effective C++*, third edition. Boston, Massachusetts: Addison-Wesley, 2005.

[19] Meyers, Scott. *Effective Modern C++: 42 Specific Ways to Improve Your Use of C++11 and C++14*. Beijing, China: O'Reilly, 2015.

[20] Reddy, Martin. *API Design For C++*. Amsterdam, The Netherlands: Morgan Kaufmann, 2011.

[21] Robertson, Suzanne and James Robertson. *Mastering the Requirements Process*, second edition. Upper Saddle River, New Jersey: Addison-Wesley, 2006.

[22] Spinellis, Diomidis. *Code Quality: The Open Source Perspective*. Boston, Massachusetts: Addison-Wesley, 2006.

[23]   Stroustrup, Bjarne. *The C++ Programming Language*, fourth edition. Upper Saddle River, New Jersey: Addison-Wesley, 2013.

[24]   Sutter, Herb. *Exceptional C++*. Boston, Massachusetts: Addison-Wesley, 2000.

[25]   Sutter, Herb. *More Exceptional C++*. Boston, Massachusetts: Addison-Wesley, 2002.

[26]   Sutter, Herb. *Exceptional C++ Style*. Boston, Massachusetts: Addison-Wesley, 2005.

[27]   Sutter, Herb, and Andrei Alexandrescu. *C++ Coding Standards: 101 Rules, Guidelines, and Best Practices*. Boston, Massachusetts: Addison-Wesley, 2005.

[28]   Wiegers, Karl E. *Software Requirements*. Redmond, Washington: Microsoft Press, 2003.

[29]   Wikipedia. Liskov substitution principle. `https://en.wikipedia.org/wiki/Liskov_substitution_principle`.

[30]   Wikipedia. Model-view-controller. `https://en.wikipedia.org/wiki/Model-View-Controller`.

Index

A

Abstract factory pattern, 173–177
Adapter pattern, 33, 37, 38
Aggregation, 125
Alternative GUI layout, 222
Analysis, 9, 17, 21–27
Architecture
    model-view-controller, 12–14
    multi-tiered, 12–14
    n-tiered, 12, 13
    three-tiered, 13–17
Author contact, xx

B

Batch operation, 195–197
Book structure, xvi
Bridge pattern, 38

C

CLI. *See* Command line interface
Cloning, 66–67, 85
Cohesion, 10–11, 16, 22, 25
Command
    binary, 71, 74–76, 78, 79
    class, 58, 60–62, 65, 66, 68, 71, 74, 76,
        78, 82, 85, 87, 91
    hierarchy, 59, 71
    pattern

        abstract, 58
        applied, 61
    registration, 88
    unary, 71–75, 78
CommandButton
    abstraction, 122–123
    design, 123–127
    interface, 127–128
Command data, 102–103
CommandDispatcher, 58, 82, 91–95
Command dispatcher, 16, 17, 21–26
Command line interface
    class, 105–112
    design, 107–112
    implementation, 97, 106, 108–112
    requirements, 97, 105–106, 111
CommandManager, 58, 76, 82, 83, 88, 89,
        91, 93, 94
CommandRepository, 58, 65, 81–87, 91
Complex numbers, 211–218
Composite pattern, 205–209
Composition, 125
Coupling, 9–12, 14–17, 28
Covariance, 67

D

Decomposition, 9–29
Dependencies, external, 225–226
Dependency inversion, 189–190

© Adam B. Singer 2017
A. B. Singer, *Practical C++ Design*, DOI 10.1007/978-1-4842-3057-2

Get the eBook for only $5!

Why limit yourself?

With most of our titles available in both PDF and ePUB format, you can access your content wherever and however you wish—on your PC, phone, tablet, or reader.

Since you've purchased this print book, we are happy to offer you the eBook for just $5.

To learn more, go to http://www.apress.com/companion or contact support@apress.com.

Apress®

Printed in the United States
By Bookmasters